REMAINS
𝔥istorical and 𝔏iterary
CONNECTED WITH
THE PALATINE COUNTIES OF
𝔏ancaster and ℭhester

Volume LI - Third Series

MANCHESTER
2013

Officers and Council Members of the Society

LPA

The Diary of Edward Watkin

David Hodgkins

General Editor: Tim Thornton
Assistant Editor: Julie-Marie Strange

MANCHESTER
2013

Published by The Chetham Society

ISSN 0080-0880

ISBN 978-0-9554276-4-0

Prepared by:

York Publishing Services Ltd
64 Hallfield Road
Layerthorpe
York YO31 7ZQ
Tel: 01904 431213

www.yps-publishing.co.uk

Printed and bound by:

Smith Settle
Gateway Drive
Yeadon
LS19 7XY
Tel: 0113 250 9201

www.smithsettle.com

Contents

List of maps

Acknowledgements

My primary obligation is to Dorothea Worsley-Taylor, Sir Edward Watkin's great-granddaughter, who discovered the notebook containing his diary from 1844 to 1846 among other papers. She asked whether it was of sufficient interest for publication and encouraged me to edit it.

I am also grateful to Terry Wyke, Michael Powell and Alan Kidd who having seen the initial transcript with editorial notes urged its publication, and more particularly to Alan Kidd for suggesting the scope of the introductory chapter.

No work of this kind can be accomplished without the help of the inconspicuous and unsung help of many archivists and librarians. I must thank particularly those in the Archives and Local History sections of Manchester Central Library. I should also thank those who helped at the British Library, the British Newspaper Library, Cambridge University Library, the National Archives and the West Sussex Record Office at Chichester. I am also grateful to the London Library which enabled me to draw on relevant books at home for long periods.

I am obliged to the British Library for permission to reproduce the transcripts of items from the Peel Papers reproduced in the Appendix.

I must also thank Tim Thornton, the general editor of the Chetham Society, for his help and suggestions. He has also overseen the work of preparing the text for the press assisted in the later stages by Glynis Harris who, as copy editor, has assiduously checked the text and raised a number of points which needed clarification.

Any errors and shortcomings remain with me as editor of the text and author of the introductory chapter.

List of abbreviations

ACLC	*Anti-Corn Law Circular*
ACLL	Anti-Corn Law League
AWJ	*Absalom Watkin: Extracts from His Journal, 1814–56*, ed. A. E. Watkin (London: T. Fisher Unwin, 1920)
BL	London, British Library
Econ HR	*Economic History Review*
Goffin	*The Diaries of Absalom Watkin: A Manchester Man, 1787–1861*, ed. Magdalen Goffin (Stroud: Alan Sutton, 1993)
MCL	Manchester Central Library
MG	*Manchester Guardian*
Pigot	*Pigot and Slater's General, Classified and Street Directory of Manchester and Salford* (Manchester: Pigot and Slater, 1841)
PP	Parliamentary Papers
TNA	Kew, The National Archives of the United Kingdom
Watkin, *Cobden*	E. W. Watkin, *Alderman Cobden of Manchester: Letters and Reminiscences of Richard Cobden, with Portraits, Illustrations, Facsimiles and Index* (London: Ward, Lock, 1891)
WSRO	Chichester, West Sussex Record Office

The Manchester area in the mid-1840s

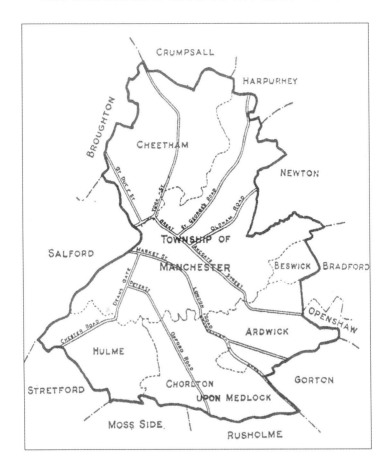

The Manchester area in the mid-1840s

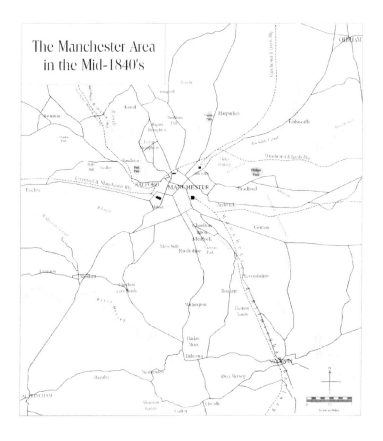

CHAPTER I

Introduction

Edward Watkin

Edward Watkin was born in 1819, the son of Absalom and Elizabeth Watkin. His father was a cotton merchant in Manchester, then living in Ravald Street, Salford. Edward was one of four children, the others being Elizabeth, the eldest, and his two younger brothers, John and Alfred. The three boys all began their working lives in their father's business, which in the period covered by the diary was at 26 High Street. Absalom was described as a commission agent and dealer in worsted yarn, warps and weft.[1] Until his marriage in 1845 Edward Watkin lived with his parents. Much of the evidence for Edward's early life comes from his father's diary, which has been extensively published in two versions. The first, edited by A. E. Watkin, contains extracts from the diary; the second, edited by Magdalen Goffin, contains extracts which are linked by passages describing the background to the entries.[2]

The family moved in 1822 from Ravald Street to Broughton Lane. In 1834, when Edward was already working in his father's business, they moved their home from Broughton to Rose Hill, a house in Northenden (or Northen), then a small village on the Mersey in the Cheshire countryside. Little is known of Edward's formal education. His two brothers attended schools in the Nantwich area where the family had close relations, but the only reference in his father's diary to Edward's education is to his attendance at a day school in September 1829, the month in which he was ten.[3] Indeed he told Cobden that he

1 Pigot, p. 260.

2 *AWJ*; Goffin.

3 I am grateful for this information to Magdalen Goffin who examined the unpublished parts of Absalom's diary in her possession. David Hodgkins, *The Second Railway King: The Life and Times of Sir Edward Watkin, 1819–1901* (Cardiff: Merton Priory Press, 2002), p. 9, discusses the sparse information on Watkin's schooling and date of starting work.

had worked since he was a little over nine years old, though this probably should not be taken to imply that his school attendance ceased at that age.[4] It is clear both from his diary and from his speeches and writings in later life that he was well read. Whatever schools Edward attended, no doubt he owed much to his father's library which he later inherited and for which he was to publish a catalogue.[5] His father's diary records him as working in the family warehouse in 1834 before his fifteenth birthday[6] and this was to be his employment for the next eleven years, including the major part of the period to which the surviving diary relates.

Edward Watkin's diary – the document

As a young man Edward Watkin kept a diary. Although most of his personal papers were destroyed in the 1940s, one volume of his manuscript diaries was found a few years ago by his great-granddaughter, Dorothea Worsley-Taylor, among papers in her possession. It covers the years 1844, 1845 and the first half of 1846. It was drawn on in *The Second Railway King: The Life and Times of Sir Edward Watkin, 1819–1901*[7] but is now reproduced here in full, together with a number of other writings of his relating to the campaign for public parks which form the Appendix.

The diary consists of a single small, hard-backed, ruled notebook. It starts with a loose page without any heading and in mid-sentence, but this is certainly part of Watkin's entry reviewing 1843 and looking forward to 1844. That the first part of the review is now missing is confirmed by the fact that it contains no references to his father or to other members of the

---

4 WSRO, Cobden Papers, CP9, Watkin to Cobden, n.d. (probably Mar 1857).

5 *Catalogue of the Library of Sir Edward W. Watkin MP, Rose Hill, Northenden* (Manchester, compiled and printed for private use by J. E. Cornish, 1875; 2nd and enlarged edn Manchester: Henry Blacklock, 1889).

6 Goffin, p. 167.

7 Hodgkins, *Second Railway King*, pp. 38–54.

Watkin family. He refers to an entry 'a page or two back' but it is likely that this was in a separate volume of the diary for 1843 which has not survived. The entries which follow are usually made at weekly intervals.

This transcript replaces some, but not all, of the abbreviations used by Watkin with the full word or words to assist the modern reader. Many of his entries were punctuated with dashes rather than commas or full stops and the use of capital letters is not in line with modern practice. In many cases the sense seems to demand the use of commas or stops rather than repeated dashes.

Illegible words are indicated. Almost all the names of the people to whom Watkin referred are identified in the footnotes, but a few have not been traced and the identification of some is uncertain. This is particularly the case with those referred to by their surname only and which are not recognisable as the name of a person with whom Watkin was likely to have been in contact, but which is a name common in Manchester. A further problem arises with names which are well known but which may indicate members of the family who were contemporaries of Watkin's rather than their well-known fathers, though Watkin was well acquainted with many Mancunians of his father's generation.

Watkin himself published extracts from his diaries of 1841 and 1843 in *Alderman Cobden of Manchester*[8] relating respectively to the Operatives Anti-Corn Law Association and the visit of Charles Dickens to Manchester to speak at the Athenaeum soirée. These extracts are printed as Chapters 2 and 3.

Edward Watkin's diary as a record

The diary is a record of Edward Watkin's life in his twenties in Manchester. At a personal level it deals with major events which were to shape his life, particularly his courtship of Mary Mellor leading to a marriage which lasted until her death in 1888, and describes the start of his career in railways, chosen because of his

8   Watkin, *Cobden*.

need for a job rather than any strong interest in railways, but an industry in which he was to remain for almost half a century. The diary records his social life in Manchester, his concerns about the family business and his part in it, closely connected with uncertainties about his ability to earn a more satisfactory and sure income than that likely to arise from the cotton trade, especially after he had met Mary, and also his preoccupations with his health. There are a number of references to the state of his bowels which he thought might account for his laziness. The strains were aggravated by his differences with his father, other family illnesses and problems, and his own inability to concentrate on business, particularly when public life in Manchester was taking so much of his time and interest.[9] The tensions in the Watkin household between Absalom and his wife, and with his sons, especially Edward, are also set out in some detail in Absalom's diary though A. E. Watkin did not include these passages which he doubtless thought would be as embarrassing to the family as they had been to Absalom himself. He explained to George Wilson in 1841 that his wife, who had in fact taken part earlier in Anti-Corn Law League (ACLL) activities, had been in so dangerous a state of health for nearly two years that she would have to decline membership of the ladies committee for the ACLL bazaar.[10]

The accumulated stress and tensions of Edward's busy life culminated in his breakdown in 1846 which he described in the diary and at greater length in his *Recollections*, published in 1887.[11] It seems he suffered a mild precursor of this in July 1844.[12] There is no indication that Watkin suffered from any organic illness such as thyroid or diabetes. It seems likely that he was suffering from an anxiety-related disorder which on occasions became acute, leading to panic attacks which resulted

9   His woes reached a crescendo in the diary entry for 16 Jan 1845.
10   MCL, M29/4, Absalom Watkin to George Wilson, 29 Sep 1841.
11   Diary entry for 31 May 1846; E. W. Watkin, *Canada and the States, Recollections, 1851–1886* (London: Ward, Lock, 1887), pp. 320–9.
12   Diary entries for 6 Jan, 27 April and 20 July 1844; 16 and 27 Jan, May 30 and 6 June 1845.

in physical weakness and subsequently to depression, which later in the nineteenth century physicians would describe as neurasthenia.[13] Full recovery was not to come until 1851 when he took leave from his employment with the London & North Western Railway to go to the United States and Canada. In later life Edward was one of the leading figures in the British railway industry, the long-serving chairman of three major companies – the Manchester, Sheffield and Lincolnshire, the South Eastern and the Metropolitan – as well as the leading protagonist of the Channel Tunnel in the 1870s and 1880s, and president of the Grand Trunk Railway of Canada in the 1860s.

At another level the diary is an account of political and public life in Manchester at a time when Manchester and all it stood for was at the centre of a number of issues in national politics. Watkin was a young man – only 21 when he made the entries for 1841 and nearly 26 when the diary closes – who was trying to make his way in the world and who was also a closely involved and active participant, albeit in a junior capacity, in the Anti-Corn Law movement, the Athenaeum, and the campaign for public parks. Indeed, as he later put it, 'in those days I was almost perennial "Honorary Secretary" to movements big and little'.[14] His diary therefore sheds light on the workings of the voluntary institutions in Manchester and the reform movements. He moved not only in the world of his contemporaries but also in that of the leaders of Manchester and through them came to meet leading national politicians such as Disraeli and Peel. Even following his marriage in 1845 and his appointment as secretary to the Trent Valley Railway he continued to be active in Manchester public life as one of the founders of the *Manchester Examiner*. He also played a part in the Stafford by-election in March 1846, described in his diary. Later he was a member of the Manchester City Council from 1859 to 1862, and was closely involved in Canadian politics during the period preceding Confederation in 1867. He was

13   I am indebted for advice to Professor Simon Wessely of the Institute of Psychiatry, London.

14   Watkin, *Cobden*, p. 98.

Liberal MP for Stockport from 1864 to 1868 and MP for Hythe in Kent from 1874 to 1895, though tending to support the Conservatives on foreign policy in Gladstone's 1880 administration and effectively a Unionist from 1886.

England in the 1840s

The diary relates to a crucial time in British society. The period of Lord Liverpool's Tory Government following the Napoleonic Wars was a time of fears lest the revolutionary spirit, defeated on the Continent, would be resurgent in Britain and consequently associated with repression. It left an indelible mark on Manchester in the shape of Peterloo. This was succeeded by the more liberal Tory administrations at the end of the 1820s. The Reform Act of 1832, secured by Lord Grey's Whig administration in the face of opposition from the Tories and above all the House of Lords, increased the number of voters by 50 per cent and in England and Wales removed 64 seats from small boroughs and gave them to industrial towns in the Midlands and North such as Manchester as well as to populous districts of London. This Act was followed by the new Poor Law of 1834 and the Municipal Reform Act of 1835.

When Watkin made the entries in his diary for 1841, Lord Melbourne was still Prime Minister, but he was succeeded in September 1841 by Sir Robert Peel, who remained Prime Minister until July 1846. For much of this period British politics were dominated by three groups of issues which were to some extent interrelated: free trade and more particularly the Corn Laws; Chartism and questions posed by the working classes, including the Factories Acts; and Ireland. These issues were seen especially sharply in Lancashire, and Manchester in particular. As Anthony Howe has written, 'No subsequent political issue generated the same passion and collective angst in Lancashire as the Corn Laws and the Factories Acts. These were issues which served to define and to resolve the tension between the new industrial elite and the traditional aristocratic state.'[15] A theme

15   Anthony Howe, 'The business community', in Mary B. Rose (ed.), *The Lancashire Cotton Industry: A History since 1700* (Preston: Lancashire County Books, 1996), pp. 94–120, at p. 114.

which is explored later in the context of Watkin's activities is how far the Anti-Corn Law movement and Chartism could work together. The Corn Laws, which imposed duties on imported grain, came to be seen as both an obstacle to the export of British manufactures and a tax on the price of bread. The absolute ban on imports unless the price was at least 80s a quarter – the law of 1815 – had been replaced by a sliding scale in 1828, but in times of scarcity this encouraged hoarding by suppliers until the price rose and the duty fell. Good harvests in the 1830s meant the Corn Laws were not a major issue, but the bad harvest of 1838, the worst since 1816, brought the matter to the fore again. Extra-parliamentary campaigning on this issue was very important with the Manchester manufacturers and merchants in the lead in the Anti-Corn Law League. At Westminster Melbourne's cabinet was divided in 1839 on whether there should be some modification, but the Prime Minister was against such a fundamental change. In 1841 the Melbourne Government favoured a modest fixed duty, but their defeat in the 1841 general election meant this was not carried out.[16] In 1842 Peel introduced an income tax, but at the same time reduced import duties to encourage consumption, later abolishing many of them. By 1845 higher consumption meant the loss to the revenue was almost offset.

In 1842 the Corn Laws were modified to temper the effect of the sliding scale to discourage delays in importing corn when the price was nearing the duty-free level, but this did little to appease the repealers. On the other hand those with protectionist views like the duke of Buckingham became much more vocal, responding to the League's attacks on the aristocracy by criticising the motives of the repealers whom they saw as exploiting their employees, especially as many were opposed to the extension of the Factories Acts. The issue effectively split the Tory party. Following the failure of the potato crop in Ireland in 1845 and with the Whig leader, Lord John Russell, coming out for repeal, Peel tried to get his cabinet to agree to suspension and ultimate repeal. This resulted in resignations from his

16 Diary entry for 16 May 1841 refers to a meeting in Manchester to support this proposal.

cabinet and concerted opposition to his proposals particularly from the landed aristocrats in the party, who were supported by Disraeli.[17] It was only in June 1846 that Peel carried the day on this issue, but his adversaries defeated him the same evening on a coercion bill for Ireland. Repeal and Peel's resignation were recorded by Watkin in his diary on 12 July 1846.

Apart from the protectionists such as the dukes of Buckingham and Richmond, Peel's Conservative party also contained a number of aristocratic young men who believed in a new feudalism of a paternalist aristocracy and that there was a chance of avoiding revolution if the upper and lower classes came together to resist the radicals and the manufacturers. They were a very small group led by George Smythe, son of the 6th Viscount Strangford, and John Manners, son of the duke of Rutland, both still in their twenties, who were joined in 1842 by Disraeli. All three were to attend the Manchester Atheneum soirée in October 1844.

The years 1838 to 1842 also saw the great Chartist demonstrations. The People's Charter drawn up in 1836 demanded universal manhood suffrage, vote by ballot, equal electoral districts, annually elected parliaments, payment of MPs and no property qualification for them. Their fundamental demands meant that the Whig Government became more determined to resist pressures for further constitutional reform. Chartism itself was split between the moral force wing epitomised by the London Working Men's Association and the Birmingham Political Union, and the more radical wing led by Feargus O'Connor, found particularly in Leeds, where O'Connor had his mouthpiece in the form of the *Northern Star*, and in Manchester. In 1839 Parliament refused to consider the petition for a charter and the call for a general strike met with virtually no response. A further petition in 1842 with 1,200,000 signatures also did not secure consideration by Parliament, but the economic depression of that year led to substantial unemployment and strikes and riots in the industrial North – the Plug Plot. Meanwhile opponents

---

17   Disraeli had still held no government office. He was Conservative MP for Shrewsbury, 1841–47.

of the Corn Laws had tried to win over the working classes to the cause of repeal, a move with which Watkin was closely associated.[18] However, despite some support in Manchester from Irish followers of Daniel O'Connell, a free trader, the Chartists generally were not prepared to give priority to Corn Law repeal over their political aims. They distrusted the manufacturers who led the League, many of whom were opposed to proposals for legislation to limit working hours. The Factories Act of 1833 had established a regime of inspection and limited the hours of children from 9 to 13 years of age to nine hours a day, and under 18s to twelve hours, but, although there were improvements in 1844, it was 1847 before there was a ten-hour day for women and young persons.

The Act of Union of 1800 meant that Ireland was fully part of the United Kingdom with representation in the Westminster Parliament, but a Viceroy in Dublin. Ireland was poor, with a growing population. It was also largely Catholic, but Catholics could not sit as MPs until the Catholic Emancipation Act of 1829 and thereafter the Anglican Church of Ireland still received the tithes. Daniel O'Connell, who had formed the Catholic Association in 1823, was, following emancipation, a Westminster MP and leader of the Irish party. The Melbourne administration, dependent on the support of Irish MPs, had been relatively accommodating to Irish demands, passing the Tithes Act in 1838. However, with the return to power of Peel in 1841 O'Connell relaunched his campaign for the repeal of the Act of Union, a campaign which got increasingly out of his control with the rise of the Young Ireland movement. Although O'Connell had avoided incitement to force, Peel made it clear that he would not countenance repeal of the Act of Union. A mass meeting at Clontarf was forbidden in October 1843 and led to O'Connell's arrest and conviction. Watkin records a debate on Ireland in the Literary Society and a borough meeting in January and February 1844. He visited O'Connell, whom he knew from the Anti-Corn Law campaign which O'Connell

18   See pages 66 to 79 below.

supported, in prison in Dublin in September 1844, but before he returned to Manchester he was able to witness his triumphal procession from prison, when his appeal to the House of Lords succeeded.[19]

Manchester

Edward Watkin's diary relates to a period when Manchester was not only at the height of its economic importance; it was also at the centre of much that was going on in Britain socially and politically. In 1845 the prospectus for the new newspaper, the *Manchester Examiner*, of which Watkin was a founder, described Manchester as 'the nucleus of the most active and enterprising district in the Empire' and also asserted that 'Manchester was the heart of the kingdom',[20] a statement with which most people in Manchester would have agreed. Interest in the town was intense. It attracted some of the first surveys analysing the social conditions and the health of the urban poor. Some were generated by residents of the town like James Kay, and Joseph Adshead with whom Watkin visited the New Bailey prison in 1844. The town was also the subject of wide-ranging description and analysis from outsiders like Faucher and Engels. The latter only arrived in Manchester two years before he wrote *The Condition of the Working Class in England in 1844*, one of many immigrants from Europe like Paul Willert, Lascaridi, Dilberbogue and Sichel who are mentioned in the diary.[21]

19 Diary entries for 6 Jan, 2 Mar and 13 Sep 1844.

20 The quotations are from the prospectus for the *Manchester Examiner* (*Manchester Times*, 9 Dec 1845).

21 Engels was a manufacturer, but the 1840s saw a marked growth in the number of foreign merchants in Manchester. In 1840 there were 110, mainly German, while in 1850 there were 183, 55 of whom were described as Greeks but this group included Egyptians, Turks and others from the Levant (Stanley Chapman, 'The commercial sector', in Rose (ed.), *Lancashire Cotton Industry*, pp. 63–93, at p. 80, derived from John Scholes, 'Foreign merchants in Manchester, 1784–1870', MCL, MS FF 382 S35). An association, The Greek Community in Manchester, was formed in 1843: Sophocles Chr. Andreades, *A Personal History of the Greek Community in Manchester and its Church, 1843–1990* (Manchester: S. Chr. Andreades, 2000).

Others, like John Byng, de Tocqueville and William Cooke Taylor, commented, sometimes only briefly, on conditions in the course of their accounts of their travels. Manchester also featured in novels of the period, particularly those by Disraeli and Mrs Gaskell who later in the 1840s was to write *Mary Barton*, the first full-length novel by a Manchester resident to deal with the working class and its problems, treating them as individuals but placing them in a culture.

Since the sixteenth century Manchester had been an important town which combined the manufacture of woollen and linen cloth with trade. Its importance increased during the first part of the eighteenth century, in part as a result of improvements to water transport which meant that the Mersey and Irwell were navigable up to Hunt's Bank, and turnpike trusts. By mid-century cotton was being added to linen cloths. The population, estimated at 10,000 for Manchester and 2,500 for Salford in about 1717, grew to 17,000 by 1758 (Manchester township) and 24,000 in 1773–74. This was a decade after the opening of the duke of Bridgewater's canal which brought coal from Worsley to supplement the supply drawn from the pits at Bradford in east Manchester, and immediately before the canal was completed to Runcorn on the Mersey, so giving access to the port of Liverpool and also to the Midlands. It was also before the coming of the powered cotton spinning mills following Richard Arkwright's mill on Shude Hill in the early 1780s where water power was supplemented by a Newcomen-type steam engine. In 1786 a stranger approaching the town only saw one high chimney which was that of Mr Arkwright's mill.[22] This was the beginning of the revolution in the techniques of spinning manufacture. By 1802 there were 52 spinning mills in Manchester and by 1830, 99. However recent analysis has shown that the growth was in medium-sized firms with from 151 to 500 employees rather than in the smaller or larger ranges.[23]

22 W. David Evans in evidence to the Select Committee on the State of Children Employed in the Manufactories, PP 1816 (397) III, 317.

23 The medium range accounted for 27 per cent of employees in 1815 and 56 per cent in 1841. Roger Lloyd Jones and A. A. Le Roux, 'The size of firms in the cotton industry: Manchester, 1815–41', *Econ HR*, 2nd ser., XXXIII (1980), 72–82, at pp. 75–6.

The power loom was improved and was widely adopted from the mid-1820s. In addition the finishing industries, dyeing, bleaching and printing, developed. In part because of the need for textile machinery Manchester became a major engineering centre. Sharp, Roberts and Fairbairn, who are mentioned in the diary, were central figures in the industry and iron foundries and engineering works congregated along the banks of the Ashton and Rochdale canals. The textile machinery firms were expansive and outward-looking and were among the leading advocates of lifting the mercantilist restrictions on the exports of machinery, the removal of which was achieved in 1843.[24]

At the first census in 1801 Manchester's population was 75,000; that of Salford 14,000. Rapid growth continued so that by 1841 the populations of Manchester and Salford were respectively 235,000 and 53,000. After 1811 the rate of growth each decade was well over twice that for Great Britain as a whole. It was fuelled, not by a declining death rate, but by migration, initially mainly from the agricultural areas, but increasingly from Ireland – there were some 30,000 Irish in Manchester in 1841 who were highly concentrated in a small number of areas. Partly because migrants were young there was also a very high marriage rate.[25] This startling growth was achieved at considerable social cost. The mills dominated the landscape, and the slums in which the poor lived attracted the attention and, with justification, the opprobrium of visitors concerned with the health and welfare of the workers, particularly the children. However, recent historians have emphasised that though manufacturing was important, by the 1840s Manchester was less a centre of manufacturing production than 'a provincial,

24   George Saxonhouse and Gavin Wright, 'Technological evolution in cotton spinning, 1878–1933', in Douglas A. Farnie and David J. Jeremy (eds), *The Fibre that Changed the World: The Cotton Industry in International Perspective, 1600–1990s* (Oxford: Oxford University Press, 2004), pp. 129–52, at p. 138.

25   Roger Scola, *Feeding the Victorian City: The Food Supply of Manchester 1770–1880* (Manchester: Manchester University Press, 1992), p. 17.

commercial and retailing capital'.[26] Manchester remained the commercial centre of the rapidly growing cotton industry, which by 1852 was supplying 45 per cent of the world's cotton cloth. This gave rise to a wide range of occupations. Although by 1841 there were 19,651 persons working in Manchester in all branches of cotton manufacture, nearly as many as in Oldham, Blackburn and Ashton-under-Lyne combined, cotton only accounted for 18 per cent of the workforce as opposed to 50 per cent in Ashton and 40 per cent in both Blackburn and Oldham. The Tuesday market for textiles, later formalised under the auspices of the Exchange, built as early as 1729 by the lord of the manor, Sir Oswald Mosley, as a public market, had long attracted manufacturers from the smaller cotton towns of Lancashire. On Tuesdays the Exchange was transferred from a state of listlessness into a community of dancing dervishes as bargains were made and deals struck.[27] It was rebuilt in 1809 by a private association of merchants and closed to all but subscribers. It served primarily as a meeting place between Manchester merchants themselves and also with the country manufacturers of Lancashire, with a coffee house, newsroom and above all a trading floor. By 1825 the Exchange had 1,600 members.[28] When enlarged in 1841 it was the largest trading floor in the world. In 1851 it was to become the Royal Exchange in recognition of its value to the area's economy.

Trade had continued to grow in both yarn and cloth or cotton goods. By 1825 there were over 1,800 warehouses in the

26 Simon Gunn, 'The "failure" of the Victorian middle class: a critique', in John Seed and Janet Wolff (eds), *The Culture of Capital: Art, Power and the Nineteenth-Century Middle Class* (Manchester: Manchester University Press, 1988), pp. 17–43, at p. 23, quoting from chapter 1 of V. A. C. Gattrell, 'The commercial middle class in Manchester, 1820–57' (unpub. PhD thesis, University of Cambridge, 1971).

27 Quoted in Simon Gunn, *The Public Culture of the Victorian Middle Class: Ritual and Authority and the English Industrial City* (Manchester: Manchester University Press, 2000), p. 74.

28 D. A. Farnie, 'An index of commercial activity: the membership of the Manchester Royal Exchange, 1809–1948', *Business History*, 21 (1979), 97–106, at pp. 97–8.

town. In 1815 Absalom Watkin's had been one of 57 in Cannon Street, many of which were sublet. His premises were small as they had a rateable value of only £18, though 71 per cent of warehouses in the town had a rateable value of less than £50.[29] Despite the small size of many warehouses, by 1825 warehouses in total already had twice the rateable value of manufactories. Manchester merchants were the leaders in Britain's greatest export business and their number was increasing at a faster rate than exports of cotton manufactures.[30] It was a trade which was an important vehicle of social mobility to which entry was relatively easy, needing warehousing and office space and access to floating but not fixed capital. Though very large warehouses came to be built in central Manchester, mainly after 1850, and warehouses were replacing houses in Mosley Street by 1840, the cheapest location was a basement warehouse below street level. It has been claimed that such sites played a far more important role in the economic history of Manchester than the cellar-dwelling did in the social history of the city.[31] Edward Watkin does not describe business on the Exchange but he illustrates its importance as providing a venue where merchants could discuss municipal and other public business or even sign petitions as when, in the immediate aftermath of the repeal of the Corn Laws, the Prime Minister, Sir Robert Peel, was asked to stand for South Lancashire at the next general election. Watkin was introduced to William Brown there, when the latter was fighting the South Lancashire by-election and with James Atherton took Disraeli to the Exchange to introduce him to various

29   Roger Lloyd Jones and M. J. Lewis, *Manchester and the Age of the Factory* (London: Croom Helm, 1988), pp. 34–5, 218. By 1841 Absalom's business was at 26 High Street. By 1855 Absalom had moved the business to Nicholas Street. Edward's brother Alfred became a partner in that year and the warehouse was purchased for £3,250. Absalom then put £1,000 of additional capital into the business. Goffin, pp. 355, 361.

30   Douglas A. Farnie, 'The role of merchants as prime movers in the expansion of the cotton industry, 1760–1990', in Farnie and Jeremy (eds), *Fibre that Changed the World*, pp. 15–55, at p. 30.

31   Farnie, 'Role of merchants', pp. 31–2.

members.[32] William Cooke Taylor described the Exchange as 'the parliament of the lords of cotton', but any implication that this was a political body as opposed to one where informal deliberations could take place would be mistaken.[33]

Cotton and fluctuations in trade

The consumption of raw cotton in Britain, which can be taken as a proxy for total output of the industry, 90 per cent of which was in Lancashire and the neighbouring parts of Cheshire, almost trebled from 1825 to 1840, though greatly increased productivity meant that this was not reflected in the value of production. Capacity was expanded after the 1836 boom. Total horsepower in the Lancashire cotton industry was 23,000 early in 1835 but as much as 38,500 at the end of 1841, though the rate of expansion had slowed after 1838. In the cotton industry 1841 and 1842 were years of depression – the consumption of raw cotton fell for two consecutive years, the only instance between the Napoleonic Wars and the cotton famine of the 1860s.[34] The export trade was not good; the home market much worse. The volume of production did not fall severely but the depression saw the lowest output by value since 1832. By late 1841 there was only investment in labour-saving devices as firms struggled to spread costs, putting other firms into difficulties. The banks, particularly the recently created joint-stock banks, had advanced credit too readily in the late 1830s and were now in no position to help.[35] The result was bankruptcies and complete stoppages of mills, throwing

32 Diary entries, 25 May and 4 Oct 1844; the correspondence with Peel is included in the Appendix.

33 W. Cooke Taylor, *Notes of a Tour in the Manufacturing Districts of Lancashire* (London: Duncan & Malcolm, 1842), p. 10.

34 R. C. O. Matthews, *A Study in Trade Cycle History: Economic Fluctuations in Great Britain, 1833–42* (Cambridge: Cambridge University Press, 1954), pp. 129, 140–1, 151.

35 S. D. Chapman, 'Financial restraints on the growth of firms in the cotton industry, 1790–1850', *Econ HR*, 2nd ser., XXXII (1979), 50–69, at pp. 60–2.

operatives out of work. Consequently, while 1839 had been a poor year, the effect was then largely felt in underemployment; 1841 and 1842 were years of unemployment. In May 1842 116 factories had ceased working and 681 shops and offices had been closed; butchers, grocers and drapers said their daily sales were down by 40 per cent and over 5,000 houses were unoccupied. The value of mill buildings and machinery had lessened fully one half.[36] Adshead wrote: 'many sure indications of increasing poverty – comfortably furnished houses rendered desolate by the disappearance of one article of furniture after another; the once decently dressed family now but half clothed in worn out rags and instead of enjoying a wholesome meal barely supporting life on a scant supply of the most meagre diet'.[37]

It was immediately noticeable to visitors. Thomas Carlyle wrote: 'poor Manchester looked far too clear; there was not the third part of the smoke that is usual there; the mills being, so many of them, out of work. Numbers of idle people were visible in the streets.'[38] The effect was increased by continued immigration, by a tendency for the labour force in cotton mills to consist of an increasing proportion of children and young people and by the final victory of the power loom over handloom weavers. This was the economic setting for the Plug Plot in the summer of 1842.

By 1844, when the main part of Watkin's diary commenced, trade was better. He records in his entry for 10 February 1844 that the cotton market was terribly excited, though six days later Absalom noted that when the boys returned from town they brought a note from Greenwoods stating that they had

36   Leon Faucher, *Manchester in 1844: Its Present Condition and Future Prospects* (translated by a member of the Manchester Athenaeum, London: Simpkin, Marshall, 1844), p. 146.

37   Joseph Adshead, *Distress in Manchester: Evidence of the State of the Labouring Classes in 1840–2* (London: Henry Hooper, 1842), p. 50.

38   Thomas Carlyle to Margaret A. Carlyle, 6 May 1842, *Collected Letters of Thomas and Jane Welsh Carlyle*, ed. C. R. Saunders *et al.* (38 vols, continuing, Durham, North Carolina: Duke University Press, 1970–), xiv. 181.

sold several thousand bundles of their twist 'at ten pence while we cannot get more than nine pence halfpenny'. He adds this made him sad, especially as Edward was as usual insolent and altogether unable to meet this proof of his inattention.[39] In general Edward's notes in 1844 suggest trade was fair, but in July he notes that 'we did a great deal last week... and prices are rather on the advance'. Later that month he notes in two consecutive weeks that business was good, and in the second entry adds that the only fault is that 'we have sold too much' (i.e. stocks had been run low). In the same week his father described himself as 'extremely feeble and much depressed at the warehouse'.[40] Father and sons do not seem to have given the business sufficient priority. Both Absalom and Edward in their diaries frequently note their black moods, and Absalom writes of the unhelpful attitudes of his sons, especially Edward. It is hard therefore to be sure of the extent to which fluctuations in the level of business at the warehouse reflected industry-wide trends or the weakness of the Watkins' approach to business, distracted as they were by literature and the public life of Manchester, and badly affected by their moods.

Curiously, in their diaries neither Absalom nor Edward give the reader any clear description of the finances of their business or how it was conducted. In 1835 Absalom reckoned that his total property amounted to at least £5,000, mostly in houses, with Rose Hill accounting for £1,600, and the business. In the late 1830s and early 1840s Absalom gives his fixed property as worth about £4,000, but gives no figures for the business. Edward said they had made £900 in commission in 1844, but this seems to be the gross figure.[41] Edward never mentions any employees, and though presumably he and his brothers did not act as porters, they may well have carried out at least some of the duties of clerks. The successful campaign for a half-day holiday for clerks in warehouses in 1843 meant that the Watkin warehouse closed on Saturday afternoons, but the only mention

39   Goffin, p. 239.
40   Diary entries for 6 and 27 July 1844; Goffin, p. 240.
41   Goffin, pp. 170, 270; diary entry for 16 Jan 1845.

in the diaries of employees is in Absalom's diary for 1823 when he states that two of his warehousemen came to inform him of a suspected burglary.[42]

The working classes

By the 1840s commentators on Manchester had long focused on two aspects of society – the living and working conditions of the poorer people and the divide between the workers and the middle classes who ran Manchester politically and economically. Byng in 1790 saw it as a great nasty manufacturing town and asked 'who but a merchant could live in such a hole, where the slave working and drinking a short life out, is eternally reeling before you from fatigue and drunkenness?'[43] The initial impression of Benjamin Robert Haydon, the painter, when he lectured in Manchester in 1837, was that he was not happy in Manchester. The association of those hideous mill prisons for children destroyed his enjoyments in society: 'The people are quite insensible to it, but how they can go on as they do in all their luxurious enjoyments with huge factories overhanging the sky is most extraordinary.' Haydon largely resiled from this comment in a subsequent entry in his diary where he said he had examined factories with 2,000 children in a room and found them healthy and strong and the room well aired. He clearly had been to one of the best employers, though in 1841 factory inspectors reported only four factories with over 1,000 workers, with 1,303 in the largest.[44] Dickens, however, on

42 Goffin, p. 60. This was long before Edward or his brothers worked at the warehouse.

43 John Byng Torrington, *The Torrington Diaries*, ed. C. B. Andrews (4 vols, London: Eyre & Spotiswoode, 1935), ii. 206, 209.

44 Haydon was then in Manchester to lecture, but also attended a meeting to advocate a school of design which was later established. His son, Frank, was apprenticed to William Fairbairn (see n. 78) at his engineering works in 1839, though his father wrote, 'I almost fear the vice of a manufacturing Town'. An inveterate opponent of the Royal Academy, dogged by debt, who shot himself in 1846: see diary entry for 12 July 1846 below (*Diary of Benjamin Robert Haydon*, ed. Willard Bissell Pope (5 vols, Cambridge, Mass.: Harvard University Press, 1960–63), iv. 417, 549). For numbers of employees, see Lloyd Jones and Le Roux, 'Size of firms'.

paying his first visit to Manchester in the following year, said that what he had seen disgusted and astonished him beyond all measure. 'I mean to strike the heaviest blow in my power for these unfortunate creatures.' He added he had seen the worst cotton mill and then saw the best: 'Ex uno disce omnes. There was no great difference between them.'[45] The heaviest blow was to come in 1854 when Dickens' *Hard Times* was published with its portrait of the employers Gradgrind and Bounderby of Coketown, the town of machinery and tall chimneys with the black canal and purple river, and where there was nothing which was not severely workful. Carlyle also paid his first visit to Manchester in 1838 and heard the rushing off of its thousand mills starting at 5.30 a.m. like the boom of an Atlantic tide as sublime as Niagara. Cotton spinning was the clothing of the naked in its result: the triumph of man over matter in its means. Soot and despair were not the essence of it; they were divisible from it, and were now crying to be divided.[46]

Disraeli, soon after his visit to the Manchester Athenaeum in October 1843, when Dickens was the principal speaker (described in Chapter 3), began to write *Coningsby*, published the following year. Coningsby, on expressing a longing to see Athens, received the response, 'the age of ruins is past. Have you seen Manchester?' Disraeli describes it as the Metropolis of Labour, and explains that rightly understood it was as great a human exploit as Athens, but the inhabitants were not as conscious of who they were or of what they had done as the Athenians were. In Manchester Coningsby finds himself among illumined factories with more windows than Italian palaces, and smoking chimneys taller than Egyptian obelisks. He admires the machinery and above all machines making machines. He does not comment adversely on the working conditions and sees a thousand or fifteen hundred girls working in a room in their coral necklaces.[47] His view of the interior of

45   *The Letters of Charles Dickens*, ed. Madeline House and Graham Storey (12 vols, Oxford: Oxford University Press, 1965–2002), i. 483–4.

46   Thomas Carlyle, *Chartism* (London: Holerth Press, 1924 reprint), pp. 70–1.

47   Benjamin Disraeli, *Coningsby* (London: J. M. Dent, 1911), pp. 95, 126–9.

the factory then resembled Haydon's rather than Dickens'. In *Sybil*, however, published only a year later, Disraeli's attitude is very different. Based in part on his study of the report on children's employment of 1842, he takes a bitter view of the two nations of rich and poor, in the setting of Chartism. He sees the solution in a regenerate aristocracy – the idea which was to motivate the Young England group.

Richard Parkinson, a canon at the collegiate church,[48] wrote: 'there is far less personal communication between the master... and his workmen... than there is between the Duke of Wellington and the humblest labourer on his estate'.[49] Engels said, 'the town itself is peculiarly built so that a person may live in it for years, and go in and out daily without coming into contact with a working-people's quarter or even with workers, that is, so long as he confines his business to pleasure walks'. This, he argued, was because the working people's quarters were sharply separated from the sections of the city reserved for the middle class. The central commercial district was surrounded by a girdle of unmixed working people's quarters averaging a mile and a half in breadth. Beyond this lay the middle bourgeoisie and beyond them the upper bourgeoisie with gardens in Chorlton and Ardwick, or on the breezy heights of Cheetham Hill, Broughton and Pendleton. 'I have never seen so systematic a shutting out of the working men from the thoroughfares, so tender a concealment of everything which might affront the eye and nerves of the bourgeoisie, as in Manchester.'[50] Engels was by no means the first to make this point. In 1841 the Manchester Statistical Society had said that 'all the families of the comfortable class' had moved 'to the outer townships; whereby large tracts of the town remain occupied solely by operatives'.[51]

48   Later the cathedral.

49   R. Parkinson, *On the Present Condition of the Labouring Poor in Manchester* (London: Simpkin, Marshall; Manchester: Sims & Dinham, 1841), p. 13.

50   Frederick Engels, *The Condition of the Working Class in England in 1844* (London: Swan Sonnenschein, 1892), pp. 45–7.

51   Quoted in T. S. Ashton, *Economic and Social Investigations in Manchester* (London: P. S. King, 1934), p. 57.

The poor were less well known to their wealthy neighbours 'than the inhabitants of New Zealand or Kamtschatka', William Cooke Taylor wrote.[52] Cobden emphasised another aspect of class division:

> It is well understood … that if the shopkeeper's family is not formally interdicted from entering our public assemblies they will not be consulting their own interest or enjoyment by attending them, and the retailer would find it probably almost as difficult to gain admission to our clubs and concerts as he might to obtain the privilege of 'entrée' to the Queen's court. The wholesale dealer in fustians or fents, whose bundles occupy a garret or cellar from which they only issue in the gross, however vulgar in mind or ill-bred in manners, are admitted without difficulty to places of privileged resort from which the mercer or the jeweller, with perhaps ten times the wealth and whose vocation demands some refinement of manners and cultivation of mind, would find himself excluded.[53]

Taylor also said that the factory operatives were badly lodged and the dwellings of the class below them were the most wretched that can be conceived. This was particularly the case in the township of Manchester: its narrow streets, its courts and cellars, had been abandoned to the poorest grade of all.[54] The contrast was brought out in the mortality statistics. P. H. Holland, a surgeon reporting in July 1844 on the public heath of Chorlton-on-Medlock over the five years ending in June 1843, said that a low rate of mortality had constantly accompanied a good condition of streets and dwellings and a high rate the contrary condition. There was a striking difference with a rate of mortality of 1.9 per cent in first-class streets and houses and 4 per cent in the third or worst class of streets and houses,

52 Taylor, *Notes of a Tour*, p. 12.
53 Richard Cobden, *Incorporate Your Borough*, 1837, reproduced in W. E. A. Axon, *Cobden as a Citizen: A Chapter in Manchester's History* (London: T. Fisher Unwin, 1907), p. 148.
54 Taylor, *Notes of a Tour*, p. 12.

inhabited exclusively by the poor, where the worst-lodged, the worst-fed and the most overworked part of the population lived. Moreover they were severe sufferers from the pressure of poor trade and bad food.[55]

Whether the living standards of the workers were deteriorating is a question on which historians have tended to place different emphases. The historian of Manchester's food supply, Roger Scola, points out that in Lancashire it appears that there were significant though highly variable wage increases between the 1820s and 1840s, while within the cotton industry pressure on spinners' piece rates was offset by higher productivity, leaving wages fairly stable. However, for the most part real wage gains were underpinned by moderate prices. Potatoes, carrots and substantial imports of Irish butter, bacon and ham as well as livestock after 1839 led to improvements. He concludes that the Manchester evidence seems to lend support to the more optimistic view of living standards in these years and warns that the impression of a total catastrophe to which a casual reading of Adshead might give rise is not altogether warranted since there were numerous wage earners who held on to their employment and would have been able to ride these difficult years, although even a partial loss of earnings could affect dietary standards. The main political protests like Peterloo and the Plug Plot were associated with distress and occurred in periods of business depression. When the cotton trade was in the doldrums and/ or commodity prices were high, living standards deteriorated materially. In more normal times the cotton industry afforded its operatives reasonable prosperity.[56] However, nationally, most recent new research findings have given increased, though not unambiguous, support to more pessimistic views, particularly taking account of further work on prices: real wages only

55   Printed as an appendix to the First Report of the Royal Commissioners for Inquiry into the State of Large Towns and Populous Districts, PP 1844 (572) XVII, 1. (*MG* 31 July 1844 contained a lengthy report.)

56   Scola, *Feeding the Victorian City*, pp. 261, 275; Richard K. Fleischman, *Conditions of Life among the Cotton Workers of Southeastern Lancashire During the Industrial Revolution, 1750–1850* (New York and London: Garland Publishing, 1985), pp. 353–4.

rose by small amounts, and some of the gains were probably made at the cost of more intensive work performed in more dangerous and more unhealthy workplaces, and many lived in crowded and unhygienic buildings which kept infant mortality high. Observers no doubt generally described what they saw accurately. For some life was extremely hard. The numbers adversely affected grew in 1841 and 1842.[57]

The living conditions of the workers in Manchester had been brought to public notice by the report on *The Moral and Physical Condition of the Working Classes of Manchester* largely by Dr J. P. Kay, medical officer at the Ardwick and Ancoats Dispensary, but also secretary of the special board set up following the cholera epidemic of 1832. Not confining the remit to cholera and its causes, he found that near the centre of town, a mass of buildings, inhabited by prostitutes and thieves, was intersected by narrow and loathsome streets, and close courts defiled with refuse. In Parliament Street there was only one privy for 380 inhabitants which was placed in a narrow passage, whence its effluvia infected the adjacent houses, and must have provided a fertile source of disease.[58] Ten years later the courts behind the lower part of Long Millgate contained the most horrible dwellings which Engels had seen:

> He who turns to the left from… Lower Millgate is lost; he wanders from one court to another, turns countless corners, passes nothing but narrow, filthy nooks and alleys, until… he… knows not whither to turn… rarely a wooden or stone floor is to be seen in the houses, almost uniformly broken, ill-fitting windows and doors and a state of filth. Everywhere heaps of debris, refuse and offal; standing pools for gutters and a stench which alone would make it impossible for a human being in any degree civilised to live

57   Hans-Joachim Voth, 'Living standards and the urban environment', in Roderick Floud and Paul Johnson (eds), *Cambridge Economic History of Modern Britain* (3 vols, Cambridge: Cambridge University Press, 2004), i. 268–94, at pp. 273, 293.

58   James P. Kay, *The Moral and Physical Condition of the Working Classes Employed in the Cotton Industries of Manchester* (London: James Ridgeway, 1832), p. 23.

in such a district. Nearby was a chaos of small one-storied one roomed huts, kitchen, living and sleeping room all in one, a whole collection of cattle-sheds for human beings.[59]

This was precisely the area which Watkin visited in late July 1844, first with Archibald Prentice and then with Ross, his fellow secretary on the Public Parks Committee, when he recorded his shock at the people looking as if they had risen out of the dung to life, like maggots. Strange, he commented, that within five minutes' walk of the Exchange this should exist.[60] Watkin does not explain the reasons for his visit, but given that he went first with Prentice, the editor of the *Manchester Times*, and had described some of the living conditions of the workers in his article in the *Times* advocating the establishment of public parks in Manchester which appeared two days prior to his visit, Prentice may well have suggested he should see for himself. Watkin later took Ross, his fellow secretary on the Public Parks Committee, to make sure that he too had seen the situation.[61]

Although this was the only visit to such an area that he recorded, and almost all his social and business contacts were with people of his own class (and perhaps sometimes of a higher class), he was familiar with working men, if not their homes. He was secretary of the Operatives Anti-Corn Law Association, attended meetings in the Queen Anne public house, itself in Long Millgate, and visited various districts to recruit signatures for the requisition for the meeting in Stevenson Square in June 1841. He also went to Kennedy's engineering works in Cable Street. In November 1844 when seeking support and subscriptions for public parks he addressed meetings of workmen at Sharp Bros & Co. and at Whitworth & Co., but the employees at these engineering establishments were likely to have been at the upper end of the working class. He did, particularly after his attachment to Mary Mellor, mix with

59 Engels, *Working Class*, pp. 50–1.
60 Diary entry for 3 August 1844.
61 The article is reproduced in the Appendix, together with other articles on public parks.

mill-owners and also attended with her a tea party of female operatives, but there is no reference in the diary to working conditions in the mills. However, his articles in the *Manchester Times* and *Manchester Guardian* advocating public parks make it absolutely clear that he was well aware, if for the most part from secondary sources, of the living and working conditions of the working classes and saw the provision of parks as something which would improve the lot of the poor, though not attack the causes.

That Watkin was not oblivious to the conditions of workers in cotton mills in Manchester is also shown by his comments on the mills of Massachusetts in the course of his tour of the United States and Canada in 1851. He then visited Lowell, the Manchester of America as he called it, where he thought the mills well and tastefully built with more air, room and space for moving about than he usually saw in Lancashire. At the Massachusetts Manufacturing Company's works, which manufactured a range of textiles, he said much of the machinery, all steam powered, was new and about 1,000 hands were employed, many of them young women, who lived in boarding houses under strict surveillance. The carpet looms were 'attended by a posse of as good looking damsels as I ever saw together, (straight, tall, clear complexions and high foreheads), and all the hands certainly had a better look, both in person and in dress', than Lancashire hands usually had. 'They are looked after like the members of a family and well paid, hence the appearance they make.' He added that the English and Irish young ladies among them made a great contrast.[62]

Local government and parliamentary reform

In 1835 de Tocqueville not only noted the prevalence of the Irish, the crowded and dreadful housing, the unclean and unpaved streets, and the disastrous separation of classes, but added that 'everything in the exterior appearance of the city attested to

62   E. W. Watkin, *A Trip to the United States and Canada: In a Series of Letters* (London: W. H. Smith, 1852), pp. 91, 93.

the individual powers of man; nothing to the directing powers of society. At every turn human liberty shows its capricious creative force. There is no trace of the slow continuous action of government.'[63] Certainly Manchester in the eighteenth century lacked the structures present in most towns. Defoe had called it one of the 'greatest, if not the greatest meer village in England. It is neither a wall'd town, city or corporation; they send no member to parliament; and the highest magistrate they have is a constable or head borough.'[64] Indeed until 1765 the township of Manchester had the status of a village. It was governed by the Court Leet of the lords of the manor, the Mosley family. Every year the Court Leet chose unpaid officers who administered such municipal services as existed at the time: the borough reeve, the day police etc. It is, however, debatable whether Manchester would have been better served by the kind of governmental structure which existed in towns with charters of incorporation. Aiken, a contemporary observer, wrote that Manchester 'remains an open town, destitute (probably to its advantage) of a corporation, and unrepresented in Parliament'.[65] However, while Manchester's development may have benefited by not being shackled by an old-fashioned corporation, it suffered because nothing effective took its place. When powers were obtained in the first Manchester and Salford Police Act of 1765 under which Cleansing and Lighting Commissioners were established, they were not effectively exercised, and when further powers were obtained in 1792 they made little difference. The lord of the manor had a monopoly of markets and incurred strong criticism on this and other grounds in the late eighteenth century and again in the 1820s and 1830s, even though in practice his rights were being eroded. 'The markets

---

63 A. de Tocqueville, *Journeys to England and Ireland*, translated by G. Lawrence and K. P. Mayer, ed. J. P. Mayer (London: Faber & Faber, 1955), p. 105.

64 Daniel Defoe, *A Tour through the Whole Island of Great Britain*, ed. G. H. D. Cole (2 vols, London: Peter Davis, 1927), ii. 670.

65 J. Aiken, *A Description of the Country from Thirty to Forty Miles Round Manchester* (London: John Stockdale, 1795), p. 191.

are not such as a town of great wealth and magnitude might be expected to possess', wrote Wheeler in his history of Manchester in 1836.[66]

The lack of an adequate system of local government was reflected in the want of representation of Manchester in Parliament, a situation which became increasingly anomalous as Manchester grew in size. Prentice listed a large number of boroughs returning two members of Parliament which were much smaller than Manchester, and one of the key objects of the Manchester reformers was to secure representation for the town. In the 1790s Thomas Walker, to whose memory Watkin raised a toast at the St Anne's Ward Reform Association dinner in 1844,[67] had founded the Constitutional Society with a number of merchants, manufacturers and professional men. The only specific demands were for better representation of the people in Parliament and a shortening of the life of parliaments below seven years. Though Walker had been borough reeve in 1790 the movement aroused much hostility from the Church and King Club particularly because of visits to France by some associated with the Society where they praised the Jacobins. Walker's house was attacked and he was tried for conspiring and confederating by force of arms to overthrow the constitution and government and to help France. The jury, however, acquitted him.

In the first decades of the nineteenth century there were some improvements in local government. In 1816 and 1817 the commissioners introduced gas lighting and established a municipal gasworks using the profits for paving and refuse disposal. In 1829 they greatly increased the number of watchmen and reformed the organisation. Nevertheless by the 1830s the system was regarded by many as unsatisfactory. Only about 2.5 per cent of the population could vote for the commissioners. Manchester politics from the 1780s, especially following the victory of Church and King in 1792, had been dominated by

---

66   Scola, *Feeding the Victorian City*, pp. 150–61; James Wheeler, *Manchester: Its Political, Social and Commercial History, Ancient and Modern* (London: Simpkin, Marshall & Co., 1836), p. 347.

67   Diary entry for 30 Mar 1844.

the Tory and Anglican groups which largely overlapped. Their dominance was such that the Literary and Philosophical Society founded in 1781 had originally exhibited a philosophical and political bias in its proceedings, but scientific investigation came to predominate in the prevailing political atmosphere. The opposition to the Corn Law in 1815 was one of the first occasions in the new century when the liberals attempted to take a stand. In the coming years the nucleus of Manchester's respectable reformers was provided 'by a small but determined band' who, though not a formal group, were as individuals involved in most of the reform movements. The band consisted of Archibald Prentice, Thomas and Richard Potter, J. E. Taylor, John Shuttleworth, F. R. Atkinson, Edward Baxter, Joseph Brotherton, William Harvey, J. B. Smith and Absalom Watkin.[68] In 1819 Peterloo, when the Manchester Yeomanry

68   The phrase 'by a small but determined band' is Richard Potter's, quoted in A. Prentice, *Historical Sketches and Personal Recollections of Manchester* (London: Charles Gilpin, 1851), p. 74. Prentice was successively editor of the *Manchester Gazette* and the *Manchester Times* and an influential member of the ACLL. Thomas Potter, head of Potter & Norris, leader in the campaign for Manchester's incorporation, was the town's first mayor 1838–40. Knighted 1840. His brother, Richard, known as Radical Dick, was MP for Wigan from 1832 where he was nominated by the cotton interest to counter the dominance of the earl of Crawford. Resigned 1839 because of ill health. Died 1842. Taylor was a partner in John Shuttleworth's business dealing in cotton, twist and warp until 1823 when he became full-time editor of the *Manchester Guardian* until his death in 1844. Shuttleworth was later a police commissioner, the local distributor of stamps, and alderman. Fenton Robinson Atkinson was a lawyer with literary and artistic tastes; 'an able lawyer with a thorough hatred of oppression', he was Taylor's solicitor at his libel trial (Prentice, *Historical Sketches*, p. 73). Like his friend James Crossley, he was a book collector. Baxter was a cotton merchant of considerable wealth who built up a large art collection. Brotherton was a cotton manufacturer in partnership with Harvey, his brother-in-law, until 1819 when he retired with a modest fortune. MP for Salford from 1832 to 1857. Harvey continued as a cotton spinner, constable of Salford in 1834 and later twice mayor. J. B. Smith was a cotton spinner who like Brotherton retired early (1836) and became a leading member of the ACLL and from 1847 to 1874 successively MP for Stirling and Stockport. More detailed biographical descriptions of the members of the band are included in Michael J. Turner, *Reform and Respectability: The Making of a Middle-Class Liberalism in early Nineteenth-Century Manchester*, Chetham Society, 3rd ser., XL (Manchester: Chetham Society, 1995), pp. 7–31.

(led by the Tory Major H. H. Birley) charged a reform meeting in St Peter's Field and at least eleven people were killed and over 600 injured, was a devastating setback, but Prentice and Taylor immediately sent accounts to the London papers establishing the radical view of events. Both were involved in the setting up of reformist newspapers in the 1820s supported by other members of the band, who also organised successive campaigns against church rates and police commission powers. Gradually they and their allies challenged the entrenched conservative oligarchy, though with few major successes before 1832.

It was only then that representation of Manchester was secured, after Manchester reformers, including Absalom Watkin, played a substantial part in the campaign leading up to the Great Reform Act. As a result Mark Philips and C. E. Poulett Thomson were elected as the first MPs for Manchester.

Meanwhile Manchester reformers had supported the passage of the Municipal Corporations Act of 1835 – Absalom had been asked to draw up a petition to the House of Lords in favour of the bill, and also a Memorial to Lord Melbourne, the Prime Minister.[69] However, the direct application of the provisions of the Act was limited to existing municipal corporations. It was 1838 before Manchester seriously attempted to change the position, the lead being taken by Richard Cobden. He was born in 1804 and so was of a different generation from that of the members of the band who were contemporaries of Absalom, all born between 1773 and 1794. It was the Municipal Corporations Act which first brought him into prominence in public life in Manchester where he had a calico-printing business. Partly because he was incensed by the power of the Mosleys, the lords of the manor, to penalise William Nield who did not wish to take up the appointment of borough reeve when it fell to him, he published a pamphlet, *Incorporate Your Borough*, advocating adoption of the provisions of the Municipal Reform Act to Manchester, and took the lead at the town meeting in February 1838 which agreed to petition the Queen in council for incorporation. He was quick to make the

69   Goffin, p. 174.

comparison between the smaller Stockport, a longer-standing incorporated town reformed under the Act, where he had stood unsuccessfully for Parliament in 1837, and its much larger neighbour, Manchester. However, the Tory and Anglican group who had largely controlled local government in Manchester counter-petitioned. It was when commissioners appointed by the Government found that their petition was supported by many bogus signatures that the reformers succeeded. A royal charter creating a municipal borough was therefore granted in November 1838. This was the real breakthrough with the reformers' victory enhanced by the refusal of the Tories to take part in the first elections for the new borough council. Initially the new council was dominated by large proprietors, so that municipal affairs were directed by the economic elite.[70]

In the 1830s the fear of public disorder and riot was reinforced by Kay's work on *The Moral and Physical Condition of the Working Classes* which, while rightly drawing attention to the physical filth and squalor of the slums, also attributed moral degeneracy to the slum dwellers. Consequently in 1839, particularly with a view to the police taking a more proactive role, a new borough police force was set up and all police in the borough were placed under the control of a single police commissioner, Sir Charles Shaw, succeeded by the first Chief Constable only in 1842.[71] Nevertheless the police commissioners formally continued in existence until 1841 and the Court Leet lasted until 1845 when the Corporation purchased from Sir Oswald Mosley the lordship of the manor and the right to hold markets and take tolls. Thus Edward Watkin's diary relates to a period when the

---

70   Alan J. Kidd, 'Introduction: the middle class in nineteenth-century Manchester', in Alan J. Kidd and K. W. Roberts (eds), *City, Class and Culture: Studies of Social Policy and Cultural Production in Victorian Manchester* (Manchester: Manchester University Press, 1985), pp. 1–24, at p. 14.

71   For a discussion of the various pressures leading to the establishment of the new police, see S. J. Davies, 'Classes and police in Manchester 1829–1880', in Kidd and Roberts (eds), *City, Class and Culture*, pp. 26–47, at pp. 30–2.

old system of government and the maintenance of order had virtually been superseded.

However, as historians have made clear in recent years, the fact that Manchester Tories supported an anachronistic system of town government did not mean that they differed in many respects from the reformers, particularly the less radical. The Tories too included great manufacturers like the Birleys, as well as many smaller ones, and when it came to economic policy, on matters of principle, particularly free trade, they were little different from the reformers, having a largely shared set of values in business and co-operating in many cultural and philanthropic activities. They were, however, a less cohesive group, largely Anglican, lacking the common educational and religious background of the leading liberal families of the Manchester and York academies and Cross Street chapel, who intermarried, and they were less attached to Manchester by family ties, often regarding themselves as county rather than Manchester families. However, religious, economic and social institutions all served similar functions as regards business networks and information flows.[72]

Moreover, to see the town of Manchester as a manifestation of a new industrial age with social and health problems on an unprecedented scale and run by middle-class manufacturers and merchants with little contact with the workers through an out-of-date system of government is to ignore the significant steps taken by that same middle class for scientific, cultural

72   The contrasts and similarities in and between the Reformers and the Tories are described in detail in V. A. C. Gattrell, 'Incorporation and the pursuit of liberal hegemony in Manchester 1790–1839', in Derek Fraser (ed.), *Municipal Reform and the Industrial City* (Leicester: Leicester University Press, 1982), pp. 15–60, at pp. 24–31. For networking, see J. Seed, 'Unitarianism, political economy and the antinomies of liberal culture in Manchester, 1830–50', *Social History*, 7 (1982), 1–25; and 'Theologies of power: Unitarianism and the social relations of religious discourse', in R. J. Morris (ed.), *Class, Power and Social Structure in British Nineteenth-Century Towns* (Leicester: Leicester University Press 1986), pp. 25–46; Anthony Howe, *The Cotton Masters, 1830–1860* (Oxford: Clarendon Press, 1984), esp. pp. 86–9; and also Gattrell, 'Incorporation and the pursuit of liberal hegemony', esp. p. 25.

and other ends, including the education of the workers. That they did so was in part a matter of civic pride, as will be seen in the example of the provision of public parks, and in part a fear that, unchecked, the disease, poverty and illiteracy could undermine their economic success. There was also a genuine philanthropic element, in part arising from the culture of dissent and particularly Unitarianism. Revd John Robberds, minister at Cross Street chapel for 43 years from 1811, told his congregation that to despair of bringing about beneficial changes in society was a kind of impiety: 'The individual was the trustee and steward of wealth in the management of which he is to keep in view the honour of God and the service of his fellow men.'[73] Philanthropy was also a matter of status as a high public profile of giving patronage to charity served to underpin the leaders' role as a middle-class elite. From the establishment of the Infirmary in 1752 to 1850 at least 49 voluntary charities were established. By the latter date involvement in charity had become one of the criteria necessary for Manchester Man, and analysis of membership of the boards of the Infirmary and two other charities has shown how dominant in numbers were those with a business background. Some clearly spent a considerable time in activities with little or no connection with their businesses.[74] Benjamin Braidley calculated that he spent over 36 hours a week 'on matters totally unconnected with my own business', including committee meetings, correspondence, social calls, and charitable and educational work.[75] Moreover the strength of the professional members of the middle class should not be forgotten. By 1851 there were 214 lawyers and barristers, 381 physicians and surgeons, 16 bankers and nearly 1,500 working as merchants, brokers, agents, accountants etc.

73   Quoted in Seed, 'Unitarianism', p. 5.

74   Peter Shapely, *Charity and Power in Victorian Manchester*, Chetham Society, 3rd ser., xliii (Manchester: Chetham Society, 2000), esp. pp. 23, 27, 63, 137.

75   Robin Pearson and David Richardson, 'Business networking in the Industrial Revolution', *Econ HR*, LIV (2001), 657–79, at p. 674, quoting Benjamin Braidley's *Memoirs*. Braidley was a cotton manufacturer, Tory and borough reeve in 1832. He published a work on Sunday Schools.

The professionals were often deeply involved with industry, and manufacturers and merchants like J. B. Smith and John Brooks were involved in banking or as directors of insurance companies. Manufacturing, commercial and professional functions were socially articulated in complicated but largely unexplored ways.[76] Watkin's diary is therefore useful in shedding light on these networks, as his contacts included lawyers, newspaper owners and editors, politicians and actors as well as merchants and manufacturers.

The institutions and recreations

Manchester's best-known voluntary society is perhaps the Literary and Philosophical Society, founded in 1781 with Dr Thomas Percival, a physician, and Thomas Henry, an apothecary and chemical manufacturer, both Fellows of the Royal Society, among the prominent members. From 1794 John Dalton was a member and the effective leader of the scientific community in Manchester, and the papers and discussions took a more scientific bias. By the 1840s in Dalton's declining years the Lit and Phil was not flourishing: it was to revive with Joule[77] as secretary from 1847, and Fairbairn and Hodgkinson were of considerable influence.[78] But this did not

---

76 John Seed and Janet Wolff, 'Introduction', in their *Culture of Capital*, pp. 1–15, at pp. 6–7. However, Stuart Jones, 'The Manchester cotton magnates move into banking, 1826–1850', *Textile History*, 9 (1978), 90–111, shows that manufacturers and merchants played a major part in banking.

77 James Joule: eminent physicist who came to the fore from 1840 with work on the measurement of electric current; president Lit and Phil 1860.

78 William Fairbairn set up an engineering works in Manchester with John Lillie in 1817, from 1824 in Canal Street. Built bridges, boats, steam engines, boilers and locomotives. President of the Institute of Mechanical Engineers, 1854. Member of Cross Street Chapel. Baronet 1869. Eaton Hodgkinson worked on the strength of metals, particularly cast iron. FRS 1840. President Lit and Phil 1848–50. Robert H. Kargon, *Science in Victorian Manchester: Enterprise and Expertise* (Manchester: Manchester University Press, 1977), p. 45.

mean that membership was confined to scientists. Four of the group of reformers – Prentice's 'band' – were members: Prentice himself, Shuttleworth, Taylor and Absalom Watkin. The last became a member in 1822. Indeed, as one historian put it, the Lit and Phil was perhaps more important as an instrument of social rather than industrial change, providing as it did the means through which a new wealthy urban elite could express themselves and legitimise their status in English society.[79] Many of this elite were undeserving of being regarded as philistines, the term which has often been levelled at hard-nosed northern manufacturers. Indeed some had substantial art collections, and Agnews had a thriving business.[80] The Chetham Society was founded in 1843 at the height of the ACLL's campaign with an overlap of membership.[81] However, if scientific interests and the Lit and Phil, like art exhibitions and concerts, as well as property, could unify the middle class and transcend party, urban bourgeois culture was also confined and exclusive, directed by self-selecting urban elites based on the home or clubs and societies, membership of which was bounded by high annual subscriptions.[82]

Other scientific bodies were founded. In 1821 the Manchester Society for the Promotion of Natural History was set up. Two years later the Royal Manchester Institution was established under George W. Wood's leadership to establish an art gallery, to provide facilities for public lectures in the arts and sciences and to provide technical instruction for the labouring classes.[83] At

79 Michael E. Rose, 'Culture, philanthropy and the Manchester middle classes', in Kidd and Roberts (eds), *City, Class and Culture*, pp. 103–17, at p. 110.

80 John Seed, '"Commerce and the liberal arts": the political economy of art in Manchester, 1775–1860', in Seed and Wolff (eds), *Culture of Capital*, pp. 45–81, at p. 45.

81 Seed and Wolff, 'Introduction', p. 7.

82 Gunn, *Public Culture of the Victorian Middle Class*, pp. 26, 28.

83 George W. Wood, merchant, MP for Lancashire and then Kendal. A Whig, prominent in Manchester reform circles. Helped finance the *Manchester Guardian*. Also a Unitarian (Mosley St. and Brook St. Chapels).

the preliminary meeting Wood declared that such an enterprise would allow Manchester to show the world that England was not merely a nation of shopkeepers. The venture was widely supported by leading Mancunians who soon subscribed enough to erect a building in Mosley Street designed by Barry. However Wood found that his plan to provide technical instruction for workers was not widely supported, probably because the upper middle class in Manchester was not willing to support by donations or personal attendance any organisation which provided for the mixing of the classes.

William Fairbairn and Richard Roberts, two of Manchester's leading engineering employers, with Wood, Benjamin Heywood[84] and others, therefore established the Mechanics' Institute. In the first place it offered mechanics and artisans the opportunity to attend classes of a scientific and technical character. It was not a complete success. For some years it had to withstand competition from the New Mechanics' Institute set up and managed by artisans and mechanics themselves though its own management became more democratic. In the 1830s other mechanics' institutes were founded at Miles Platting and Salford, that at Miles Platting being a development from the working-class housing and mission established by Benjamin Heywood.[85] But their limited success led to the introduction of Lyceums from 1838 with lower membership fees, a more democratic ethos, if not working-class control, and the provision of news rooms. The classes mainly provided more basic instruction in reading, writing and arithmetic, and sewing and knitting. By the 1840s the Mechanics' Institutes themselves had adjusted their sights and were providing enrolments of clerks, warehousemen and shopkeepers for basic

---

84   Roberts, inventor of the self-acting mule and owner of engineering works. Benjamin Heywood, eldest son of Nathaniel Heywood and his wife, the daughter of Thomas Percival, who opened Heywood's Bank in Manchester in 1778. Succeeded father in management of bank 1828. MP for Lancashire 1831. Created baronet 1838, FRS 1843. Prominent member of Cross Street Unitarian Chapel where he and two of his brothers were trustees.

85   Seed, 'Unitarianism', p. 15.

grammar, reading, writing and arithmetic who outnumbered the mechanics attending science classes. Watkin went to a meeting at the institute at Bury in October 1844 where 'we got them out of debt by a little arrangement' and he attended an exhibition at the Oldham Lyceum.[86] However, there was also an exhibition in 1840, open to the working classes and organised by the Manchester Mechanics' Institute, of paintings loaned by Manchester collectors, including ones by Turner, West, Landseer and Eastlake.[87] More generally there was a growth of educational provision in the later 1830s and 1840s and an increase in activities such as missions and home visiting, in part because the Anglican Church diverted money to parish work in working-class areas.[88]

Two other learned societies were flourishing in the 1840s, the Manchester Statistical Society and the Manchester Geological Society. The former was founded in 1834 when it began to collect data on social conditions in Manchester. The latter was started in 1838. What was remarkable was how far these societies relied on the initiative and financial support of the same group of leaders of Manchester society. Benjamin Heywood was the banker for the Geological Society. James Heywood[89] was one of the principal founders of the society and a founder member of the Statistical Society. William Langton[90] was also a founder member. Shuttleworth was an active member.

---

86 Martin Hewitt discusses the extent to which the middle-class elite retained control of the mechanics' institutes and similar bodies as a form of 'moral imperialism', and the role of workers in *The Emergence of Stability in the Industrial City: Manchester, 1832–67* (Aldershot: Scolar Press, 1996), pp. 66–91; diary entries for 18 Oct 1844 and 24 Mar 1845.

87 Seed, '"Commerce and the liberal arts"', p. 69.

88 Seed, 'Unitarianism', pp. 15–16.

89 Youngest of five sons of Nathaniel Heywood. After a legacy from his uncle, Benjamin, also a banker, went to Cambridge University and was called to the Bar. Took up scientific and literary pursuits. Liberal MP for N. Lancs. 1847–57, FRS.

90 William Langton worked in Heywood's Bank. Later managing director of the Manchester and Salford Bank. At the time of the diary was Treasurer of the Athenaeum.

Both Heywoods and Langton were to play prominent parts in the Athenaeum Club for the Advancement and Diffusion of Knowledge in 1836. Lord Francis Egerton[91] was president of the Geological Society. He was to serve as president when the British Association met in Manchester in 1842. Dalton and Benjamin Heywood were vice-presidents, and James Heywood one of the secretaries.

One of the reasons for the founding of the Statistical Society was the recognition that analysis of living and health conditions was necessary following the cholera epidemic of 1832. This also gave rise to the Manchester and Salford District Provident Society set up in 1833 of which Kay was a founder member as were Langton and the two Heywoods.

Edward as well as Absalom was a member of the Manchester Literary Society, which is to be distinguished from the Manchester Literary and Philosophical Society. The Literary Society was founded by a group of Manchester Whigs in about 1815 and 'prudently suspended its meetings' in 1817 because of the Tory Government's crackdown on public meetings. It was revived in 1826.[92] The diary contains frequent references to the meetings in which Edward was actively involved as a presenter of papers and as a debater.

Cobden, when he was in the United States in the 1830s, had seen the big crop of institutions there, but on his return found nothing in Manchester except the Mechanics' Institute. There was nothing for the 'middling classes', 'including our clerks and helpers in warehouses and stores'. A proposal to remedy this went ahead under the presidency of James Heywood, with Cobden initially the chairman of the directing committee. The Athenaeum Club for the Advancement and Diffusion of

91 Lord Francis Egerton, son of the marquess of Stafford (later first duke of Sutherland), Eton and Christ Church, Oxford. MP for S. Lancs. from 1835. He lived at Worsley House. An early promoter of free trade and of London University. Also president of the Manchester Botanical and Horticultural, and Agricultural Societies. Fellow of the Geological Society of London. Poet. Created earl of Ellesmere 1846.

92 Thomas Baker, 'An account of the Manchester Literary Society' (MCL, MS 373–4273C1) *c.*1868.

Knowledge was founded.[93] The opening meeting was held at the Royal Institution on 11 January 1836 when Absalom seconded a vote of thanks to the directors.[94] The foundation stone for the new building for the Athenaeum in Princess Street, on a site next to the Royal Manchester Institution in Mosley Street (both now form the City Art Gallery), was laid on 26 May 1837 and it was opened in October 1839. The building, also designed by Charles Barry, was costly, and the Athenaeum's success as an institution was limited as it became an area of conflict between Cobdenite and other liberals, perhaps because of Cobden's involvement but also because it chose to open on Sundays. Consequently the directors were forced to borrow. Edward was only involved in the management after the finances got into difficulty, becoming a director in April 1843. He was the honorary secretary, with Peter Berlyn,[95] for the great bazaar held to raise funds and for the literary soirée in October 1843 to which they invited Charles Dickens.[96]

The extracts from Watkin's diary for 1843 record the visit of Dickens for the soirée in October 1843. Watkin invited Charles Dickens to preside, approaching him through his sister, Fanny Burnett, who lived in Higher Ardwick, her husband, the singer Henry Burnett, having moved to Manchester in 1841.[97] Dickens was then 32, and had just returned from America. He

93 Watkin, *Cobden*, p. 115.

94 *AWJ*, p. 184.

95 'I did my best [for the Athenaeum] with the able aid of my secretarial colleague, Peter Berlyn' (Watkin, *Cobden*, p. 114). Peter Berlyn was almost an exact contemporary of Watkin. Of German birth, he was for some years connected with Salis Schwabe, calico printers. He became a member of the Athenaeum in 1837 and with Watkin was elected a director in 1843. He was very active in the Athenaeum Essay and Discussion Society. He resigned in 1846 in circumstances 'which conveyed no blame to him individually except in following a system in which others were deeply engaged with him' (*MG*, 31 Jan 1846). He died in 1885, aged 67.

96 Shapely points out that the fund-raising techniques of the Atheneum, and indeed of the ACLL, were typical of those adopted by charities in Manchester: *Charity and Power*, p. 31.

97 Watkin, *Cobden*, pp. 114, 123; *MG*, 5 July 1843.

had published *American Notes for General Circulation* but not yet *Martin Chuzzlewit*. He had visited Manchester in 1838 and 1839 with Harrison Ainsworth, when at Gilbert Winter's house he met William and Duncan Grant on whom he modelled the Cheeryble brothers in *Nicholas Nickleby*.[98] Dickens conceived of the idea of *A Christmas Carol* when hurrying through the streets of Manchester. He said he came to Manchester to be victimised on the altars of the Manchester Athenaeum[99] and spoke on a matter which was always nearest his heart, the education of the very poor, protesting against calling a little learning dangerous. He described taking Longfellow to see the poor in the nightly refuges of London and contrasted this with the unspeakable consolation and blessings that a little knowledge had shed on men of the lowest estate and most hopeless means. Dickens told Watkin that he was pleased with his visit and that the proceedings were remarkably well reported.[100] Disraeli happened to be in Manchester and at Cobden's suggestion he was invited at short notice and spoke. While Watkin simply records that Cobden had asked him to call and they invited him accordingly, Mrs Disraeli said that Disraeli declined to attend when asked by the original deputation, but they then sent a deputation of ladies whom he could not refuse. In his speech he denounced as vulgar and superficial the prejudice which associated with commerce and industry an inability to sympathise with the fair inventions of art or the poetic creations of the human intellect, and held up the examples of the merchants of Venice, the Medici and the manufacturers of Flanders.[101]

98   F. R. Dean, 'Dickens and Manchester', *The Dickensian*, 34 (1938), 111–18, at p. 111. Gilbert Winter was a Manchester merchant, borough reeve in 1823–24. A Tory. The Grant brothers of Ramsbottom were well known for personal acts of giving to the needy. Dickens believed Daniel Grant to have given away £600,000 in his lifetime – 'extravagantly perhaps', commented Howe, *Cotton Masters*, pp. 274, 302.

99   F. Kaplan, *Dickens: A Biography* (London: Hodder & Stoughton, 1988), p. 159, quoting Dickens' letter to Fanny Burnett of 5 June 1843.

100 Dean, 'Dickens and Manchester', p. 111.

101 William Flavelle Monypenny and George Earle Buckle, *The Life of Benjamin Disraeli, Earl of Beaconsfield* (2nd edn, 3 vols, London: John Murray, 1929), i. 581–2.

By early 1844 the fortunes of the Athenaeum had revived. The annual meeting on 31 January 1844, over which Absalom presided and at which Edward briefly spoke, heard that membership, over 1,100 in 1837, had dropped to 700 in 1841, but was then 1,500 and the debt nearly liquidated. Edward, however, was disappointed not to head the poll in the election of directors, doubtless a case of unrealistic youthful expectations.[102] The diary records his participation in debates, his attendance at directors' meetings and above all the preparations for, and the visit of, Disraeli and his wife to the soirée in October 1844. In 1845 he was busy with the attempt to pay off the mortgage debt, though on 6 July he records that his canvassing had met with some rebuff and he thought the members and directors were not giving their wholehearted support. The profits from the soirée in October 1845 were devoted to the reduction of the mortgage but, although Watkin was one of the instigators and attended, his duties with the Trent Valley Railway doubtless prevented his playing any major part in the preparations, though he did not sever his links completely and was re-elected to the committee in January 1846.[103]

The Saturday half-holiday

At the beginning of his diary for 1844 Watkin referred to his achievements in 1843. These include his 'talking and services' which 'in one way or another' had aided in 'gaining the half-holiday since that regulation, provided it be permanent, bids fair to be the fruitful parent of happiness and good to the vast number of sensible people and at no harm to the fools'. This did not benefit factory workers. The campaign was on behalf of clerks in warehouses. It began with a public meeting on 28 August 1843 when William Marsden, a contemporary of Watkin's and the leading spirit in the campaign, was elected to the chair.[104]

102 *MG*, 3 Feb 1844; diary entry for 1 Feb 1844.
103 *MG*, 31 Jan 1846.
104 Marsden, the only son of .Henry Marsden of Marsden & Chappell, Cannon Street, died in 1848, aged only 29. A memorial in St John's Church, Deansgate, now demolished, commemorated his life and achievement.

Marsden claimed that there were fewer holidays in England than in any other country in the world. William Harvey, one of the band, well known as a charitable and philanthropic employer, moved the main motion which was seconded by Watkin. He denied it was an assemblage of idle people to protest against work. Labour was honourable and he respected the men who laboured at however mean an occupation more than those who did nothing for the public good.

At the second meeting there was some discussion as to whether the half-day should be on Friday, which was then the custom in some solicitors' offices, or Saturday, but the meeting decided on the latter. Watkin later argued that a Saturday half-holiday would protect the Sabbath. At this meeting it was agreed to approach employers. Despite considerable opposition and a reluctance to be first in the field, in November it was reported that 441 firms as well as over 40 carriers had agreed to the half-holiday which began forthwith. Absalom wrote on 4 November: 'today, the giving of a half-holiday on Saturdays to people employed in warehouses, etc., commenced. About 500 warehouses were closed at 1, 2, or 3 o'clock.' On 29 November there was a soirée to celebrate the weekly half-holiday 'liberally conceded by the employers of Manchester to their salesmen and clerks and as a mark of respect to the committee'.[105] Watkin in his speech at the soirée told how the victory had been won. In his account there was utter and entire objection to a Friday half-holiday on the part of all the members of the influential Croaker family (presumably an after-dinner allusion to those he termed 'the great guns' in his diary), when Alderman Armitage, 'an ever constant friend of his less fortunate fellowmen', invited to dinner a number of his fellow tradesmen – the aristocracy of the town – and after dinner forcefully put the case. The company agreed that more leisure was needed and, provided Saturday was asked for, no serious objection would be raised.[106]

105 *MG*, 30 Aug, 27 Sept and 29 Nov 1843; *Manchester City News*, 8 Feb 1930; and Leo H. Grindon, *Manchester Banks and Bankers* (Manchester: Palmer & Howe, 1877), pp. 174–5.

106 Elkanah Armitage, cotton manufacturer and merchant. Manchester alderman. Mayor 1848, when knighted.

Parks

In his speech at the half-day holiday soirée Watkin also went on to venture on new ground by introducing the subject of providing parks at public expense in order for the proper use of leisure time. Manchester should ask for the return of a small portion of its contribution to public funds devoted to the formation of a park with a public playground with a public pond in which Her Majesty's lieges might bathe in summer. This would become one of Watkin's main interests in 1844, and is recorded in the diary. Watkin was both organiser and publicist, acting as joint secretary to the committee and writing articles for the Manchester newspapers which are reproduced here, together with the submission Watkin wrote as briefing for the meeting with Peel in 1845.[107]

Even in the 1830s and 1840s many of the houses of the merchant and professional classes were quite near the open country. When the Gaskells moved into 121 Upper Rumford Street their home was only one and a half miles from the very middle of Manchester, but they looked into fields, 'not very pretty or rural fields … but in which the children can see cows milked and hay made in summer time'.[108] But this was less and less possible for most of the poor who lived in the inner areas, though the Greenheys Fields, near the Gaskells, were the resort of factory girls and young men as well as John Barton and George Wilson and their wives and families. However, this was an unplanned remainder of an earlier society. In the early nineteenth century, with increasing urbanisation and the creation of squalid towns, most workers lived near the factories at which they were employed. As towns grew they were less able to reach open spaces and the fresh air of the countryside. This was a long-standing problem in Manchester. Nationally Robert Slaney, then MP for Shrewsbury, obtained, and subsequently

---

107   For Watkin's speech at the soirée *see Manchester and Salford Advertiser*, 2 Dec 1843. For his articles on the campaign for parks see the Appendix.

108   *The Letters of Mrs Gaskell*, ed. J. A. V. Chapple and Arthur Pollard (Manchester: Manchester University Press, 1966), p. 81.

chaired, a Select Committee of the House of Commons in 1833 on the means of providing open spaces in the vicinity of populous towns as public walks and places of exercise, calculated to promote the health, happiness and comfort of the inhabitants. G. W. Wood, MP for South Lancashire, and Sir Oswald Mosley, then MP for North Staffordshire, were members of the committee. The committee found that there were not enough open spaces. However, despite evidence on the needs of Manchester from Mark Philips, Benjamin Braidley, then the borough reeve, Richard Potter, Joseph Brotherton and J. P. Kay, particular recommendations were largely confined to London. Kay, who gave written evidence, said the entire labouring population was without any season of recreation and was ignorant of all amusements. Were parks provided recreations would be taken with avidity, and one of the first results would be a better use of Sunday and a substitution of innocent amusements at all other times for the debasing pleasures then in vogue.[109] Although the committee accepted that as respects those employed in the three great manufactures of the kingdom, cotton, woollen and hardware, creating annually an immense property, no provision had been made to afford them the means of healthy exercise or cheerful amusement on their holidays or days of rest, only London was the subject of specific recommendations. The need for a park to serve the East End was identified. Victoria Park in Hackney, Bow and Bethnal Green was developed, the purchase of the land paid for by a royal grant from the sale of the lease of York House to the duke of Sutherland. The committee's report made much less impact on provincial towns, where provision was less and the need was often greater.[110] Although Manchester had its pleasure grounds – Pomona in Hulme, Vauxhall Gardens in Collyhurst and Belle Vue at Longsight – these were not free.

109 PP 1833 (448), XV, Report from the Select Committee on Public Walks, 4.

110 Susan Lasdun, *The English Park: Royal, Private and Public* (London: Deutsch, 1991), pp. 137–8, for the debate on public walks – the committee is usually known as the Committee on Public Walks.

Although both Braidley and more strongly Richard Potter had told the 1833 committee that a public subscription could be raised for a park, nothing was done in Manchester for ten years, and elsewhere there were few developments. Derby's Arboretum, the gift of Joseph Strutt, and Norfolk Park, Sheffield, donated by the duke of Norfolk, were exceptions. In 1842–44 Princes Park in Liverpool was developed as a combined housing and park development on land purchased by Richard Vaughan Yates, an iron merchant and philanthropist, from the earl of Sefton for £50,000, though in Derby and Liverpool access for the general public was restricted. In 1844 considerable publicity was given to the cause and a campaign got under way. When writing in 1843 to decline an invitation to speak at an Athenaeum soirée Thomas Carlyle told Watkin:

> I have regretted much in looking at your great Manchester, and its thousand industries and conquests, that I could not find, in some quarter of it, a hundred acres of green ground with trees on it, for the summer holidays and evenings of your alert enquiring industrious men; and for winter season and bad weather quite another sort of social meeting places than the gin shops offered! May all this and much else be amended.[111]

Perhaps Carlyle's letter was Watkin's inspiration for his remarks at the half-holiday soirée in December 1843. On 30 March 1844 he wrote, 'I have commenced endeavouring to obtain a public walk or ground in the suburbs of Manchester.' He notes on 6 April that he was busy with a requisition to the mayor, Alexander Kay, for a public meeting on the subject, and writing some little matters for the *Manchester Times* and *Manchester Guardian*.[112] On 10 May he and T. H. Williams[113]

111 Carlyle to Watkin, 26 Jan 1843, Watkin, *Cobden*, p. 136.
112 Published in the *Manchester Times* on 6 Apr.
113 T. H. Williams: an agent who lived in Victoria Park. Member of the Literary Society. Auditor to the Council of which he was a member. Later chaired the Council's Public Parks Committee.

presented the petition to the mayor. There were over a hundred signatures, headed by Sir Benjamin Heywood and Sir Thomas Potter.[114] Watkin's pamphlet *A Plea for Public Walks* in which he argued for four parks of not less than 20 acres each on each side of the town at a cost of £25,000 was published on 18 May. Unfortunately no copy has been traced, but the substance was certainly reproduced in a number of articles Watkin wrote for the *Times* and the *Guardian* in the spring and summer of 1844, on occasion producing different articles for each paper for publication on the same day. The first on 15 May, which can probably be attributed to Watkin, asked whether the inhabitants of Manchester were going to establish public walks or whether they were going to look quietly on as Oldham and Stockport did so. Manchester should apply for a portion of the government fund of £10,000 established in 1841 before it was too late. On 25 May he argued that this great city of 300,000 souls of incomparable importance and untold wealth did not boast of a single yard of park ground upon which the feet of the poor man as of right might be planted, and did not possess a single tree or bush set apart to refresh the gaze and revive the heart of the weary prisoner in the town. This compared most unfavourably with continental villages and cities, even with Rouen, the Manchester of France. In Manchester comparable shade and verdure were forbidden by the smoke, but surely they could plant and water beyond the influence of tall chimneys. In a longer article on 20 July he claimed that Manchester was the only town of prominence in the kingdom entirely destitute of parks, promenades or grounds for the free use of its population. London had its magnificent parks, Derby its arboretum, Liverpool its parade and Glasgow its green.[115] The parks campaign had been given added weight by the publication earlier that week of the *First Report of the Commissioners of*

---

114 Published with the mayor's consent in the *Manchester Times* on 29 June 1844.

115 These and subsequent articles on parks are reproduced in the Appendix.

116 PP 1844 (572) XVII, 1, with a report by P. H. Holland, surgeon of Chorlton-upon-Medlock, 570–82.

Inquiry into the State of Large Towns and Populous District[116] and Watkin emphasised that deaths in Broughton, where there was a garden to every house, were 1 in 63, while in Manchester itself the rate was 1 in 28. The average life expectancy of professional men, gentry and their families was 38, of mechanics, labourers and their families only 17 years.

Further articles by Watkin appeared in the *Manchester Guardian* and *Manchester Times*. That in the *Guardian* on 27 July emphasised the advantages to all classes of public grounds with easy access from the town and the likelihood that parks would reduce social exclusiveness of which there was still too much in Manchester. On 3 August he explained the need for the effort to be worthy of Manchester. The geography of the city meant a single public resort would not suffice. Readiness of access was very important. He called for four parks, one on each side of the borough. They needed to be sufficiently large, citing London, Edinburgh and Dublin where parks covered thousands of acres. He appealed for the landowners whose estates surrounded Manchester – the Wiltons, Egertons, Clowes, Ducies and Stamfords – to aid with donations of land. On 8 August Carlyle wrote to Thomas Ballantyne, then with the *Manchester Guardian*,[117] 'you are right to try for four parks', and in the climate of Manchester advocated roofed spaces kept under mild but strict order in which the poorest man that would behave himself might have the means of securing access like a man.[118]

Watkin attended two preliminary meetings immediately before the public meeting on 8 August with the mayor in the chair and Watkin prompting him and seeing to speakers.[119] Many of the wealthy manufacturers and merchants attended,

---

117 Thomas Ballantyne was a journalist, a former editor of the *Bolton Free Press*, who joined *the Manchester Guardian*. He later left to edit the *Examiner*. His brother John was the first secretary of the Manchester Anti-Corn Law Association and later editor of the *ACLC*.

118 *Carlyle Letters*, xviii. 171.

119 Diary entry for 9 Aug 1844. Shapely points out that the mayors were expected to be philanthropic and generous leaders in the community: *Charity and Power*, p. 30.

particularly the liberal reformers. Lord Francis Egerton and Canon Clifton[120] moved and seconded the principal resolution on the need for parks, supported by Sir Thomas Potter; Mark Philips moved that the meeting declared its determination to adopt suitable measures without delay; while Robert Gardner moved a resolution calling upon the Government to make a contribution to the cost, though he also said that many of those present had the working class to thank for the creation of their wealth and social position. In return they should donate liberally – it was an obligation they owed to the community. The sum of £7,000 was then subscribed.[121] 'Quite full and steam up' was Watkin's comment.[122] The Committee on Public Walks, Parks, Gardens and Playgrounds was then set up to raise money for the provision of parks and to select and purchase sites, decide on their layout and convey the properties to the borough for the free use and enjoyment of the inhabitants in perpetuity. At its first meeting on 14 August Watkin was appointed joint secretary with Malcolm Ross.[123] In the afternoon they were successfully 'cadging', as Watkin put it, from Sir Thomas Potter and Alderman Kershaw.[124] On 22 August the mayor issued a public appeal for funds and the secretaries wrote to the Prime Minister on 30 August asking for his financial assistance. They enclosed a subscription list, having referred to the liberality of Egerton, a non-resident who, like Sir Benjamin Heywood,

120   Revd Robert Cox Clifton, a canon of Manchester, 1843 until his death. Also rector of Somerton, Oxon. Later trustee of Owen's College.

121   *Manchester Times*, 10 Aug 1844.

122   Diary entry for 9 Aug 1844. Absalom attended the meeting, but was annoyed that, on being introduced by the mayor to Lord Francis Egerton, he omitted to thank him for the great and enduring pleasure which he had derived from Egerton's translation of Schiller's *Song of the Bell* (*AWJ*, p. 234).

123   Malcolm Ross, a merchant at Cromford Court, Market Street. He lived at Moston House, Moston. He came to Manchester from Scotland in 1832 as a representative of Oswald Stevenson & Co. by whom he had been employed in Glasgow and then became partner and subsequently senior partner. Later president of the Manchester Chamber of Commerce.

124   Diary entry for 14 Aug 1844.

Mark Philips and Jones, Loyd & Co., had pledged £1,000. The Prime Minister replied that although he no longer had any personal connection with Manchester, it was the metropolis of the industry to which he and his family were under a very deep obligation. He too subscribed £1,000, most heartily approving of the wish to provide those doomed to almost incessant toil with the means of healthful recreation and harmless enjoyment.[125]

Money continued to be subscribed – £2,700 in one week in September, at the end of which month the total was £20,688. On 10 September an 'aggregate meeting of operatives' of Manchester and Salford was held in the Free Trade Hall under the chairmanship of Thomas Taylor and John Watts. A committee of working men was formed. In contrast to his usual enthusiasm for public affairs and ambivalent attitude to business, Watkin on 1 November complained that public parks had taken much of his time. It was a sad bore to have an object of this kind interfering with business. Indeed the advertisements in the press in the autumn referred to the secretaries attending the Town Hall every morning at 10 a.m. However, this mood passed and that month he went to meetings at both Sharp Bros and Whitworth & Co. to seek help from the workers.[126] The clerks at the Town Hall subscribed £19, and a number of industrial workplaces made similar contributions. At the end of the year the fund stood at £28,824. In late February and March 1845 he was engaged in searching for sites, going out to Bradford to see some land and then with the mayor and Campbell of the Botanical Gardens to see a number of other possible sites.

By March 1845 the fund had reached £30,000. Watkin wrote to Egerton that the sites for which they were negotiating would cost about £60,000 and to complete the effort successfully a grant from the Government would be necessary. He proposed that Egerton should lead a deputation to Peel. The accompanying memorandum set out plans for the purchase of five plots. The

---

125   Reproduced in the Appendix (BL, Add MS 40550, ff. 347, 351, Ross and Watkin to Peel, 30 Aug, and Peel's reply of 7 Sept 1844).
126   Diary entries for 1, 8 and 21 Nov 1844.

total cost of £86,600 included not only the purchase of the land but also the cost of its conversion into public parks. The memorandum explained that two were on the south side of the city which was greener and where land was in any case dearer, and the imperative was to find £52,000 for the purchases in other areas. The special claims of Manchester were urged, including its lack of corporate property in land and the debt still outstanding for the purchase of manorial rights.[127] Watkin and Ross both accompanied the mayor to see Peel on 9 April. Because of an attack of gout Egerton was not able to meet Peel, but three other local MPs were present: Entwistle, the recently elected MP for South Lancashire; Milner Gibson, one of the two MPs for Manchester; and James Brotherton, MP for Salford. Peel offered a grant of £3,000 from the Government's fund, provided a government surveyor inspected the way the money was spent and that the local subscriptions were forthcoming. The smallness of the grant took the committee by surprise. Watkin saw this as a rebuff as they had wanted £80,000! He and the committee might have been more grateful had they known that Peel had overruled advice from Lord Lincoln, First Commissioner of Woods and Forests, not to consent to a grant at all, as he was concerned that other towns would make similar and possibly stronger claims. Parliament had only voted £10,000 for public walks which had been doled out by the Treasury in small sums, as Lincoln put it, though £750 had been authorised for Sunderland. Manchester had no corporate funds but it had revenue from its gas supply and also from water.[128] The mayor, who had reserved the position of the Manchester delegation at the meeting with Peel, later accepted the £3,000 offered but indulged in the hope that it might only be a portion of the assistance Manchester might reasonably expect.[129]

127 Purchased in March that year, though payment was spread over a period of years.

128 BL, Add. MS 40563, ff. 292, 295–6, 306, 309, 313, Egerton to Peel, 26 March, Ross and Watkin to Egerton, 22 March, and to Peel, 26 March, all reproduced in the Appendix; Add. MS 40563, f. 302, memorandum from Lord Lincoln, later 5th duke of Newcastle, to Peel of 8 April 1845.

129 MCL, MS 352.7 M5, letter of 26 May 1844.

Watkin continued to be closely involved. However, at the end of May he wished that 'public parking' was over so that he could 'settle with all my soul to business'. In all, three sites were purchased, one in Salford and two in Manchester itself. The first purchase for £5,000, the Lark Hill estate from William Garnett, which became Peel Park, was concluded in March 1845.[130] Land from the Walness estate, belonging to John Fitzgerald, was added to this and cost £5,481. The Hensham Hall estate at Harpur Hey was bought for £7,250 from Jonathan Andrew and became Queen's Park, and part of the Bradford estate was bought from Lady Hoghton for £6,200 to form Philips Park.[131] In all £32,127 had been subscribed. On 30 April a letter appeared in the *Guardian* signed Pro Bono Publico proposing names for the three parks. The suggestions were Peel Park, because Peel had stayed at Lark Hill on his last visit to Manchester, Philips Park because Mark Philips, Manchester's first MP, was in ill health and had said he would retire from Parliament, and Queen's Park because it was claimed there were a number of King's Parks in the country but no Queen's Park. The committee accepted these suggestions on 13 May.

Immediately before his marriage and taking up his railway career Watkin, with his joint secretary, Ross, was able to present the trusts to the Town Council. They were plentifully praised by the mayor and Nield and loudly applauded.[132] By August a competition for laying out the parks, all three of 30 to 31 acres, was advertised, and Joshua Major, a landscape gardener of Knowstrop, near Leeds, won the first prize.[133] The parks were opened on 22 August 1846 and conveyed 'for the free use and enjoyment of the inhabitants in perpetuity' to the Manchester Council which then formed a Public Parks Committee.[134] Peel

---

130 £4,500 was paid as Garnett gave £500.

131 Diary entry for 20 May 1845.

132 Diary entry for 5 Aug 1845.

133 George F. Chadwick, *The Park and Town: Public Landscape in the 19th and 20th Centuries* (London: Architectural Press, 1966), pp. 97–8.

134 Thomas Swindells, *Manchester Streets and Manchester Men* (5 vols, Manchester: J. E. Cornish, 1906–08), v. 69, and Chadwick, *English Park*, pp. 97–8. For a discussion of the policies of the Public Parks Committee and the use made of the parks, see Theresa Wyborn, 'Parks for the people: the development of public parks in Victorian Manchester', *Manchester Region History Review*, 9 (1995), 3–14, at pp. 7–13.

Park was transferred to Salford Council in 1851. Watkin seems to have continued to act as joint secretary until the opening of the parks.

One of the features of the successful appeal was the large number of very small donations received – there were 537 of five shillings, 481 of one shilling and 173 of sixpence, as a result of the workers' committee and no doubt in part Watkin's visits to firms. The appeal to the aristocracy for donations of land went unheeded by Lord Wilton, Sir Oswald Mosley, the Ducies, the Stamfords and the Clowes.[135] Indeed most of the old landowners had left the area, the family seats taken over by merchants and manufacturers.[136] Apart from Lord Francis Egerton who resided at Worsley and represented South Lancashire, and who played an active part in Manchester affairs, but not in its politics, they were not among those listed as subscribing £100 or more. Andrew and Garnett, who sold their houses and land, were both merchants, perhaps not inappropriately as Manchester must take the credit for being the first of the major industrial centres to acquire a municipal park.[137]

Newspapers

Manchester's newspapers had long been partisan politically. Reformers had been strongly supported in the 1790s by the short-lived *Manchester Herald* and Cowdroy's *Manchester Gazette*, founded in 1791, counterbalanced by Wheeler's *Manchester Chronicle*, a Tory paper founded in 1781, and the *Manchester Mercury* of 1751. In the years following the Napoleonic Wars Manchester's newspapers had undergone considerable changes. The impetus for many of these came

135 Revd John Clowes, a noted gardener and botanist, resided at Broughton Hall. He died in 1846 and was succeeded by his brother William Legh Clowes. The Clowes were benefactors of churches in Broughton, and developed Broughton Park, a villa estate for the middle classes laid out from 1840 to 1845.

136 Gattrell, 'Incorporation and the pursuit of liberal hegemony', pp. 22–3.

137 Hazel Conway, *People's Parks: The Design and Development of Victorian Parks in Britain* (Cambridge: Cambridge University Press, 1991), p. 49.

from the reformers. As Michael Turner put it, 'The examples set by the *Herald* and the *Gazette* suggested that a well-conducted newspaper with a vigorous, explicitly reformist editorial line could be the most powerful weapon in the Manchester liberals' arsenal.'[138] J. E. Taylor, who had written extensively for the *Gazette* and established his radical credentials, became the first editor of the *Manchester Guardian* when it was founded in 1821 as a weekly. It was intended to be an organ that would give a greater news coverage and act as the voice of reform to a wide readership. However, many of the reformers soon thought that the *Guardian* did not live up to these expectations and from the start business considerations had seemed more important than political content. It was this dissatisfaction with what Prentice and others regarded as the less than wholehearted support given by Taylor's *Guardian* to radical causes which led to Archibald Prentice's purchase of Cowdroy's *Manchester Gazette*. Prentice's financial situation was such that in 1828 he had to give up the *Gazette* but a joint stock company was formed in the same year to publish a new paper, the *Manchester Times and Gazette*, and Prentice was made editor. 'Gazette' was soon dropped from the title and Prentice became the main owner. As something of a counterpoise to the *Gazette* and *Guardian*, Thomas Sowler, a Manchester bookseller, started the *Manchester Courier* in 1825 and it became the leading Conservative paper, more right-wing than the *Chronicle*, the only surviving paper from the eighteenth century. Meanwhile the *Guardian* had purchased Harrap's *Manchester Mercury* and the *British Volunteer*, also owned by the Harrap family in 1825 following the younger Harrap's death, and continued the former for a few years as a midweekly counterpart to the *Guardian*. The *Manchester and Salford Advertiser* was founded in 1828 by the licensed victuallers on non-political lines, but by the late 1830s it was owned by Mrs Jane Leresche, who was a printer and also ran a patent medicine warehouse, and George Condy, a barrister.

Wheeler's *Manchester Chronicle*, which for a long time had enjoyed more advertising revenue than its rivals, succumbed to

138 Turner, *Reform and Respectability*, p. 63.

competition at the end of 1842, so that for most of the period covered by Watkin's diary the principal newspapers published weekly or more frequently in Manchester were the *Advertiser* on Saturdays, the *Courier* and the *Guardian*, both Wednesdays and Saturdays, and the *Times* on Saturdays. All cost 4d except the *Times* which was 4½d. Only Thomas Sowler's *Courier* was Conservative. The others reflected different shades of Liberal opinion. Prentice's *Times* was particularly strong in its support for the Anti-Corn Law League. The *Guardian* was still regarded as somewhat suspect by the more radical reformers as being the voice of industry and more interested in maintaining circulation and profits than in backing causes. In terms of circulation, in the early 1840s the *Guardian* (some 800,000 copies a year, but twice weekly) was increasing its lead over the *Courier* (200,000), with the weekly *Times* and *Advertiser* rather over, and about, 100,000 respectively.[139]

What triggered Watkin's interest in newspapers is not clear. Early in 1844 he reviewed Thomas Hood's new magazine for the *Manchester Times*.[140] In proposing 'the people' at a dinner when Jeremiah Garnett, the proprietor of the *Guardian*, was present, he scoffed at the recent timeserving of the *Guardian*. In May 1844 he wrote that in conjunction with James Edwards[141] he had tried to get a meeting of the 'great guns' to consider the propriety of supporting the *Advertiser* as a check upon the *Guardian*, but without success. The fact that Mrs Leresche, by this time the sole owner of the *Advertiser*, sent for him to enquire about parties willing to engage in the newspaper trade and more particularly to help manage her business, suggests that Watkin must already have been acquainted with several of the key people in Manchester newspapers. In June he notes that

139 The figures are only intended as a rough guide. They are derived from the graph in Donald Read, 'North of England newspapers (*c.*1700 – *c.*1900) and their value to historians', *Proceedings of the Leeds Philosophical and Literary Society*, 8 (1956–59), 200–15, at p. 211, and are based on the number of copies on which newspaper stamp duty was paid.

140 Diary entry for 13 Jan 1844.

141 James Edwards, a calico printer, Dalgish Falconer & Co. A leading member of the ACLL. On the Athenaeum Committee.

Joseph Pollock, a Manchester barrister, and he had been trying to induce some of the bigwigs, as Watkin described them, to unite the *Advertiser* and the *Times*, presumably a response to Mrs Leresche's request.[142] Probably one of the bigwigs was John Bright, as he wrote to Watkin in November that he was fully conscious of the need to do something with the *Times* and *Advertiser*, but was puzzled how it was to be done. He could not advance a large sum himself and thought it unlikely that they could persuade others. 'Newspaper property is proverbially insecure and Manchester people like what is certain better than what is hazardous.' Bright thought that the *Guardian* had recently been more reasonable, but to depend upon it was most unsatisfactory – 'he will probably betray us when we want him most'.[143]

Many of the reformers thought the betrayal came in 1845 when the *Guardian* backed those members of the Chamber of Commerce who were dissatisfied at the way it was run almost as an adjunct to the Anti-Corn Law League. Though the Chamber was nominally non-political, it had become increasingly dominated by ACLL members. In 1845 a new Commercial Association was formed by breakaway members of the Chamber of Commerce. The catalyst was the exclusion of Richard Birley, a Conservative, from office in the Chamber after he took the chair of the Conservative Entwistle's committee in the South Lancashire by-election. The new association included Whiggish Liberals like James Aspinall Turner, John Potter, Malcolm Ross and William Nield as well as Conservatives like Birley.[144] Both bodies, however, supported free trade.

By March 1845 Watkin was busy with a project for a new newspaper, noting the desire for one had much increased since Jeremiah Garnett most sillily backed Mr Birley in the Chamber

142   Diary entries for 12 May and 16 June 1844.
143   MCL, M219/2/5, Bright to Watkin, 25 Nov 1844.
144   Richard Birley, Conservative cotton spinner, had been chairman of the Athenaeum. Son of H. H. Birley. J. A. Turner of Pendlebury House, cotton manufacturer and merchant, Liberal MP for Manchester 1857–65. William Nield, calico printer, mayor 1840–42.

of Commerce affair. Tom Potter had asked him to go into it and he seemed to be thought by many as a likely man to manage it. He was attracted particularly after talking it over with Thomas Ballantyne, then the sub-editor of the *Guardian*, but with his usual despondency confided in his diary that to sell calicoes would be the highest office he would fulfil in this life.[145] There is a lack of detail in his next references to a new newspaper. He notes fiddling about in it in May and he had to see Bright in August.[146] By November he had embarked on the 'Newspaper line' and he records the amount of capital subscribed by each of the partners – Bright £1,000, Revd William McKerrow £1,000, Thomas Ballantyne, who had left the *Guardian*, £500 and Watkin £250 – in a new venture, the *Manchester Examiner*. It is not clear how or when McKerrow became part of this project, though as minister of the Presbyterian Lloyd Street Chapel to which he was appointed, aged 24, in 1827, he had taken an active part in public life in Manchester. He was an active supporter of the ACLL and prominent at the four-day convention of all denominations on the Corn Laws held in August 1841. He was elected to the first Manchester School Board and was later to be active in wider educational movements.

The *Examiner* advertised its prospectus in December 1845. It promised free trade without sham, mistake or compromise, and attention to railways, perhaps an indication of Watkin's influence. 'To a great practical subject, the railway system, the *Examiner* will be found devoting its careful attention, supporting all that it is safe and advantageous to the public, yet exposing the delinquencies of sordid speculation.'[147] The first issue appeared on Saturday 10 January 1846 when Bright called on Watkin to ask him to leave the railway business to go into the paper, an invitation he renewed in April.[148]

---

145 Diary entry for 17 Mar 1845.
146 Diary entries for 9 May and 8 Aug 1845.
147 *Manchester Times*, 9 Dec 1845.
148 The paper was published weekly on Saturdays. Entries for 11 Jan and 12 April 1846.

Meanwhile Watkin was engaged in sorting out printing problems at the newspaper office and on one occasion Bright and he kept Ballantyne company at the office until 12.30 a.m. writing and correcting. By April the circulation was about 5,700 a week. Watkin's influence can be detected in the *Examiner's* promise of earlier London news through an arrangement with the London & North Western Railway. By use of the railway's telegraph they had the Queen's speech at 6 p.m. on the day it was delivered. The original partnership did not last. Watkin soon left, probably because the purchase of the Trent Valley by the London & North Western meant that his office was in London from September 1846, and Bright retired on being elected MP for Manchester in 1847.[149] Alexander Ireland, who had moved to Manchester in 1843 as a representative of a Huddersfield firm, became the publisher and business manager. George Wilson and Henry Rawson bought the *Times* and in 1848 they bought up the *Examiner* and amalgamated it with the *Times*.

Railways

Although after 1845 Watkin's major interest was to be railways, his entries in his diary show that following his engagement to Mary Mellor he would have been well content to have taken up any occupation which would have secured to him a greater and steadier income than he was likely to obtain from the business his father had founded and which his younger brother Alfred, later an alderman and Lord Mayor of Manchester, was to continue. He records no particular interest in railways and there is nothing to compare in his diary with the excitement recorded in his father's diary on the occasion of the opening of the Liverpool & Manchester Railway in 1830 which Edward had

---

149 F. Leary, 'History of the Manchester periodical press' (MCL, MS f052 L161, 1889–1898), pp. 240–72; James Muir McKerrow, *Memoir of William McKerrow, D.D., Manchester* (London: Hodder & Stoughton, 1881), pp. 147–9. Watkin did not move his home to London until 1848.

witnessed as a boy when his father had taken him to the railroad in Oldfield Lane. His railway journeys were recorded as a matter of fact for by the early 1840s railways were established as an essential means of transport, though the network which began to take shape in the 1830s was still developing. The Liverpool & Manchester Railway had surprised even its promoters, most of whom were Liverpool rather than Manchester based, by its success with passenger traffic. The Bridgewater Canal interests, despite the substantial investment by the marquess of Stafford in the Liverpool & Manchester, had only agreed late in the day to the railway crossing the Irwell to Liverpool Road station, and for some years resisted extension eastwards. A journey by rail from Manchester to London became possible in a not very direct way in 1838 with the linking of the Liverpool line to the Grand Junction at Earlestown which ran to Birmingham to join the London & Birmingham. Access to the capital was made easier in 1842 when the Manchester & Birmingham Railway was opened, providing a direct line from London Road station to Crewe on the Grand Junction. Meanwhile the Manchester & Leeds Railway had opened. The terminus was for some years at Oldham Road, but a new passenger station, Victoria, was built at Hunts Bank and opened in 1844. This also served the line to Bolton opened in 1838 and a link was made through Salford to the Liverpool & Manchester. In contrast to the 1820s, in the 1830s and 1840s Manchester capitalists were instrumental in financing several of the major railways, contributing, for example, some 40 per cent of the capital of the London & Southampton (later London & South Western) and of the Manchester & Birmingham, and nearly 20 per cent of the London & Birmingham.[150] It was the growth of the market in railway shares which led to the creation of the Manchester Stock Exchange in the railway boom of 1836.

Watkin became secretary of the Trent Valley at the height of the next boom – the Railway Mania of 1845, which began

---

150 Malcolm C. Reed, *Investment in Railways in Britain, 1820–1844: A Study in the Development of the Capital Market* (London: Oxford University Press, 1975), pp. 135, 141, 149.

with an upsurge in railway promotion following economic recovery in 1844–45 after the very depressed period of the early 1840s. As commercial confidence grew railway shares were soon in great demand as an apparently easy way for individuals to make capital gains on a rising market. Expectations became increasingly unrealistic, and more speculative, sometimes fraudulent, schemes attracted subscribers. Even rich men, like Robert Gardner, himself a director of the Trent Valley, encouraged by those more closely involved in the prospective companies, became worried about the extent of their commitments, as Watkin records.[151] Many schemes did not reach the parliamentary stage. Other lines, though approved by the legislature, were not built as in the ensuing recession even the stronger companies could not raise funds for construction. The mania was at its height in the summer and autumn of 1845. Watkin, urged on by his impending marriage, seems to have bought a mixed bag of shares with the intention of making a quick profit rather than investing for the longer term. We do not have sufficient information to judge his success though his diary entries suggest initial gains followed by losses. His investments were not among the wilder schemes, but neither did they turn out to be sound investments for the long term, though this was not his aim. The Great Northern of France, largely owned by the Rothschilds, and the Sheffield & Lincolnshire proved viable, the latter as part of the Manchester, Sheffield & Lincolnshire, of which Watkin became the general manager in 1854. The West Lancashire and the Manchester, Wigan & Southport were

151 Diary entry for 17 Oct 1845. Gardner by the 1830s was one of Manchester's leading cotton entrepreneurs in partnership with Thomas Bazley and William Atkinson. Edward Tootal had succeeded him as Atkinson's partner. Gardner has been described by S. D. Chapman as 'probably the most successful of Manchester's self-made men of the post-war generation': Stanley Chapman, *Merchant Enterprise in Britain from the Industrial Revolution to World War I* (Cambridge: Cambridge University Press, 1992). Went bankrupt in 1847 when his debts were over £100,000 but he had assets of £350,000, £90,000 in freehold property and much of the remainder in goods shipped to North and South America (Lloyd Jones and Le Roux, 'Size of firms', p. 63).

to fail in committee in 1846 and had to be revived in more limited forms before securing parliamentary authorisation; the Manchester & Southampton failed in the Lords; the Fleetwood & Preston Junction never exercised the powers it obtained; and the Leicester & Tamworth quickly came to nothing. It is likely that Watkin's most substantial gain was achieved in 1846 in the shares of the Trent Valley Railway as he most certainly acquired, or was allotted, shares on taking up the secretaryship and by the spring of 1846 it had been sold to the London & Birmingham at a large profit as he records in his entry for 27 February 1846. The line became an integral part of the main line to the north-west bypassing Birmingham; Mrs Gaskell recorded in December 1847 leaving 'Manchester at 26 minutes to 10 and from that time till we got to [London] last night we never stirred out of the Railway carriage. For we went through the Trent Valley which does not pass through Birmingham.'[152]

Watkin owed his appointment to the Trent Valley to James Atherton[153] and Edward Tootal. The latter was the largest shareholder and epitomised the new age. He was a Manchester silk manufacturer, and from 1842 a partner in Atkinson Tootal, manufacturers of white cotton goods, who invested his profits in railways. By the 1850s he had virtually abandoned textiles for railways and was an increasingly influential director of the London & North Western Railway. He had lost £10,000 in an earlier attempt to get the Trent Valley Railway started and invested heavily in other shares at the time of the Railway Mania. Watkin, particularly initially, was highly critical of Tootal in his diary, so much so that he seriously thought of giving up his post with the Trent Valley and concentrating on newspapers. Tootal does seem to have been a difficult man to get on with. His manner of speaking was very abrupt and he was impatient of any hesitation in reply to his rapidly put

---

152 *Letters of Mrs Gaskell*, p. 49.

153 Atherton was president of the Athenaeum and an ACLL supporter. A muslin manufacturer – Horrocks, Jackson & Co. Later chairman of the Union Bank. He was also vice-chairman of the Committee on Public Parks and was probably impressed with Watkin's work as joint secretary.

questions. R. B. Dockray, an engineer with the LNWR, referred to getting through a meeting 'very pleasantly' with Mr Tootal 'with his sneers and suspicions' not present.[154] Some at least of Watkin's hostility arose because Tootal thought he ought not to be pursuing ventures other than the Trent Valley such as the Manchester *Examiner* and the Oldham, Manchester, Liverpool & Birkenhead Junction Railway in which his wife's family had major interests. The Trent Valley, though it did not serve Manchester, had its office in that town, reflecting the predominance of Manchester textile men on the board, like Henry Newbery and Robert Gardner mentioned in the diary.

In the autumn of 1845 and early 1846 Watkin devoted a lot of attention to the Oldham, Manchester, Liverpool & Birkenhead Junction Railway, a grandiose title for a line from Manchester London Road station, via Newton, Failsworth and Hollinwood to the centre of Oldham with an extension to Saddleworth. The capital was £220,000. Both Jonathan Mellor senior and his son, Jonathan, were on the provisional committee. It was a rival to the Oldham District which was backed by the Manchester & Leeds, with John Hawkshaw as engineer, and was projected to connect Ashton-under-Lyne, Stalybridge and Stockport with Oldham, Shaw, Royton and Rochdale with a branch to Saddleworth to join the Manchester & Leeds main line. Watkin records the rivalries between the two lines, and in the final entry for 12 July 1846 the defeat of the Oldham District and the success of the Oldham & Birkenhead in the Commons. However, the latter was subsequently defeated in the Lords, and, though the two companies then came together to form the Oldham Alliance, this in turn did not come to anything.

---

154   George P. Neele, *Railway Recollections: Notes and Reminiscences of Half a Century's Progress in Railway Working, and of a Railway Superintendent's Life, Principally on the London and North Western Railway* (1904; Wakefield: E P Publishing, 1974 reprint), p. 125; Michael Robbins, 'From R. B. Dockray's diary', *Journal of Transport History*, 1st ser., vii (1965–66), 1–13, 109–19, 149–59, at p. 2.

Suburbs

The preference for the well-off in Manchester to live away from the central areas was well known to both contemporaries and historians. By the 1840s the tendency was very apparent. It was commented on by Engels, and some of those whose houses Edward Watkin visited lived in the newer more distant parts of Manchester – Thomas Potter in Buile Hill in Pendleton where John Spencer also lived, James Atherton in Swinton Park, William Evans in Crumpsall Grove, and T. H. Williams in Victoria Park, where the earliest houses were built from 1837 to 1840. Nevertheless all these residences were within three miles of the centre; few lived further out, though Mark Philips was at The Park, Prestwich, and H. H. Birley in Eccles. Some affluent merchants and manufacturers occupied large country houses, like Samuel Marsland whose daughter Mary Mellor visits at Baguley Hall, and by 1849 James Watt was at Abney Hall, Cheadle. Absalom notes that in 1842 Robert Gladstone had bought a house with 14 acres at Withington.[155] Nevertheless, by the standard of the 1840s the Watkins at Northenden, almost six miles out, were far from the centre. Movement to places in Cheshire had only just begun with the opening of the railway line to Crewe in 1842 with stations at Wilmslow and Alderley Edge. The numbers at first were small. Building on the hill at Alderley started in 1845 but by 1850 there were only about thirty very handsome residences there which the railway company had encouraged by its season ticket policy though hardly providing a service for commuters as the first train arrived in Manchester at 9.00 and the second at 10.30.[156] The line to Bowden and Altrincham only opened in 1849.

By the 1840s omnibuses were advertised as running frequently during the day from Market Street to Ardwick, Broughton, Cheetham Hill, Didsbury, Eccles, Longsight, Pendleton, Stretford and other suburbs, while coaches ran to

155 *AWJ*, p. 215.
156 Jack Simmons, *The Railway in Town and Country, 1830–1914* (Newton Abbot: David & Charles, 1986), p. 113.

Oldham and less frequently to Altrincham.[157] Both Edward and his father record using the omnibus to Northenden. His father kept a sociable – an open four-seater carriage – but this seems to have been used mainly for the family and not for routine journeys into town, though on one occasion Edward drove Mary to Northenden in the sociable. He also records taking the omnibus to Cheadle and then because it was wet taking a phaeton home.[158] One feature of the diary which may occasion surprise to the modern reader is the distances walked by Edward Watkin, not on country rambles but in order to get to business or social events. These included from Cheadle station to Northenden (over three miles), from Northenden to Urmston (about five miles), from the warehouse to Northenden (about six miles) and on one occasion apparently from Northenden to Failsworth (about ten miles). These are not vast distances for a healthy young man but are less expected as they were clearly not country walks for the purpose of leisure. However, perhaps in this habit he was following the example of his father, a founding member of the Society for the Preservation of Ancient Footpaths, who once complained, following a Sunday afternoon walk on Kersal Moor with Spencer and J. E. Taylor, that they 'did not walk fast enough or far enough for me. The walks I take with them are not exercise, only sauntering.'[159]

The Watkins

There can be little doubt that Absalom Watkin was a big influence in shaping his son. In many ways Edward was following in his footsteps. Absalom had taken over his uncle's business in 1807, when he was only 20, but he always took an interest in matters unconnected with the workplace, forming with five friends for mutual improvement the Sciolous Society, which ceased to meet in 1813, probably because of the political

157 Pigot, pp. 150–1.
158 Diary entries for 9 May and 5 Aug 1845.
159 *AWJ*, p. 133.

restrictions of the day.[160] Soon a Literary and Scientific Club took its place. Absalom's interest in politics developed slowly, but in February 1815 he attended a meeting to oppose the Corn Bill, at which Archibald Prentice and Thomas and Richard Potter were present. Prentice said that the manufacturers opposed the bill because they believed that raising the price of food would increase the price of labour and thus prevent them competing with other countries.[161] Absalom became, as Prentice put it, one of the carriers of the principles of reform down to another generation – the small band, several of whom feature in Edward's diary such as Thomas Potter, Archibald Prentice, F. R. Atkinson, John Shuttleworth, Joseph Brotherton and J. B. Smith. They and other members of the band were Dissenters. Turner notes that Watkin was the only member of the band who was not a Dissenter but an Anglican. Certainly, from the time of his removal to Northenden he attended, though not every Sunday, the parish church of St Wilfred's and not the Methodist chapel, and his son, John, became an Anglican clergyman.[162] Absalom, however, in his younger days had been a member of the Methodist New Connexion and an active lay preacher. To this he probably owed much of his ability as a public speaker. According to Slugg he and John Shuttleworth were regarded as the most effective speakers in Manchester.[163]

Edward, in his sketch of his father's life, said that there was reason to believe that Absalom drew up the public remonstrance against Peterloo, but there seems to be no other evidence for

---

160 E. W. Watkin, *A Sketch of the Life of Absalom Watkin, Fragment No 1* (Manchester: Alex Ireland, 1874), p. 25.

161 Prentice, *Historical Sketches*, pp. 68–9.

162 Turner, *Reform and Respectability*, p. 30; *AWJ*, pp. 101, 133; Goffin, p. 238.

163 Prentice, *Historical Sketches*, pp. 73–4; J. T. Slugg, *Reminiscences of Manchester, Fifty Years Ago* (facsimile reprint, Shannon, Ireland: Irish University Press, 1971), p. 174. 'The New Connexion Methodism of [Absalom] Watkin's youth faded into a sort of low church eclecticism': Howard M. Wach, 'Civil society, moral identity and the liberal public sphere: Manchester and Boston, 1810–40', *Social History*, 21 (1996), 281–303, at p. 302.

this.[164] Absalom was in this period, in Prentice's phrase, 'giving himself more to literature than to politics', and calculated that he could leave business as he and his family could live comfortably on an income of £150 a year. Nevertheless when urged to do so he asked, 'Why leave a trade in which my success (considered in relation to the means) has been extraordinary?' The tug between business and literary and political activities was a constant tension in Absalom's life. He asserted that genius, learning, skill, strength and ability of every kind were legitimate sources of value. A picture by Lawrence, or a poem by Byron or Southey, was a saleable article in every country in Europe, as much a portion of the national wealth as a spinning jenny or a steam engine.[165] There are no signs in Edward's diary that he found literature or the arts a distraction from business but certainly public life and politics were. It may be that some of Absalom's annoyance with his son for not attending more to business was in part a reflection of his own guilt at staying up reading in the early hours and being late for the warehouse in consequence. Even as late as 1841, when Absalom had long been active in Manchester's public life, he displayed a measure of diffidence and was conscious he was not one of the Manchester plutocracy. He wrote to George Wilson to say that 'upon reflection it appears to me that some gentleman of more weight than myself in pounds sterling should move the resolution which you wish me to take'.[166]

Absalom developed wider interests and commitments in Manchester in the 1820s. He was on the committee of the Commercial Clerks Society, a benevolent institution. He was elected to the Literary and Philosophical Society of Manchester. He became a special constable for Broughton in 1823. In 1827 Thomas Potter suggested to him that he become editor of the

164 Watkin, *Sketch*, p. 19.
165 *Manchester Iris*, 5 Apr 1823.
166 MCL, M20/4, letter of 14 Sep 1841. The meeting on 16 Sep was to draw up a memorial to the Queen not to prorogue Parliament until the cause of the distress and the restrictive laws had been considered. In the event he moved the resolution (Goffin, p. 218).

Manchester Gazette. Potter had backed the paper financially but had now lost confidence in Prentice, the editor and proprietor. Potter soon abandoned the idea, apparently preferring Prentice's more radical approach, though Absalom thought it was because they believed he would be too independent.[167] Absalom also met reformers other than the respectable Manchester town leaders. He knew Joseph Johnson, one of the leaders at Peterloo, though then much less radical in his opinions, Richard Carlile and William Cobbett. Johnson by the late 1820s was living at Northenden, and it was he who told Absalom that the property, Rose Hill, which he bought in Northenden was for sale. The parliamentary reform crisis of the early 1830s brought Absalom much more into the political world. He drew up the petition from Manchester in 1830 and the following year drafted the resolutions and the parliamentary petition and address to the King. He was similarly employed on several occasions during 1832 and was also a member of the reform committee in Manchester. He was an early supporter of the Ten Hours Bill, attending and speaking at the public meeting in Manchester in April 1833, and, as will be seen, he was very much involved in the Anti-Corn Law campaign. About 1840 he wrote 'The Voice of Dearth', a poem which was both an expression of his own fears of revolt by the people maddened with hunger and a warning to the despots who scorned and mocked the voice of dearth and left the people's woes and people's will unheeded.[168] Edward thus grew up in a household where the reform tradition was very much alive, and as a boy of twelve saw the procession in Manchester in honour of the passing of the Reform Bill in August 1832.

Edward's political interests

Relatively soon after Edward started work at the family warehouse he began to take an interest in politics and like

167 Turner, *Reform and Respectability*, p. 87; *AWJ*, 4, 15 and 20 Dec 1828; David Ayerst, *Guardian: Biography of a Newspaper* (London: Collins, 1971), p. 88.
168 Watkin, *Sketch*, p. 21.

his father was torn between the cotton trade and reforming causes. Absalom and his friends had roused his interest in the latter. In April 1835 he undertook his first public duty and acted as 'check clerk' at the by-election in Manchester caused by Poulett Thomson's appointment to the presidency of the Board of Trade.[169] Later that year Edward first saw Cobden, then aged 31, at a meeting at Hayward's Hotel to promote the Manchester Athenaeum. Cobden soon became his hero and mentor.[170] Cobden's preoccupation with municipal reform was followed in late 1838 by the start of the long campaign to repeal the Corn Laws, in which he was to play the leading role.[171] The Corn Laws had attracted little attention in the first part of the 1830s, but this was to change towards the end of the decade with the worsening of the economic situation and high food prices. In September 1838 Archibald Prentice organised a meeting in Manchester which agreed to form an Anti-Corn Law Association. The provisional committee included George Wilson, John Benjamin Smith, Thomas Potter, Prentice and Absalom. Cobden joined them on his return from Eastern Europe where he had been collecting evidence of the stifling effect of the laws on international trade. He asked Absalom, with Smith and Prentice, to draw up an address explaining the nature and objects of the association.[172] The Anti-Corn Law Associations held their first and not very successful meeting in London in February 1839, which led Cobden to write to J. B. Smith: 'My hopes of agitation are anchored in Manchester.'[173] The National Association was set up with its headquarters in Manchester. In March Absalom spoke to an audience of 3,000 in the Manchester Corn Exchange.

169 *AWJ*, p. 177. Until the early twentieth century all MPs becoming ministers were regarded as holding an office of profit under the Crown and so had to seek re-election.

170 Watkin, *Cobden*, p. 115.

171 Simon Morgan, 'Cobden and Manchester', *Manchester Region History Review*, 17 (2004), 28–37, for a recent assessment of Cobden's role in the town.

172 Cobden to A. Watkin, 3 Dec 1838, Watkin, *Cobden*, pp. 60–1.

173 Quoted in N. McCord, *The Anti-Corn Law League, 1838–1846* (London: George Allen & Unwin, 1958), p. 44.

However, the birth of the Anti-Corn Law movement was virtually simultaneous with that of Chartism. In 1838 working men's associations all over Britain adopted the Charter. In Manchester the Chartists held a huge meeting on Kersal Moor on the same day as the associations met in London. Manchester Chartism was not so much in the London or Birmingham mould, the 'moral force' wing, as that of Leeds, the 'physical force' wing, led by Fergus O'Connor and his newspaper, the *Northern Star*, a national voice for working-class radicalism.

Working-class radicals saw the Corn Laws as increasing the price of bread to the poor so repeal of the Corn Laws and parliamentary reform had been frequently associated. The Peterloo meeting had called for both, but enfranchisement of the middle classes in 1832 changed the position. In Manchester many in the the League were not interested in further reform but wanted to build up working-class support for repeal while defeating the political aims of Chartism. They also saw pursuit of the Charter as diverting attention from repeal, while many Chartists saw the League's campaign as a diversion, deliberate or otherwise, from the pursuit of the Charter. There was no common front, in part because for the Chartists the priority was political reform from which other benefits would flow, but above all the Chartists were as hostile to the middle (and employing) manufacturing class of League supporters (who themselves were at best uncomfortable with working-class radicalism) as to the aristocratic Government to which the League was opposed. In their view a cheaper loaf would just lead to lower wages and drive farm labourers into the towns, further depressing their standard of living. Northern Chartists in particular were understandably suspicious of the League when so many of its leading lights were hostile to factory reform and their movement drew much of its strength from depression following the 1836 boom. The two movements soon came into conflict. In February 1839 the Chartists disrupted a meeting of the Manchester Association at the Corn Exchange, when 'the respectable persons' had to withdraw from the meeting.[174]

---

174 Archibald Prentice, *History of the Anti-Corn-Law League* (2 vols, London: W. & F. G. Cash, 1853), i. 116.

However, the demonstration on Kersal Moor on 25 May 1839 was peaceful. In August the 'sacred month' of National Holiday (a general strike), planned by the Chartists to follow the rejection of the Charter by Parliament, did not develop into anything serious despite the alarm engendered before the event.

Nevertheless the League wished to gain support from among the working classes to show that their cause was not a sectional one and to add to their numbers. They firmly believed that both groups would benefit from the removal of the Bread Tax. An Operatives Anti-Corn Law Association (OACLA) was formed in Manchester as well as in other towns such as Leicester, Leeds and Huddersfield. According to McCord, a few days after the League's defeat by Chartists in Manchester at the end of February 1839 Cobden gave Edward Watkin the task of organising this body, and he was busy at this task throughout 1840 and the early months of 1841.[175] The Manchester Operatives had their own officers under the chairmanship of Frederick Warren, himself a Chartist, and by the beginning of April 1839 were meeting regularly on two evenings a week. In its second issue the League's own newspaper, the *Anti-Corn Law Circular*, contained a column entitled 'The Operative' which set out to dispel workers' misconceptions. On the effect of repeal on wages, it said the stimulus which repeal would impart to Britain's foreign trade would so increase demand that wages would fall less than the price of the necessities of life.[176]

Watkin was only 20 in 1839 and it is hard to see quite what role he had in that year or in 1840, especially as we only have his diaries for May and June 1841, but he was addressed as 'Our Edward' by George Wilson and J. B. Smith.[177] Certainly the Operatives Association extended. They organised events to complement those of the League, though the form these events took made it all too clear to the operatives that they were there in a subordinate capacity. When in January 1840 the Manchester Association held a banquet for 3,000 people,

175 McCord, *Anti-Corn Law League*, pp. 80–1.
176 *ACLC*, 30 Apr 1839.
177 *The Looking Glass*, 1 Apr 1878.

200 places were reserved in the gallery for the operatives. The latter had their own dinner in the same hall the following night for which tickets were 1s. Five thousand operatives sat down to dine. Frederick Warren presided. Thomas Potter, the mayor, was present and many of the League leaders spoke as did Daniel O'Connell who had given his support to the League in its early days.[178] OACLA was only a limited success. Twenty-three branches have been identified, mostly in the industrial districts of Lancashire, Cheshire and Yorkshire.[179] In May 1840 the Operatives Association held their first big rally, and the Chief Commissioner of the Manchester police, Sir Charles Shaw, reported that there were at least 4,000 operatives present and it was impossible to describe the quiet and regularity of this meeting. Nevertheless the core of the organisation was still small, and the Chartists were tending to dominate the series of joint meetings set up between their representatives and the operatives. As Pickering has shown, Warren was an unreliable ally, and like many of the operatives not prepared to detach himself from supporting Chartism.[180] Subsequent meetings of operatives in 1840 were much less successful. Watkin's work with the Operatives Association took place in Manchester itself, but he also campaigned in the area near Northenden, still largely agricultural and not yet a suburb, and lectured on behalf of the League in Gatley, Wilmslow and Cheadle. Earlier Edward had written to Sir Robert Peel on the Corn Laws. His father, not slow to praise as well as criticise, noted that it was a fair and conclusive reply to a very artful shuffling speech, and did great credit to Edward's industry and argumentative powers.[181]

In May and June 1841 there was a series of rowdy and sometimes violent events, as rival meetings were held by the Operatives and the Chartists. These are described in Watkin's

178 *ACLC*, 31 Dec 1839 and 16 Jan 1840; *AWJ*, p. 206.

179 Paul A. Pickering and Alex Tyrell, *The People's Bread: A History of the Anti-Corn Law League* (London: Leicester University Press, 2000), p. 144.

180 TNA, HO 40/43; Paul A. Pickering, *Chartism and the Chartists in Manchester and Salford* (Basingstoke: Macmillan, 1995), pp. 100–1.

181 Goffin, p. 211.

diary for those months. He shows how he worked at the task of organising for the League an efficient and well-drilled body of workers. The town was split into numbered sections each with its own officers and banners, and a branch formed in each.[182] The Operatives' tactics then adopted were only possible because many of the 30,000 Irish in Manchester were strong supporters of Daniel O'Connell, who often appeared on ACLL platforms. Many of the Chartists disliked O'Connell, who had quarrelled with Feargus O'Connor, a much more radical Irish nationalist. The extremists regarded him as a sham radical, particularly on account of his support for the new Poor Law.[183] The situation became more complex when the Chartists came to an agreement with one wing of the Tories. Edward Nightingale's antipathy to the Whigs was such that he was prepared to support the Tories in opposing J. B. Smith at the Walsall by-election when he stood unsuccessfully as a free trade and anti-Corn Law candidate. In Walsall Chartists broke up League meetings and the League's supporters forced the Tories to hold their meetings in private. These tactics were now used in Manchester. As Watkin put it fifty years later: 'We who were in a peaceable way advocating the unrestricted importation of food to starving people – that importation leading to more exports, more work and more wages also – were for a long time described as "Moral Force Whigs" in contrast with the "Physical Force Chartists." They discovered that the Duke of Buckingham's Protection or in other words "Unjust Rents" Association[184] was devoting its funds to ruffling and their indignation grew. They concluded "Why should we not test this physical force?"'[185]

O'Connell now agreed with Watkin and Tim Duggan, one of the leaders of the Manchester Irish, to join their forces

---

182   McCord, *Anti-Corn Law League*, pp. 98–9, 171.

183   D. Read, 'Chartism in Manchester', in A. Briggs (ed.), *Chartist Studies* (London: Macmillan, 1959), pp. 29–64, at p. 51; Pickering, *Chartism*, p. 96, points to the importance of the division in the Irish community in Manchester between supporters of O'Connell and O'Connor.

184   Properly the Central Society for the Protection of Agriculture.

185   Watkin, *Cobden*, p. 67.

to break Chartist control of public meetings in the area. The Operatives were well organised and could draw on the resources of the League. The Irish were tough and could be rough. Michael Donohough, 'Big Mick', an 'uneducated common labourer of humble parents', one of the many Irish in the OACLA for which he was officially a collector, who played a big part in the joint campaign, denied on numerous occasions that he was paid by the League (the national body), but he was in fact paid by the Manchester Anti-Corn Law Association.[186] That Cobden and others in the ACLL were prepared to countenance the use of physical force is evident from Watkin's diary entries. The OACLA waited upon the League and 'got all our requests as to the public meeting granted. We are to have plenty of flags etc.' and it seems the 'etc.' included good blackthorn sticks by which equipment the men understood the real meaning of their office – Anti-Corn Law police rather than flag-bearers.[187] And of course Sir Thomas Potter, John Brooks[188] and Cobden were present in Stevenson Square. When he was arranging the meeting in the Carpenters' Hall on 17 May Edward noted, 'We have to summon our forces to the battle. A strong one no doubt it will be', and afterwards, 'we had as pretty a row as I have ever witnessed and regularly thrashed them and passed our own resolutions'.[189] The Operatives had further complete victories before the climax in Stevenson Square on 2 June. For several days before the meeting the walls were placarded with

---

186   McCord, *Anti-Corn Law League*, p. 99.

187   Diary, entries for 23 May and 5 June.

188   John Brooks, banker of Cunliffe & Brooks, partner in Butterworth & Brooks, calico printers and merchants. A Tory in 1832 and borough reeve in 1839–40. Became a radical and a prominent ACLL activist, who succeeded J. B. Smith as president of the Manchester Association when the latter's difficulties in the Bank of Manchester compelled his resignation. Brooks 'collected good causes with as much ardour as he cultivated his business empire', and was said to renounce bed and sleep in his carriage between engagements. Pickering and Tyrell, *People's Bread*, pp. 18–19. See diary entry for 18 Feb 1845 and footnote for his financial affairs.

189   Diary, entries for 16 and 23 May.

Chartist denunciations of the millionaires and announcements that leading Chartists would address the meeting. O'Connell himself was invited but he did not come.[190] The repealers issued rival placards headed 'More Nightingales – Remember Walsall – Caution' and asking who had paid the Chartists' expenses. An agent of the duke of Buckingham was present at the Royal Hotel and Wilkins[191] was reported as having presented a cheque drawn by Buckingham for £150.[192] Cobden thought that the exposure of this treachery on the eve of the meeting in Stevenson Square fortunate, as it made the crowd unwilling to hear them. Moreover, while Watkin's account might have been discounted as youthful euphoria, his attitude was entirely shared by Cobden who in letters written in the week after Stevenson Square applauded the tactics of the Anti-Corn Law party and thought that it now had absolute possession in Manchester, and that the Chartist leaders had been annihilated.[193]

The description of the events in Stevenson Square is the last of the surviving entries of Watkin's diary for 1841. By 1844 when the main diary begins Corn Law repeal was not one of his main preoccupations. However, he continued to engage in Anti-Corn Law activities in 1841 and 1842. He spoke at the conference for ministers of religion of all denominations organised by Colonel Thompson in September 1841 when he presented an address on behalf of the Operatives Association.[194] Between then and March 1842 OACLA sponsored 38 lectures, two tea parties and five large public meetings. However, despite

---

190 Duggan to O'Connell, 25 May 1841, *The Correspondence of Daniel O'Connell*, ed. Maurice R. O'Connell (8 vols, Dublin: Blackwater for the Irish Manuscripts Commission, 1978), vii: *1841–1845*, p. 73.

191 Charles Wilkins, the clever but erratic barrister, then perhaps better known as a Tory agent than in any other character, according to Watkin, *Cobden*, p. 30.

192 Prentice, *Anti-Corn Law League*, i. 214.

193 Cobden to Charles Villiers and his brother Frederick Cobden 10 and 16 June 1841 (WSRO, Add. MS 6014, and BL, Add. MS 50750, ff. 43–4).

194 *The Corn Laws: The Formation of Popular Economics in Britain*, ed. Alon Kamish (6 vols, London: William Pickering, 1996), iv: *Free Trade and Religion*, p. 143.

Cobden's view in the afterglow of Stevenson Square, it was but a temporary victory. Subsequent meetings in the summer of 1841 can best be regarded as holding operations, achieved at the cost of alienating Irish and radical Chartist opinion, when the control of the repealers was achieved at times by physical means. A meeting in September 1841 ended with cheers for O'Connell and Cobden, but neither Watkin nor Cobden thought the position sustainable and discussed how best to secure firmer working-class support. In 1841 Cobden had seen that parliamentary success was a prerequisite of repeal, but despite his own victory in Stockport and gains by a few other League candidates, including Walsall, Peel and the Conservatives had won the 1841 general election decisively. This made working-class support more important but from Cobden's correspondence with Watkin in 1841 and 1842 it is apparent that he had no consistent strategy for securing their support or acquiescence when the priorities of the two groups continued to be fundamentally different. Consequently he considered possible steps largely from a tactical point of view. One possible route was to win over the Chartists to repeal and form an alliance. Another was to create separate effective working-class support possibly through the universal suffrage movement which was to gain ground that autumn. A third was to agree a stand-off.

Watkin initially seems to have thought some common front with the Chartists was possible and sent Cobden an account of an Operatives meeting at which Colonel Thompson spoke: 'your Conciliatory Meeting', as Cobden put it. But he warned Watkin against a partnership. Fraternisation would mean that the Chartists would probably want to incorporate Corn Law repeal with their five points.[195] Watkin also told Cobden that the only way of putting down O'Connor was by finding a universal suffrage leader who possessed the confidence of the people. He thought that Cobden should take this on personally and promised an association of 10,000 in Manchester by

---

195 Cobden to Watkin, 9 and 24 Oct 1841, Watkin, *Cobden*, pp. 79–83.

Christmas.[196] Cobden still felt a working-class movement independent of the Chartists was necessary, with a leader of firmness and character. He canvassed Watkin's opinion as to who might undertake this, as he was unwilling to take this on himself as Watkin had suggested.[197] Nothing came of this. He took Watkin seriously enough to tell him in early October that he and his little band were doing wonders by keeping alive the Anti-Corn Law agitation and also canvassed Watkin's views on starting another universal suffrage newspaper either in London or in Manchester on the lines of the *Weekly Dispatch*. Later in the autumn they discussed the possibility of an alliance with Sturge's Complete Suffrage Union. Cobden thought that the Union would be something in the League's rear to frighten the aristocracy and would take the masses out of the hands of their present rascally leaders,[198] but that Union members failed to grasp that the Corn Law issue was a working men's question primarily, and when it was settled, the middle-class leaders of the League would be able to concentrate on securing the rights of the unfranchised, a precise reversal of the Chartists' order of priorities.

Although the League Council had decided not to support the Daily Bread Society's scheme for importing grain by mass action, when in November 1841 there were Operatives meetings to consider the best means to be adopted by the working classes to obtain total repeal it was decided to support the Daily Bread Society in Manchester. Watkin and Warren were appointed to the committee. On New Year's Day 1841 a conference of working-class deputies was held with Watkin in the chair and later that month Cobden was urging Watkin to draw out the trades on the Corn Law question.[199] Nothing

196 WSRO, Cobden Papers, CP1, f. 44, Watkin to Cobden, 27 Sept 1841.

197 Cobden to Watkin, 9 Oct 1841, Watkin, *Cobden*, p. 81.

198 Cobden to J. B. Smith, 4 Dec 1841, quoted in Lucy Brown, 'The Chartists and the Anti-Corn Law League', in Briggs (ed.), *Chartist Studies*, pp. 342–71, at p. 366.

199 *Anti-Bread Tax Circular* (formerly *ACLC*), 18 Nov 1841 and 13 Jan 1842. For the Daily Bread Society more generally, see Pickering and Tyrell, *People's Bread*, pp. 152–3. Cobden to Watkin, 19 Jan 1842, Watkin, *Cobden*, pp. 86–7.

came of the Daily Bread Society, but the meetings seem to have led Cobden to suggest a stand-off – a public meeting between Chartists and repealers, amongst other things, to agree not to interfere with the agitation of either question on its own merits. 'This would be far better than to tie yourselves neck and heels for the rest of your lives to the O'Connorites which would be trumpeted in the Star as another victory.'[200] Any idea of a stand-off seems to have been made impossible by clashes at the Hall of Science in March, when O'Connor accused Watkin of inciting the Irish to attack the Chartists, charges Watkin denied personally to O'Connor. Cobden wrote to Edward, 'by the way I see that Feargus was upset at the Hall of Science; what was the secret of it?', and added that while he had no objection to ACLL members turning Chartist, 'we must not turn the League into a suffrage party'.[201] Watkin again told Cobden that what was wanted was a popular leader and compared disparagingly several of the possibles, including Hume, Fielden and Roebuck, with Cobden himself. 'We have no shepherd.'[202]

Edward had attended the Anti-Corn Law conference in London on 8 February 1842 and a week later was on the platform at a meeting at Manchester Town Hall. In the spring of 1842 Absalom was concerned about Edward spending too much time in politics and neglecting the family business so he arranged for his son to go to Italy with his friend George Wall and wrote to Cobden for advice on whom Edward should contact in Italy. Cobden replied that 'he would be very glad to render any service to your son for whose character, talents and energy I have great respect'. He assumed Absalom had a prudent desire to withdraw him for a short season from the vortex of political excitement into which his ardour had plunged him.[203] Absalom himself had never been to the Continent and the trip to Italy was probably an unusual experience for

200 Cobden to Watkin, 19 Jan 1842, Watkin, *Cobden*, pp. 86–7.
201 Cobden to Watkin, 11 and 16 Mar 1842, Watkin, *Cobden*, pp. 89–90.
202 *AWJ*, 12 Mar 1842; WSRO, Cobden Papers, CP1, f. 39, Watkin to Cobden, n.d., 'Northen, Sunday Morning'.
203 Cobden to Absalom Watkin, 22 Apr 1842, Watkin, *Cobden*, pp. 92–3.

someone in Edward's position for though in the 1830s the sons of Manchester employers like Thomas Ashton had attended German universities, holidays on the Continent were only taken by all sections of the well-to-do in the industrial cities after 1850 with the establishment of the railway networks.[204]

The Universal Suffrage movement seemed to carry more and more risks for the repealers and in any case its support was faltering. In June 1842, following a meeting of shopkeepers called to discuss repeal which had ended in repeal and the Charter being put cheek by jowl in a resolution, Watkin told Cobden that Sturge's movement had damaged the repealers much but as yet showed no sign of success. 'The radicals who went with us before, have now joined the charter association.'[205] Cobden agreed. It must be 'Charter' or 'Corn Law repeal', nothing between the two would do.[206]

The gap between the League and the working class widened in the spring and summer of 1842. The second Chartist petition was rejected by Parliament. Trade was stagnant and it was said the Manchester soup kitchens dispensed as much as 10,000 gallons a day. Even Cobden suggested that people should withhold taxes which would be paid into a fund to be used for the purchase of flour and bread which could be sold free of duty for the poor: a form of passive resistance which was an alternative to violence and part of Cobden's attempt 'to do all we can to increase the uneasiness of the rascals'.[207] In July someone asked Watkin whether the repealers would support a Chartist plan to put down house rent by paying only limited amounts, just as the Eccles Chartists were limiting the prices they would pay for milk, meat and bread. Watkin told Cobden that he was aware of the slippery fellows to be dealt with, but so many were

204 Gunn, *Public Culture of the Victorian Middle Class*, p. 26.
205 WSRO, Cobden Papers, CP1, f. 68, Watkin to Cobden, 22 June 1842.
206 Cobden to Watkin 22 June 1842, Watkin, *Cobden*, pp. 93–4.
207 Cobden to Bright, 21 June 1842, quoted in Wendy Hinde, *Richard Cobden: A Victorian Outsider* (New Haven and London: Yale University Press, 1987), p. 109, and Cobden to Watkin, 22 June, Watkin, *Cobden*, p. 94.

out of work that he was sure that if a united movement could be got up the scheme would be carried out well. Cobden told him sharply that his proposed plan of operation was not practicable. The attempt, said Cobden, had often been made to practise self-denial in eating and drinking for the attainment of political ends, but had never succeeded and never would. 'We have no other hope but the continued enlightenment of the people of all classes, accelerated as it will be by increased suffering.'[208]

By the time of the serious strikes (the Plug Plot) in Lancashire in the summer of 1842, the attempt by Watkin and Cobden to gain substantial working-class support for Corn Law repeal in Manchester had virtually ended. The industrial disputes began when three firms in Stalybridge threatened their weavers with a 25 per cent wage reduction. The dispute was generalised and a plan devised for workers to move from mill to mill turning out hands. This was done effectively in Stalybridge and neighbouring towns and spread to Manchester, with groups of workers marching on factories to call out their workers and pulling out the plugs of the boilers. The disputes led to disorder in Manchester itself where the disturbances lasted a week, particularly when Birleys' mill continued to work. Although John Brooks rebuked Birleys the magistrates could not stand aside. Absalom, who had been appointed a magistrate in 1839, and Edward were both involved in efforts to keep order. On 10 August Absalom drew up a notice in the name of the mayor and magistrates, warning people of the illegality of their proceedings and threatening punishment. He later went to the gasworks to relieve W. R. Callender, the magistrate who with troops had dispersed the mob from the works. He joined Edward and officers of the Rifles and Dragoons in the manager's parlour where windows and the looking glass were broken.[209] One thousand two hundred troops were sent into Manchester two days before the anniversary of Peterloo on August 16 when the planned procession by the strikers was abandoned. The strike

208 WSRO, Cobden Papers, CP1, f. 72, Watkin to Cobden, 15 July 1842; Cobden to Watkin 19 July 1842, Watkin, *Cobden*, p. 95.
209 Goffin, p. 225.

lost momentum though it lasted into September. Its failure finally destroyed hopes of a common approach between the workers and manufacturers. Cobden's attempts to enlist the trades on the side of the League gave rise to suspicions on the part of the Chartists that the manufacturers had deliberately provoked the Plug Plot, a suggestion taken seriously enough by the Government for Sir James Graham, the Home Secretary, to arrange for the publication of a dossier exposing the employers in the December issue of the *Quarterly Review*. While Bright and others wished to go some way to supporting the strikes in August, and the speeches of some League members were inflammatory, especially when they suggested that the continuation of the Corn Laws would drive workers into acts of violence, the lockouts and strikes seem to have had largely economic origins and to have started spontaneously. As has been seen trade was at a low ebb and cutting wages was the response. The League afterwards, possibly on behalf of the Government, sought evidence of those who opposed them. Cobden gave Bright a list of ACLL contacts who might help and added that Edward Watkin had given these matters some attention 'and is wise and judicious'.[210]

The League, however, had learned its lesson. While G. Kitson Clark's statement that the League changed sides when it saw that the people did not demand cheap bread but the Charter and better wages perhaps does not reflect the complexity of attitudes and events, certainly after August 1842 the League and its organ, the *Anti-Bread Tax Circular*, showed little interest in working-class needs or claims.[211] Edward's involvement was much reduced, though he took part in a number of events, including the Grand Free Trade Festival in April 1843 and, as his diary makes clear, he maintained a keen interest in the League, attending events such as the tea party at Bury with Cobden and John Brooks in January 1845, where he spoke,

---

210 Brown, 'Chartists', pp. 365–9; BL, Add. MS 43649, Cobden to Bright, n.d., but probably autumn 1842.

211 G. Kitson Clark, 'Hunger and politics in 1842', *Journal of Modern History*, 25 (1953), 355–74, at p. 368.

and commenting in July 1846 on repeal, particularly on the part played by Bright.[212]

Watkin as a witness of Manchester in the 1840s

Watkin is not to be regarded as adding significantly to our knowledge or understanding of the social problems of Manchester or of the workings of its industry. He says nothing which contradicts those who wrote on those matters and in one graphic instance – his visit with Prentice to the slums of Shude Hill – he confirms it. He personally did accept the need for some amelioration of the lot of the poor and wholeheartedly worked for one solution, the provision of public parks, which he saw as achievable. Moreover, though trying to get a grant from the Government, he saw it as the duty of the wealthy of Manchester to pay for the parks. This emerges very clearly from his articles in the Manchester papers where he implicitly accepts the criticisms of Manchester society made by the commentators and points to the lack of contact between the employers and workers, rich and poor, arguing, perhaps in a somewhat unrealistic way, that parks would provide a meeting ground for the social classes.

His diary is valuable as an account of middle-class life in Manchester in this period. In that respect the diary entries are perhaps nearer to, but in some respects very different from, the letters of Mrs Gaskell rather than her great novels. Many of her friends and correspondents were Manchester merchants and manufacturers or members of their families. They included the Shuttleworths, Langtons, Fairbairns, Marslands, Alcocks, Mark Philips and James Aspinall Turner of those mentioned in Watkin's diary and others like the Schwabes, Winkworths, Schuncks and Behrens. But his diaries have an added interest in showing the passion on the part of the Manchester middle classes for debate and discussion of the issues of the day – not only the Corn Laws where they saw a clear benefit for

212 Diary entries for 21 Jan 1845 and 12 July 1846.

themselves, but the state of Ireland, British rule in India or even the role of women in politics.[213] The entries also demonstrate the way in which the voluntary societies of Manchester worked; the institutions for learning; the appeals for charitable causes; and the various campaigns, above all that for public parks. They show how intensely some of the leading Mancunians were involved in these different activities, despite their tendency to live away from the city centre and the working-class areas. They lend support to those who argue that the middle classes in Manchester were not so engaged in money making and materialism that they ignored the interests of others, whether those affected by the fire in Quebec or the provision of parks in Manchester for the workers of Manchester and their families.[214]

213 Diary entries for 6 Jan and 2 Mar 1844. Watkin was one of 73 MPs who in 1867 supported John Stuart Mill's amendment to give women the vote on the same basis as men.

214 The *Leeds Mercury* commented on the generosity of Mancunians in 1845. It stated that £40,000 had been subscribed for the creation of churches, £70,000 for the ACLL, £3–4,000 for the Pottinger testimonial, £2,500 for the Dalton testimonial, £2,000 for Rowland Hill, £7,000 for Quebec, £2,000 for the Greeks, £10,000 for the Infirmary and £60,000 for the extension of the Exchange as well as £6,000,000 subscribed for railway shares. Report copied in *The Times*, 25 Aug 1845.

CHAPTER 2

Extracts from diary for 1841

May 9

We – the Operative Anti-Corn Lawites of Manchester – have managed to unite the repealers of the Union against the Chartists. Last Wednesday evening the latter called a meeting to pass a vote of censure on O'Connell. We sent all our men, and also the repealers, and entirely upset them. The malcontents left in an unusual hurry.

May 16

Last Monday night we had a lecture against the Corn Laws, delivered on the Green in the open air, at Cheadle by Finnigan.[1] We had an excellent meeting. On Thursday evening I went to the committee meeting of the OACLA[2] and then adjourned to the 'Queen Anne' in Long Millgate, where we formed an association for No 3 District.[3] On Tuesday next we are to have a meeting in the town hall for the purpose of backing ministers.[4] We have to summon our forces to the battle – a stormy one, no doubt, it will be.

---

1   John Joseph Finnigan had been involved with the Operatives Anti-Corn Law Association since 1839. An immigrant weaver, he became a full-time lecturer for the League in 1840. Opposed to O'Connor and the factory system.

2   *Watkin's footnote*: Operatives Anti-Corn Law Association.

3   *Watkin's footnote*: This did not mean No 3 of the fourteen districts of the old Police Commissioners, but of the districts into which we had mapped the town for the purposes of our own agitation.

4   *Watkin's footnote*: The Melbourne Cabinet was then favouring a fixed duty on corn as a measure of amelioration though not abolition.

May 23

On Monday evening last the Chartists held a meeting in Carpenters' Hall[5] for the purpose of continuing McDowall [sic] as a member of the Convention[6] a fortnight longer, and also – but this did not appear in the bills – for that of passing an address to the Chartists of Newry.

Our associates and the Irish and other repealers of the Union and the Corn Laws mustered in full strength, and we had as pretty a row as I ever witnessed. The Chartists were driven out of the hall four times. We regularly thrashed them and passed our own resolutions.

On Tuesday we mustered all up for the meeting in the town hall, where we gained another complete victory.

On Friday a public meeting took place in the town hall, Salford, which we attended and were victorious also.

On Thursday night there was a tea party in the Corn Exchange, which went off admirably. I was there, but had to leave for near an hour to attend a committee meeting of the OACLA. We resolved upon a committee to make arrangements for the public meeting to be held in the race week.

5   The hall was built in 1838 by the carpenters and joiners of Manchester to form a rallying place where working men might meet to discuss their grievances and where reformers might urge the cause of reform. Thomas Swindells, *Manchester Streets and Manchester Men* (5 vols, Manchester: J. E. Cornish, 1906–8), iii. 43.

6   *Watkin's footnote*: The Chartist Convention, that is. Dr McDowall was a noted man among them, and a very good speaker. He practised as a surgeon in the neighbourhood of Accrington, and his political sympathies seem to have been determined by what he saw of the excesses of the factory system of labour. In the cause of Chartism he suffered imprisonment. (Watkin's reference is to Dr Peter Murray McDouall, 1814–53, who became a Chartist as a result of seeing the poverty and disease in Ramsbottom, near Accrington. Topped the poll in the elections for the Executive of the National Charter Association in 1841 and 1842.)

On Saturday morning we waited upon the League and got all our requests as to the public meeting granted. We are to have plenty of flags etc, etc.

30 May

Last Monday evening I went into No 1 District where we formed an association.

On Tuesday evening I went into No 3, where we had a spirited meeting.

On Wednesday evening down into Salford, and then up to Kennedy's in Cable Street (Manchester).

On Friday evening at the Carpenters' Hall – a meeting of Requisitionists – near 2,000 there. I spoke, and agreed we should hold a meeting in the open air next Wednesday morning at 11.

During the week I have been uncommonly busy as a member of the meeting and procession committee. The procession we hope to be a great affair.

Our requisition of the working classes to the mayor was signed by 5,690. It was completed on Wednesday afternoon, 27th May and five of us went over with it. The mayor opened his eyes when he saw it, but after humming and hawing, he declined to give an answer until Friday. On Friday morning we received his reply – politely declining to call the meeting.

The Chartists threaten to give O'Connell, who is coming to Manchester on Tuesday morning, a 'welcome'. I hope they will not attempt it, as, if they do, blood will be shed. Nous verrons. They also talk of opposing us on Wednesday next.

Saturday 5 June

On Monday evening last I went into Salford, and spoke to the Salford repealers on the necessity of backing our movement on the following Wednesday. I afterwards went to Kennedy's, in Cable Street (Manchester), on the same errand.

On Tuesday morning I went to the Mosley Arms to see O'Connell and afterwards went to a meeting he addressed in the fields[7] behind Carpenters' Hall. In the evening I went to a dinner, in the hall, in honour of the 'Liberator'.

On Wednesday morning I was up before six, and went immediately to Newall's Buildings. I found Howie sending off the flags to the various districts. I went thence to Stevenson Square, where the hustings for the meeting were part erected. A few of the Chartists were there even at that early hour, and cheek by jowl with the hustings was a machine for the accommodation of the Chartist orators. I went from the square to Kennedy's in Cable Street, and thence to Timothy Mulhearn's. At this man's house I found about a score of 'boys' all ready for 'work'. These men were ostensibly 'flag-bearers', but by their being ornamented with good blackthorn sticks it was clear they understood the real meaning of their office – viz. that of A.C.L.[8] police.

7   *Watkin's footnote*: Fields since built over with the factories and cottages near the Medlock bank. Readers who know the locality may ask why it was that Manchester politicians were so used to debates and riots in Carpenters' Hall, then a suburban situation, and where the tide of politics no longer flows. The answer is that Carpenters' Hall, close to the Medlock, was then a new erection, popular as the property of a trade union, containing one of the largest rooms then to be had – one of the cheapest also (the charge was but one guinea per night) – and, what is more noteworthy still, the best Manchester meeting-room for *hearing*, till the Free Trade Hall came into being. Both the present Free Trade Hall and its chief predecessor of the League days have been remarkable in that respect. The curious in the matter may now visit the main room of the Manchester Free Reference Library, bear in mind that the central portion was the public meeting-room of the Town Hall of former days and be assured that the voices of most speakers got lost in the glazed dome of the roof. But in this, as in so many things, Mr Cobden took advantage: he was always careful to *speak down* to the ears of an audience, not to soar in the space overhead.

8   *Watkin's footnote*: Anti-Corn Law.

I took these men with me to the square, and we rather astonished the Chartists, who had increased in numbers somewhat by this time, with our appearance.

I got my horse, and we went back to Kennedy's, where our band assembled. After some preliminary preparations we marched up Oldham Road, down Livesey Street and George's Road,[9] to the 'Queen Anne' in Long Millgate. Here we took in tow the procession forming there and we went all together to Stevenson Square. We got there at a quarter to ten. The place was nearly filled with people. The Ardwick, Hulme, Salford No 1, Newton and Failsworth and Ratcliffe detachments had arrived, and were either in the square or in Lever Street and Hilton Street. We found it would be impossible to form the procession as we had intended, and we resolved to hold our meeting first. I rode about and got as many of our friends as possible to get in front of the hustings. I also got the principal part of the flags either reared against the walls of the church[10] on one side or Robertson's mill on the other, or else furled and tied to the pillars of the hustings. By this time Dr Sleigh and his son, with Charles Wilkins,[11] were come, and all the Chartist leaders were arrived. The police had taken possession of the Chartist hustings, much to the mortification of the 'Convention', all the members of which, we were told, were on the ground.[12]

At half-past ten I went on to the hustings. Almost immediately after a body of Chartists from the country, carrying two banners, one of which had inscribed on it, 'No new poor law',

9   *Watkin's footnote*: St George's Road, the present Rochdale Road.

10 *Watkin's footnote:* St Clement's, then in the Square, but afterwards removed.

11 *Watkin's footnote*: Dr Sleigh was a noted Irish barrister and Orangeman of the period, who lectured in support of the Society for the Protection of Agriculture. Charles Wilkins was the still more noted actor-barrister, Whig-Tory agent, and eventual Serjeant-at-Law.

12 Cobden told Charles Villiers that it was lucky that the police took possession of the hustings as had the Chartists done so, 'our men would probably have killed some of the vermin in their own cage' (WSRO, Add. MS 6014, letter of 10 June 1841).

and the other, 'Down with the Whigs,' made their appearance, and began to advance to the front, pushing our friends to the left and the right. This was submitted to pretty quietly, but at last from the violent conduct of the parties, and from the view of the hustings being partly hidden by the flags, an attempt was made to pull them down. This was immediately resisted, and the Chartists showed their preparation for a row by drawing forth short staves, with which they began to lay about them. Our Irish friends, made desperate by seeing this, and particularly by the brutal conduct of a fellow who nearly killed a poor man with a blow from an iron bar, rushed at the flags, tore them down, broke the shafts in pieces, and laid about them to such good effect as to drive the Chartists out of the square, leaving a kind of lane about four yards wide, next to the church, and reaching down as far as Lever Street.[13] At this moment a kind of desire manifested itself on the part of the men immediately in front of the hustings to join the affray. Seeing this, I jumped on the hustings rail, and pulling off my hat, said – 'Englishmen and Irishmen – many of you know me – you know that I am a repealer of the Union, and also a repealer of the Corn Laws. As your friend, and the unflinching supporter of the rights of the labouring millions, I call upon you to keep the peace. As you wish to see carried out the measures you are here to support, and as you value freedom for your country, remain perfectly quiet and do not be provoked to leave your places by the conduct of men who I believe, are hired to come here and disturb the meeting. Will you keep the peace? There.' 'Yes; yes,' resounded from all parts. 'Well, then' I continued, 'all of you who are determined to do so, hold up your hands.' At least three thousand hands were immediately held up. I then called for three cheers, which were given, and then I retired. On leaving the front of our hustings I was thanked by John Brooks, Sir Thomas Potter and others, for having, to use their words, 'preserved the meeting.' At precisely eleven, I rose and proposed

13   Cobden enquired at the Infirmary and ascertained that 13 cases had been taken there, none serious, merely lacerations of the scalp but no fractures (ibid.).

Cobden as chairman. McGowan[14] seconded him, and he was carried by ten to one. The Chartists, who had returned in part, voted against us, and made a slight noise, which was drowned in the cheers of the rest of the meeting.

Cobden briefly opened the proceedings, and then called upon Warren to move the first resolution. Warren not being on the hustings, I was compelled to step forward and do it myself. As the spooney[15] had the copy of the protest we intended to submit in his pocket, and as I had no copy, I was obliged to move a resolution which we never intended to put – 'That in the opinion of this meeting the Corn Laws are unchristian, impolitic and unjust.' J. Daly[16] seconded it. In moving it, I took care to pitch into Wilkins about his political harlequinism, thus in some measure preparing him for a warm reception from the meeting. When the motion had been duly moved and seconded, Dr Sleigh, Bairstow, Connor[17] and others, wanted to speak. After some little interruption, Dr Sleigh was allowed to speak. He was heard with great patience as long as he stuck to professions of regard for the working classes but as soon as he told them the Corn Laws benefited them, his voice was drowned in uproar, and he was not allowed to go on. At last he sat down, and the motion was put and carried, with twenty or thirty dissentients, out of a meeting of perhaps thirty thousand. Warren, who had just arrived, moved the protest. Finnigan seconded it, and it passed with five dissentients. McGowan[18] and Ridings[19] then moved and seconded the adjournment of

14   McGowan not traced.
15   Used in the sense of a silly or foolish person.
16   James Daly, an Irish Union repealer who joined the OACLA.
17   Probably Jonathan Bairstow, the Leicester handloom weaver who achieved prominence in the national Chartist movement and was a noted orator, and Charles Connor, an Irish Chartist repealer, but possibly John Connor, who joined the OACLA.
18   *Watkin's footnote*: When Dr Sleigh at the height of the tumult, exclaimed, 'Irishmen, hear me, I am an Irishman!' McGowan retorted, 'So was Castler-a--a-y! with prodigious effect.'
19   A working-class poet who was nicknamed 'the Byron of the Loom'.

the meeting until the effect of the protest on the votes of the Houses was seen. This was carried unanimously. The Rev. Daniel Hearne[20] then moved Cobden out of the chair, and a vote of thanks was given to C., who ably responded. We then formed a procession, and marched to the New Cross, down Oldham Street, Market Street, over Victoria Bridge, Chapel Street, over New Bailey Bridge, up Bridge Street, King Street, Mosley Street, down Oxford Road, Rusholme Road, round Ardwick Green, down London Road, Piccadilly, Market Street, into St Anne's Square – where we paused, and after sundry cheers for total repeal, the Queen, etc, etc, we separated. Thus ended one of the finest days' work Manchester ever saw.

20   Father Daniel Hearne, priest at St Patrick's, Livesey Street, Manchester, 1831–46. One of the few Roman Catholic priests to support repeal of the Corn Laws and, like O'Connell, also supported repeal of the Act of Union. Reprimanded for attending and speaking at the ACLL's Convocation of Ministers in 1841, he was removed by his bishop 'for the good of the religion and the salvation of souls' in 1846.

CHAPTER 3

Extracts from diary for 1843

No date, but probably 6, 7 or 8 October 1843

Mr Dickens wrote to us, desiring an interview for Wednesday night, October 4, at about 9 o'clock, to arrange for the meeting.

By arrangement with Mr Samuel Giles, whose brother had assisted in the education of Dickens,[1] we [Berlyn and I] took tea with him and then walked to Mrs Burnett's house, 3 Elm Terrace, Higher Ardwick. Ringing the bell, the door was opened by a youth in livery, who informed us that Mr Dickens was in the drawing-room, obtained our names, and running briskly up two or three steps, looked round and desired us to 'Please walk up.' Throwing open a door opposite the landing, our guide announced us, and we entered. Shaking hands with Mr and Mrs Burnett, we were at once introduced by Mrs Burnett to her brother, standing with one hand on the chimney-piece. He cordially welcomed us, and asked us to take some wine, and in passing the decanter upset his own glass, and deluged a very pretty book lying on the table.

Removing the book, he commenced the business conversation by asking as to the programme of the meeting. This I briefly gave him. We then spoke of the speakers, and talked of their several qualities in a free and laughing manner – Dickens elevating his eyebrows and nodding his head forward as the remarks struck him. An interjection as to the doubt he had in 'Pickwick' cast upon 'swarries' [soirées], provoked a quick, funny, glance which preluded an immediate turn of the talk to something else.

---

1   As a child Dickens had attended a school in Chatham run by the Revd William Giles, a young Baptist minister. Samuel Giles was a calico printer and joint secretary to the Manchester and Salford Town Mission for the Religious Instruction of the Poor.

'Whom do you intend to place beside me?' said Dickens. 'We thought Mr and Mrs Burnett,' I replied, 'as we imagined you would like better to have them with you than be environed by perfect strangers. Of course we wish to put off, if possible, the customary stiffness and stateliness of such meetings on this occasion. We wish to consult your comfort and your wishes.' 'No, I should not wish that,' he rejoined, 'by any means. I am obliged but I could not allow that. You must look at the result upon your object in choosing my supporters.' 'Then' we replied, 'we might place Mr Cobden on one side and the Mayor on the other.' 'That would do very well – excellently.' 'Or we might place a better mixture of parties. Perhaps we could place Mr Cobden and Mr James Crossley[2] side by side, and thus make violent political opponents for once put aside their differences for the good of the Athenaeum.' 'That would be beautiful. If you can get them to sit together, it will be excellent indeed … Then this meeting, I see, is to be held in the Free Trade Hall.' (Then followed enquiries as to the size of the room etc, etc.) 'You had 10,000 in it at the Education meeting, had you not?' said Dickens, addressing Giles.

Then we went into the history of the Athenaeum – spoke of the class to be benefited by it – of their sufferings and wants. In all this, Dickens appeared to take great interest. A remark as to opposition to such educational institutions by the bigoted, and the difficulty of reconciling all political bias, so as to make all men in this case work all together, caused Dickens to say, 'Well, we must do all we can to obtain the assistance of all classes; but if a certain party choose to oppose the education of the masses, we cannot help it. We must go on in spite of them.'

Speaking of the partial want of due sympathy with the intellectual welfare of the people, and of the necessity of bringing to the

2   James Crossley was a solicitor, and partner in Crossley & Sudlow. President of the Athenaeum, 1847–50. Built up a very large library. FSA. In 1843 founded the Chetham Society, and was president until his death.

aid of the institution a celebrity like his – superior to party predilections, and powerful with all men – he said – modestly disclaiming some of the merit we wished to attach to his visit, – 'Yes, such institutions are most necessary and useful, and there is a too general desire to get the utmost possible amount of work out of men instead of a generous wish to give the utmost possibility of improvement. I shall enforce the necessity and usefulness of such invaluable means of education. I must put it to them strong' ('or give it to them strong').

Speaking of the bazaar and its proceeds, he displayed a complete knowledge of all the history of the undertaking. He said it would not do to talk too much of the result being yet insufficient – 'I suppose I may say that the debts of the Institution are in rapid course of liquidation, eh! that will be the way.'

Mr Giles happened to hint about the utility of appealing to the audience from the chair for money. To this I objected that it would be unfair to Dickens and too much like making a marketable commodity of him. He said, 'Yes, I should not like to do that; but I will try and excite their liberality in another and equally or more useful way.'

He spoke of Lord Brougham and his note of apology. Dickens said he had received a note from his Lordship, regretting his inability to attend the soirée – 'but how would Cobden and Brougham consort or agree together?'[3] 'Oh! we have no cause to remember political differences – they are no business of ours.' 'Oh! of course not; but you should have Mr Bright there to make the set complete.'

We then spoke of miscellaneous matters – music and the taste for it among the rest. Alluding to the new systems, it was

3   Brougham, in 1832 the champion of free trade and of popular causes, had recently attacked the ACLL for appealing directly to the mob and condemned as unconstitutional its actions in raising money to buy freeholds to obtain the franchise.

mentioned that Mr. Burnett taught the singing class at the Athenaeum. 'Ah! so he tells me,' he replied, as I thought with the air of one who seemed to wish 'not too much to be said about that.'

We arranged that he should come into the hall immediately after tea. He talked of the effect. 'Get the tea all over – I must confess to a sort of horror of tea-things (or tea on a grand scale), and I think the best way to excite and keep up the interest would be to appear immediately after tea, and go to work at once.'

Berlyn handed him a number of the Bazaar Chronicle, and told him that his friend Pickwick had been helpful to that document.[4] He received the papers, slightly laughed, and turned the conversation from his works. Berlyn told him that we had taken a liberty with his portrait (by placing it upon the ticket). He praised the ticket, and declared we were welcome to make any use we liked either of the portrait or the original.

We spoke of future plans for benefiting the institution, and of our intention and hope of being able to establish others. 'The once sure success of one institution will establish others elsewhere,' he said; 'therefore the Manchester Athenaeum is not

---

4   *Watkin's footnote*: E.g. "Mr Pickwick arrived yesterday at the Bazaar ... accompanied only by Mr Tracy Tupman ... and was made to 'put in' sixteen raffles and to expend £1 4s 9¼ d in miscellaneous goods. 'They will please Sam's children' said Mr Pickwick. Handing over a handsome sum to Mrs Milner Gibson at her stall, and desiring her to lay it out for him according to her own taste, Mr Pickwick received in return for his money, twelve pincushions, four babies' slippers, two inkstands, some engravings, three ladies' caps, and a splendid large cushion, which latter he magnanimously declared he would 'notwithstanding the injuries she had attempted to do him' send as a present to Mrs Bardell. 'Put into this raffle, sir,' said a handsome young lady to Mr P. 'Raffles I don't like' said Mr Tupman; 'they are in my opinion a contrivance for cheating the public.' 'You are wrong, sir,' rejoined Mr P; 'they are a very harmless mode of exciting that more vigorous agitation of the pecuniary atmosphere which people commonly call 'raising the wind'. Put down Mr Tupman's name, my dear'" and many pages of the like.

the sole thing depending on your efforts: it is the principle of athenaeums that we are really struggling for.'

After some further conversation, we arranged to meet him at the Athenaeum in the morning at twelve, and to take him to the meeting in the evening (with James Heywood), and rose to go. While standing, the 'numerous advantages' of the Athenaeum were again dragged upon the carpet. After naming them all, he added, briskly and laughingly – 'And two balls, two concerts, per annum'. He saw us down stairs and we departed.

On Thursday morning we obtained the attendance of Cobden, the Mayor,[5] Sir Thomas Potter, Milner Gibson,[6] James Heywood, Langton and one or two others, at the Athenaeum; and on Dickens' arrival we (B and I) introduced them to him. We then all walked round the institution, talked about it in all ways, dived into its cellars, and mounted to its top, calling at the Courts of Bankruptcy on the way.[7] Then we went to the Free Trade Hall, amid sundry jokes about Crossley and Cobden, political parties etc., etc.

Dickens was much pleased with the hall; immediately on entering it he said he felt that he could make himself exceedingly well heard in it.[8]

---

5   James Kershaw, cotton spinner and calico printer, Leese, Kershaw & Callender. A Manchester alderman and mayor in 1842–43. A prominent ACLL supporter. MP for Stockport 1847 until his death in 1864, when Edward Watkin was elected unopposed to succeed him.

6   Thomas Milner Gibson was MP for Manchester. He was preferred as Liberal candidate to Cobden.

7   *Watkin's footnote*: One of our means of raising money was to let an entire floor of the building to the Bankruptcy Commission, and more than twenty years passed before the Athenaeum, even in its prosperity, flourished sufficiently to do without the rent they paid for their courtrooms.

8   *Watkin's footnote*: Not the present building, but one of its predecessors – 1840–55.

Passing near the gallery, Cobden archly pointed to the sheaves of wheat painted on the sides, and said people had tried with a microscope and been unable to find the word 'free' upon it. 'Ah! but you should send for Mr Barlow and let him try', cried Dickens.[9]

In the evening James Heywood called with his carriage at the Athenaeum and we (Berlyn and I) went to Burnett's in it with him. We found Dickens waiting, and as we had a few minutes to spare we sat down to talk. I told him that we should have invited General Duff Green, an American now in Manchester, to attend the soirée but for the exasperation felt by the Yankees ever since his 'exposure' of them.[10] 'Ah, General Green, I know. Never mind – the Americans will thank me for it themselves in ten years hence.' He spoke of Cobden – thought he had been older than he was. We then spoke of the 'manufacturing district face' and the prematurely aged appearance of the people round here, etc.

On the way to the hall we talked of Hood and Jerrold.[11] Dickens lamented Hood's ill-health and poverty, and much praised his writings; admired Jerrold and lauded Punch, which, he said he generally 'saw before it was in print.'

9   *Watkin's footnote*: Mr Dickens evidently remembered the Barlow-Peel-Velvet affair. (Elsewhere Watkin explains that one of the symbols of the Anti-Corn Law movement was known as 'The Peel Velvet'. Some of Cobden's friends, calico printers, got up a beautiful material in cotton velvet, closely covered all over with a small design of ears of corn, and a waistcoat of it was offered as a compliment to the Premier, Sir Robert Peel, by Mr Barlow of Ancoats Vale. Although Peel accepted it, probably without closely examining the cloth, someone pointed out to him the significant word 'Free' repeated in tiny letters on every binding of the corn. On learning this Peel returned the gift. A cartoon was published depicting Lady Peel in tears over a dress-piece of the velvet, which her obdurate husband was forbidding her to wear. Watkin, *Cobden*, p. 102.)

10   General Duff Green, a brigadier general in the Missouri militia. Moved to Washington. Journalist, newspaper proprietor, political operator and Southern economic promoter. President Tyler's unofficial ambassador to England, 1841–44.

11   Douglas Jerrold, playwright, journalist and wit. Constant contributor to *Punch* 1841–57.

I tried to turn the talk upon America. Heywood asked about the society of the American Universities. Dickens praised it highly – said it was of necessity a little world within itself – that its members banded themselves together in order to protect themselves from the system by the evils of which they were surrounded. He said he had formed friendships amongst them which would last his life. He praised the society of Boston, and I think of New York and Philadelphia, and said the feeling against slavery was stronger than people imagined, and was growing.

I noticed that Dickens occasionally said, when interested in conversation, 'Oh lord (or law), yes!' 'Oh law, no!' – a cockneyism.

Dickens is in appearance about thirty-five or thirty-six years of age,[12] about 5 feet 8 inches high, elegantly, compactly, but slightly made; his face is not, strictly speaking, handsome; the features are not very good, as some people say they are. His eyes are very dark and full of fire, and, when turned upon you, give a light to his rather dark countenance, such as I have seldom seen before beaming on any face. He has a good deal of the eyebrow-elevating, shoulder-shrugging and head-nodding peculiar to people who have travelled a good deal. His voice is well regulated and strong, but there is an occasional slight peculiarity, of which the defect of 'maw-mouthed' people would be the extreme caricature. He can look very expressively. When he looks 'droll', he looks very droll; when interested deeply so. His hair is dark brown and abundant.

12 *Watkin's footnote*: Actually, he was under thirty-two.

CHAPTER 4

The diary for 1844

Part of Watkin's review of 1843

[As a result of] my exertions in good measure the Athenaeum has been restored to usefulness and vigour and the £2,300 has been raised towards paying the debt. I am glad to think that my talking and services in one way or another, have aided in gaining the half-holiday, since that new regulation, provided it be permanent, bids fair to be the fruitful parent of happiness and good to the vast number of sensible people and at no harm to the fools.[1]

Minor matters I do not please myself with. But I have not minded my own business exclusively.

As to mental cultivation I have improved my speaking by frequent spouting in public and at the Lity Socy. Writing I have not followed much, having been too busy drawing up billets and statements for the Ath. Lity Bazaar.

Reading has been sorely neglected. I have had no time, or little time and no quiescence of mind, a condition all-necessary with reading to advantage. My manners, the result of mental improvement, have not yet progressed. In polish, the consequence of greater intercourse with the world I imagine I am more shining. I have had much to do with ladies and that has been of advantage. I have been less mauvaise haute.

In business ability I think I am no worse: little better certainly.

In religious matters I have I fear rather gone back. The little episode named a page or two back has made me think a little more. I hope it may continue to have that influence at least. I

---

1   The surviving diary starts with the words 'my exertions'.

make no resolves for 1844. I know what I ought to do – what duty calls for. I shall endeavour to do it. I shall try to work hard and improve in amount of knowledge and in mode of communicating it by speech and writing.

I hope I may have more cause for self-congratulation next year than I now have, and that at all counts that I may deserve it more.

Saturday January 6 1844

Monday last (New Years day) of course at home.

Tuesday in town – at the Literary Society. My father's question – spoke briefly.[2]

Thursday & Friday at home – lounging, reading and walking.

Bowels rather out of order – cannot get them to work right somehow. This makes me at once lazy, uneasy, angry.

Saturday January 13

Wednesday last (10) at the Soirée at the Athenaeum. Tea, a discussion of the spiritual character of the Inst[itution]s and literature of the middle ages as compared with the present – I spoke (very badly) – dancing from 10 to 1/2 past 4 on Thursday morning.[3]

2   This and other notes providing contextual detail for proceedings of the Literary Society are taken from the Society's minute book – MCL, MSF 062 M3. The size of the votes at these debates did not reflect the attendance as many members left before the end, some after the opening speech.
His father's question was 'Has Ireland been injured by the Union?' It was decided in the negative by 9 votes to 5.

3   The Annual Soirée of the Essay and Discussion Society (of the Athenaeum) – 'an able speech by E.W. Watkin' (*MG*, 13 Jan 1844). He opposed G. H. Cope who took a favourable view of the influence of the church in the Middle Ages which for its faith, works of charity and spirituality of character was pre-eminent over the present era. Watkin argued that for science, religion and intelligence the present age was distinguished by far beyond its predecessor.

Last night (Friday) at William Evans' at Crumpsall Grove – a pleasant party, left at 1 and staid at Whns.[4]

Business a little excited once or twice but not much doing. Sold 2 or 3 thousand pieces to come in.

Feel myself flat – an ignoramus.

On Monday at Cobden's request I wrote a placard about O'Connor and had it printed and posted. I see it is noticed in the Star this week and Leach is to lecture on it tomorrow (Sunday).[5]

I wrote a review of Hood's New Magazine on Thursday Evg: It appeared in the Times of today. I wrote to Hood yesterday.[6]

4   William Evans was a very active member of the Anti-Corn Law League Council. Later a pall-bearer at Cobden's funeral, and chairman of the Emancipation Society. A member of the Literary Society. His wife, Mary, was also active on behalf of the ACLL. 'Whns' not identified.

5   O' Connor had wanted to debate with Cobden 'Would the repeal of the Corn Laws and the establishment of Free Trade be of immediate benefit to the working classes?' Cobden prevaricated about the wording and then it was found that O'Connor owned property. According to the *Northern Star* (6 and 13 Jan 1844) the placard ran 'The Murder Out. O'Connor an avowed bread taxer. To the Working Classes – O'Connor has thrown off the mask. He is a landlord. Signed, One of Yourselves.'

James Leach was a Manchester Chartist, formerly a factory operative, but now a touring lecturer and member of the executive of the National Chartist Association. Author of *Stubborn Facts from the Factories by a Manchester Operative* (London: John Ollivier, 1844).

6   The review of *Hood's Magazine and Comic Review Miscellany* of 1 Jan 1844 appeared in the *Manchester Times* of 13 Jan. It was almost a column in length. Watkin identified Hood as associated with the department of English literature the object of which was to make men wiser by making them merrier. He distinguished between ill- and good-natured laughter, and quoted a lengthy extract from the poem *A Haunted House* and a review, he supposed by Hood, of Miss Martineau's *Life in the Sick Room*: the unfurnished mind is a more dreadful destitution than the sick room or garret. An intellectual feast with a great number of talented pieces was Watkin's verdict. Watkin later invited Hood to the Athenaeum soirée in October 1844 but he declined as for him all long journeys, save one, were over – no slight hardship while steam and rail afford such facilities for locomotion. *The Letters of Thomas Hood*, ed. Peter F. Morgan (Edinburgh: Oliver & Boyd, 1973), p. 649.

By the by on Monday evening I attended a Bazaar Committee meeting called at the request of Mr James Heywood, to investigate some reports about Miss Abraham's dishonesty at the bazaar. Was decided not go into the matter. After the meeting I went to the Essay and Discussion Socy. I took part in the debate going on – on a question of Robinson's.[7]

Tuesday evg, Jany 23

Monday evg Jany 14 at Geo Wall's.[8]

Tuesday at the Lity Socy – a question of Newall's[9] on the right and expediency of permitting associations like the repeal association to meet at any time in any number in public – I replied to him and spoke 'comme ça'.

Wednesday was at home – skimmed a little about the middle ages from Dunham's book in the Lardner Cyclopaedia.[10]

Saturday afternoon at the drawing of the Athm lottery. Stayed the night and Sunday with Berlyn – we had to draw up a

---

7   Probably Smith Philips Robinson in view of reference to S. P. Robinson on 27 July 1844, rather than Samuel Robinson, the cotton manufacturer of Manchester and Dukinfield. The former was a salesman in the print warehouse of Wright & Lees in Manchester and prominent in the ACLL and later secretary of the Lancashire Reform Union.

8   Close friend of Edward's with whom he had travelled to Italy in 1842. He married Edward's cousin – see diary entry for 27 Sep 1844 below. In 1846 became a coffee planter in Ceylon (now Sri Lanka) where he was later a leading figure in the community of British planters and merchants.

9   Probably John Newall, a solicitor of Cross Street. The question was: 'Is it legal or expedient that a body of men having recognised rulers or leaders, contributing large sums of money to a common fund, and receiving contributions to that fund from the subjects of foreign states should assemble, unnamed, on any occasion, and in any number, for the purpose of effecting a radical change in the constitution of the empire?' Decided in the affirmative, 18 to 3.

10 S. Astley Dunham wrote the volumes on the *History of Europe during the Middle Ages* (1833–34) in Lardner's *Cabinet Encyclopaedia* which was published in 133 volumes (London: 1830–49).

report for the Ath Annual Meeting. Last night, Monday, at the adjourned discussion on Cope's paper at the Athenaeum.[11] A splendid discussion. Spoke pretty well. Cope's reply really fine – sophisticated but ready, witty and truly eloquent at times.

Business moderate: sold nothing today but 1300 delaines.[12]

Saturday, Jany 27

On Wednesday at home. Rode walked and read.

Thursday night at the Athm directors' meeting.

Friday a Committee meeting at the Ath.

Business moderate.

I find John has notions of parsonifying.[13] If so I must live in Manchester and work a trifle harder.

Thursday, Feb 1

Last Monday night I staid with Geo Wall and spent rather a dull evening talking about next to nothing.

Friday at the Lty Socy[14] and then to Sheridan Knowles' lecture on the 'genius of Shakespeare'.[15]

11 C. H. Cope had presented the paper on 10 Jan (entry for 13 Jan). He was an accountant and general agent.

12 A light fabric, originally of wool but by then probably mixed cotton and wool.

13 Edward's brother, John, asked Absalom for his consent on 18 Jan (*AWJ*, 18 Jan 1844).

14 Edward Herford's question, 'Is it expedient that the votes of the electors for members to serve in Parliament should be taken by ballot?' was affirmed, 7 to 0.

15 James Sheridan Knowles, playwright and lecturer. Then lessee of the Theatre Royal. Wrote a life of David Kean.

Wednesday the annual meeting of members of the Ath. My father in the chair. I made a short speech – ineffective. Dr Vaughan who was there made a brilliant speech.

Today I learn that I am not at the head of the Poll as a director of the Athm. A suitable number, however, in the list: but 81! It is however gratifying to be 'first favourite' in a small way.[16]

Sunday, Feb 4

On Friday I had to meet Coveney (one of the late Athm directors) and someone who had told him I had been canvassing against him.[17] I met C.J. Goodwin (another ex-dir) at the Clarence Hotel. G. however perfectly exonerated me and both parties expressed themselves in the highest terms of me.[18]

Friday night the first meeting of the new board. Plenty of talk and little business.

Yesterday at home (not very well) doing almost nothing.

16 Dr Vaughan was a minister of religion and president of Lancashire Independent College, Withington, Manchester. At its opening in 1840 he said the training provided would favour an educated over an emotional ministry. His *The Age of Great Cities: or Modern Society Viewed in Relation to Intelligence, Morals and Religion* (London: Jackson & Walford) had been published in 1843. Watkin's speech was to thank the ladies whose untiring exertions had crowned the bazaar with success and to propose a reduction in their subscriptions to the library and lectures. He used the membership of the ladies, who belonged to no party, to strengthen his denial that the Athenaeum was a party institution. The membership, which had dropped to 700 in 1841, was now 1,500 (*MG*, 3 Feb 1844). Watkin's comment on the poll seems to have been the result of misplaced youthful expectations. The number of votes he received was 81.

17 William Coveney of Coveney & Hewitt, manufacturers of galloons and doubles.

18 Goodwin has not been identified. The Clarence Hotel was in Spring Gardens.

The cotton market has been terribly excited during the past week. 109,000 bags have been sold – a greater number than were ever sold before. Prices are up. The prices of yarns and cloth are very unsteady. I see there is to be a meeting of spinners and manufs at 3 to consider what to do.

Peel declares his intention of doing nothing further and Howick declares that the question will be no alteration or total repeal.[19] We shall declare for (or rather prefer) the latter. A meeting was held on Wednesday at Wakefield. Cobden and Bright were there. Lord Morpeth[20] attended and spoke. He is not just for total repeal but says he will be if nothing is done for a year. Cobden spoke after and exposed the nonsense of a fixed duty in style. His speech will do much to bring round the waverers and to encourage Morpeth to put himself at the head of this cause in the House of Commons.

Saturday, Feb 10

On Monday night at Geo Wall's.

Tuesday night Ath Committee meeting and then to Sheridan Knowles' lecture on the poets.[21]

Wednesday at home.

Thursday

Friday (last night) at a concert in the Ath. with my mother.

---

19   i.e., repeal of the Corn Laws. Howick, son of Earl Grey, had been a member of Melbourne's cabinet. Whig MP for Sunderland and succeeded to the earldom in July 1845.

20   Son of the earl of Carlisle, then out of Parliament.

21   'Readings from the British Poets interspersed with observations about their genius'.

Nothing of consequence occurred. Some business un-
pleasantness has arisen, but I suppose occasional disagreements
are inevitable.

Saturday, Feby 17

Monday night at Geo Wall's.

Tuesday – Lity Socy[22] and Com at Athenaeum.

Wednesday at home.

Thursday

Friday Com at Athm.

Some most infernal annoyances in business. I find that on
several instances in these scarce articles, we have been beaten
by other agents selling, when we could not and selling at prices
we could not obtain! All in one week. I see the infernal effects
of giving our thoughts to other things than business. I believe
that I must – if I get on at all – literally commence de novo. I
must get together a properly classified set of connections – now
broken up and in disorder for want of attention – and I must
with care and deep attention acquaint myself with the business
mysteries which I once knew but have forgotten – and again get
hold of the thread I have let drop from my fingers which must
enable me to walk safely in the labyrinths of trade. I am a fool.
Money first – distinction afterwards. I have tried to begin at the
wrong end and have earned notoriety – the thorn and curses
of fame – only – while I have lost that habit of obedience to
circumstances – that readiness to act and think which business
disciplines once made me in some part master of.

22 Philip Holland's question: 'Is it desirable that a system of medical
    police similar to that in France or Germany should be introduced
    into England and would such a system be an effective substitute for
    Coroners' Inquests?' The first clause was decided in the negative by 3 to
    1, and the second part unanimously.

My father goes to London on Monday – John Brooks action against Sowler.[23]

I was with Col. Thompson on Friday for a few moments.[24] The old boy has been dealing in rather strong language at the meeting in the Hall last Wednesday.

Saturday, February 24

My father and mother left for London last Monday morning. I expect them back the day after tomorrow.

Business has been very flat. I have worked hard but find myself less au fait than I ought to be. On Tuesday particularly I was active and industrious and I find as I have always found before that activity is the best promoter of mind as well as of bodily health. I have again felt a consciousness of power, an inborn strength, lately stranger to my experience.

I can hardly stop laughing at myself. On Tuesday excited with work I thought as I hurried up and down that there was no sorrow

23   Absalom was subpoenaed to give evidence in the action brought by John Brooks against Thomas Sowler, editor and publisher of the *Manchester Courier*, for libel. Sowler had imputed to Brooks that he had dishonourably promised a subscription to the Manchester and Eccles Church Building Society without intending to pay it, and to escape payment had picked a quarrel with the clergy who were patrons of the building society. He also alleged that Brooks had promised a subscription to the ACLL without intending payment to induce others to give. The case was settled on the first day, on the proposition of Sowler's counsel, much to Sowler's annoyance according to Absalom, as there were not sufficient grand jurors and neither counsel would pray a tales, i.e. ask the court to make up the jury from the common jury panel. Each litigant paid his own expenses (*AWJ*, 23 and 24 Feb 1844; *MG*, 28 Feb 1844).

24   An independent radical, proprietor of the *Westminster Review* 1829–36. MP for Hull 1835–37 and, after several unsuccessful contests, MP for Bradford 1847. Wrote *A Catechism of the Corn Laws* (London: Cowie & Strange, 1827) and active in the Anti-Corn Law movement as well as in other causes.

or trouble but a deal of pleasure in an active business life. The day after I thought rather differently – the day after and today hard at it again – I feel my feet once more. What a weathercock.

Geo Wall here last Monday night – old Mr Makinson and his daughter.[25]

On Tuesday night, the reverse.

Saturday, March 2

My father and mother came home on Monday night last.

On Tuesday evening I floated my question about women at the Lity Socy – a good discussion – but only three voted with me in favour of female participation in debate. How maddening.[26]

Wednesday staid with Geo Wall: attended a Committee meeting (Books and papers) at the Athm and a lecture on Complete Suffrage by Spencer[27] at the Corn Exchange.

Thursday evening a borough meeting to take the state of Ireland into consideration, the Mayor in the chair, took place in the Free Trade Hall which was crowded.[28] Sir T. Potter, Mr Heywood, Richd Gardner[29] were the speakers. The resolutions,

25 Members of Edward's mother's family.

26 His question was: 'The ladies of England would through their habitual participation in political and general discussion and in legislation, improve the character of debate, moderate angry bigotry, humanise the laws, and help elevate the ideas upon which Acts of Parliament and social regulations are founded.' It was decided in the negative by 7 to 3.

27 A meeting of the Complete Suffrage Union at which Revd Thomas Spencer spoke. Spencer was perpetual curate of Hinton Charterhouse near Bath. Moved the resolution for complete suffrage at Joseph Sturge's first Complete Suffrage Union Conference in Apr 1842.

28 Alexander Kay was the mayor, 1843–45.

29 Richard Gardner was the son of Robert Gardner. He wrote pamphlets and newspaper articles. Married the daughter of the count of Mendlesloh, the Wurtemburg Minister, and was MP for Leicester from 1852 until his death, aged 43, in 1856.

pretty strong ones, were carried unanimously and all went off exceedingly well. I have had a good deal to do with the arrangements for this meeting during the week, and I fear meetings, resolutions, tother tother have taken up too much of my time. I seconded the vote of thanks to the Mayor, but only said a few words.[30] The Guardian walks into the meeting sham Reform-like.

Last evening I went with Berlyn to a party at Mrs Wooley's. We met a Mr and Miss Rafter and a 'dollop' of other people, left at 2 and stopped with Berlyn.[31] In waking this morning find that a tremendous fire had broken out and was raging in George St. It began at 6. By 9 all the warehouses, on one side from St James Church to York St, were completely destroyed. Loss £130,000. Decidedly the largest fire for years.[32]

Business has been miserably flat. Hardly anything done.

Richd Gardner – or Dick as he is usually called – has called on me. He wants me to come out as a public person. I have had a little talk with him.

Sunday, March 10

On Monday evening with Geo Wall: met a Mr Outram.[33]

30 The *MG* (2 Mar) reported that the majority at the meeting were Irish. The newspaper could not consent to such a meeting being described by Prentice as comprising a considerable proportion of the respectability of Manchester. It ended with three cheers for O'Connell and three groans for the *Guardian*. Watkin spoke briefly recommending every man present to take a sheet of paper and during the next day to get it filled with the names of all who were opposed to the course of the present government in Ireland.

31 Probably Mrs Elizabeth Wooley who presided over a stall at the Athenaeum bazaar and was secretary of the Manchester Ladies Committee of the national Anti-Corn Law Bazaar in May 1845. Rafter and Miss Halkett Rafter were artistes closely associated with the Theatre Royal.

32 Ten mercantile and manufacturing firms suffered heavy losses (*MG*, 13 Mar 1844).

33 Possibly John Outram, a bookkeeper.

Wednesday evening Geo Wall came over here and staid till Thursday afternoon: we walked to town together.

Yesterday I should have gone to Mr Abraham Barnes to meet Mr Geo Thompson[34] but did not, going instead to Stockport (Borella[35] with me) and walking thence home. On Friday afternoon I went with my father, Joseph Adshead and Borella to look through the New Bailey. I was much pleased with the general arrangements but of course pained at so many human beings in so degraded a position.[36]

Saturday, March 16

Last Monday evening staid with Geo Wall.

Tuesday at the Lity Socy. Shawcross's question on the policy of British rule in India.[37]

34 George Thompson was a leader of the anti-slavery movement in the 1830s, then a member of the ACCL. MP for Tower Hamlets, 1847–52. Abraham Barnes lived in Ancoats.

35 Borella, a contemporary and friend of Edward Watkin's. Probably Francis Borella who signed the requisition for the public parks meeting. Borella, Harling and Berlyn were regarded by Absalom as the 'children of the Athenaeum' (*AWJ*, 10 Sep. 1843).

36 Adshead had written *Distress in Manchester: Evidence of the State of the Labouring Classes in 1840–2* (London: Henry Hooper). In 1843–44 he had given a series of lectures on prison discipline, which had not endeared him to the prison authorities, and according to Absalom, he was requested not to ask questions in the course of this visit (Goffin, p. 240). Later the author of *Criminal Manchester*. Failed in business as a merchant, but set up as an agent.

37 Edward Shawcross was a contemporary of Absalom's, a member and then president of the Literary Society. The question 'Has British rule in India been marked by sound policy?' was decided in the negative by 11 to 1.

Wednesday at a party at Mr Alcock's – the occasion Tom's coming of age.[38]

Thursday at the Athm. Dr Vaughan's lecture on Athens.

Friday at the Theatre. Miss Rafter's benefit. Artaxerxes.[39]

Business has been rather better this week. We have not sold much but a more genial feeling prevails and the India news tho' announced as bad seems to be satisfactory if one may judge by the increase in the purchases of goods.[40]

I have worked pretty well this past week. I do not however buckle to, as I ought. I really must improve. It will ne'er do to be grinding away all the days of my life without accumulating a farthing or gaining the power of doing some good for my own reputation or the world. It will never do.

Mar 23

On Monday evening with Geo Wall – learning to play at chess.

Tuesday at a lecture on the state and prospects of Christianity in India by a Church missionary named Weitbrecht.[41]

38 Family friend. John Alcock was a manufacturer of tablecloths and damasks in Gatley. Lived at Gatley Hill.

39 The Rafters' last appearance of the season. Arne's opera, *Artaxerxes*, was being performed for the first time in Manchester. Miss Rafter played Maudane. A farce, *Popping the Question*, and other entertainments were included (*Manchester Times*, 9 Mar 1844).

40 Following the battles of Maharajpoor and Punniar and the capture of Gwalior, the British troops withdrew and left sovereignty to the Maharajah.

41 John James Weitbrecht, German born, but a priest in the Church of England since 1830. He was a missionary with the Church Missionary Society in North India from 1830 to 1841. Died of cholera in Calcutta, 1852.

Thursday at the annual dinner of the St Anne's Ward reform association – Alderman Willert in the chair. Ald Shuttleworth, Jer Garnett, Ed Shawcross[42] and others were there. I proposed 'the people'. In a fair speech. Scoffed covertly at the recent time-serving of the Guardian and I believe pleased the old fogies present who are now reposing upon their 'laurels'. Afterwards, at Shuttleworth's request, I proposed the 'Memory of Thos Walker'. We had rather a jovial evening. Met Berlyn after all was over. The night or rather morning was mild and pleasant and Edwards, Berlyn and I promenaded up and down Oxford Road for an hour and then I went home with Edwards.

Business miserable. 3900p sold and a little yarn (500lb). Flat state, falling and unprofitable. However my boy, grind away – grin and abide – do your duty and leave the rest to providence. Cloth is coming down with a rattle.

Saturday, Mar 30

On Monday with Geo Wall

Tuesday at the Lity Socy – Duval's paper on Ireland – a ladies meeting – spoke.[43]

Thursday at a directors' meeting at the Athm and Vaughan's lecture – attended.

---

42 Paul Willert came from Mecklenburg and began business in Manchester, aged 27, in 1821. Skilled financier and amateur musician. A commissioner of police 1832–42. Jeremiah Garnett was one of the proprietors of the *Manchester Guardian*.

43 Lewis Duval, a Manchester lawyer who specialised in conveyancing. The question was: 'Should the appropriation of church property to state purposes and a graduated tax upon real property be the best means of relieving the distress of Ireland?' It was carried by 5 to 0. Eight ladies were present and 15 men.

During the week I have been endeavouring to sell to Mr Lensbury[44] one of the houses in Broughton on favourable terms. I have no final answer yet.[45]

I have commenced endeavouring to obtain a public walk or ground in the suburbs of Manchester.

Business flat, stale and unprofitable.

Saturday, April 6

Tuesday evg at a lecture by B.R. Haydon,[46] on the history of British art, at the Athm. The old man as usual attacks the Academy and spoke of his own high resolve to denounce it as long as his life lasted. Staid with Borella.

Wednesday – a concert by Miss Woolgar[47] and others at the Athm. Staid with Borella. I should have gone to Mr Garnett's (Guardian) after the concert, but Borella's persuasions and not my usual inclination to go to parties at all, prevented me – altho' I was dressed tailed etc – I am sorry and vexed now that I did not go.[48]

Yesterday (Good Friday) at Northen with Berlyn, Borella and Harling – a pleasant rather happy day. Better for the exercise and slight excitement.

---

44   Not identified.

45   In 1821 Absalom bought a plot then called Frog Place in Broughton on which he built three terraced houses and he and his family lived in one of them until they moved to Rose Hill in 1834 (Goffin, p. 53). Edward was now trying to sell one of them on his father's behalf.

46   A course of four lectures by Robert Haydon, the historical painter, on Painting and Design which were published. Shot himself 1846 – see diary entry for 12 July 1846.

47   Miss Woolgar organised the concert and sang, including a duet from Bellini's *Norma* with Miss Rafter.

48   Jeremiah Garnett lived at Grosvenor Place, Oxford Street

A little busy with a requisition to the Mayor to call a public meeting about public walks – also seeing people and writing some little matters for the Times and Guardian on the subject. I think we shall work it.

John went to Oxford on Friday week and came back last Monday duly admitted a member of the University.

Business moderate. I have not yet managed Lensbury. I almost fear it will fall through.

Saturday, April 13

Monday evening at Joseph Makinson's to meet a Mr Davis, who I believe is the promised swain of Hannah M., and a party – staid till 1/4 to 1 and then went away with my father.[49]

Tuesday at the Lity Socy – a dull discussion on the Factory question; then at the Free Trade Hall fetching my sister; Alfred and Miss Whitelegg home from the Festival.[50]

Wednesday a party at our house: all the Lime Place[51] and Grove House lot – Davis, Geo Wall, L Mordacque, and Mary Alcock.[52]

49 Davis came from Chester (Goffin, pp. 246–7); Joseph was Edward's uncle and Hannah Maria was Joseph's daughter.

50 Dr Satterthwaite's question was: 'Would it be wise and just to restrict by law the hours of factory labour for young persons to less than twelve?' This was decided in the negative by 4 to 3. Miss Whitelegg was a daughter of near neighbours of the Watkins in Northenden. In 1843 she was very friendly with Alfred. They had probably been to the Easter Grand Music Festival.

51 Lime Place, in the Bury New Road, Broughton, was where William Makinson, another of Edward's uncles, lived. Makinsons and Clarke, the ladies school, or academy, which he ran, was situated at Grove House nearby.

52 Louis Henry Mordacque, then at Brasenose College, Oxford, was the son of Louis Alexandre Mordacque, French teacher at Manchester Grammar School. He entered the Church of England in 1848. The Mordacques and the Alcocks lived near the Watkins.

Staid up dancing till 1.

Lensbury's affair no go – damn it.

Public walks requisition going on.

Business fair 4000 p and 2500 lb yarn.

Saturday, April 20

Wednesday evening at a Soirée at the Athm – over at 1/2 past 3 o'clock on Thursday morning: got to bed at 4 at Berlyn's and rose at 6 to set off by the first train to Whitmore[53] en route for Booth Hale farm near Cheadle where a sale of Hay, under Bower's estate, of which my father is assignee, was to take place as soon as I got there. The morning was fine and I had a pleasant trip. I got to Whitmore at 1/4 p 9 and set off from there in a gig to Cheadle passing the Trentham Lane End etc. The country is fine and the drive did me good. At Booth Hale got some dinner with a nice old farmer who holds the land and after the sale returned to Cheadle and then by gig again to Whitmore where I got into the Rail and came to Cheadle (Cheshire) at 1/4 p 9. Walked home.

Yesterday was at home.

Business flat – very little done.

Saturday, April 27

Monday at Geo Wall's.

---

53 Whitmore was on the Grand Trunk Railway (later LNWR) between Crewe and Stafford. Edward took that route because the North Staffordshire line from Stockport to Stoke on Trent only opened in 1849. Cheadle (Cheshire) on the Manchester to Crewe line was then the nearest station to Northenden. Later resited and known as Cheadle Hulme.

Tuesday very unwell – obliged to come home at noon: was at home on Wednesday and Thursday. Set potatoes, spread dung and read.

Business moderately good.

Nothing very particular occurred.

I am lazy: my bowels do not act as they should, and this nasty fact may in part account for the laziness – while I ought to be able to conquer any indisposition to do any duty that can in any way proceed from an accumulation of turds.

Sunday, 28th

Read. Hibbert here in the aftn.[54]

Saturday, May 4

On Monday with Geo Wall.

Thursday at home.

Friday at a bazaar Com meeting of the League and then to Lime Place where I staid all night.

Have about finished the Public Walk requisition.

Business poor.

Sunday, May 12

Geo Wall here last Monday.

---

54   John Hibbert is referred to in the diary entry for 24 March 1845 below. Possibly John Tomlinson Hibbert, who was then at Cambridge. He was the eldest son of Elijah Hibbert of Hibbert Platt & Sons, machinists of Oldham.

Wednesday at home. Enjoyed myself very much. I walked in the Garden – read, wrote – finishing a paper on the Lit and Scientific Institutions of Manchester for my uncle William.

Yesterday afternoon at Altrincham with my father, dining with the Literary Society, at the Stamford Arms. We had a pleasant meeting and separated at 1/2 p 9 tolerably excited.[55]

During the week I have been very busy with the Public Walk requisition. I presented this on Friday to the Mayor who is to call a preliminary meeting to put the thing in train. I imagine that all is going on well in this matter. I have likewise been seeing to the first steps for presenting information preparatory to drawing up a report of the working of the Half-holiday.

On Thursday Mrs Leresche (Advertiser)[56] sent for me and wished me to make enquiries about parties willing to engage in the Newspaper trade. She wants a man to look after the business with her and money to help her to go imperiously on. She is an astonishing woman and has toiled on for years, doing the work of three men. One of her sons is now 'sick unto death' and her spirits are becoming low.[57] She says her servants do pretty much as they like and she is so anxious and troubled that for the first time in her life she had that morning said 'she wished she was dead'.

Some time ago (in conjunction with Edwards) I tried to get a meeting of the great guns to consider the propriety of supporting the Advertiser as a check upon the Guardian. We did not succeed but must try again.

---

55 There were 23 present. 'Perhaps there was a little too much raillery, and perhaps we drank a very little too much, but there was no intoxication – no ill-nature' (*AWJ*, p. 233).
56 Mrs Leresche's co-owner, George Condy, had died in 1841.
57 Watkin later noted 'since dead' in the margin.

Saturday, May 18

On Monday evening out on horseback with Mr Watts, canvassing the Didsbury voters for Mr William Brown the free trade candidate for South Lancashire.[58] We had very poor success.

Wednesday at Geo Wall's.

Friday evening (most of) at the Albion Hotel. Brown was there.

I have during the week written a little pamphlet on public walks which is published today.[59]

I have just returned from a canvassing visit to Cheadle.

Business moderate. 4000p

Saturday, May 25

Tuesday out canvassing.

Wednesday at home: had with my sister, Alfred and Hannah Makinson[60] a pleasant out to the other part of the parish.

I was introduced to Brown on 'Change on Tuesday. He is a fine old fellow. The show of hands was yesterday declared by the Sheriff as against us. Blast it. The bullying blackguard hired by

---

58 Probably James Watts of Burnage, elected to Manchester Council in 1848, and mayor in 1855–56. A wholesale draper, who later lived at Abney Hall, Cheadle. William Brown, originally from Ulster, but who had been a merchant in Baltimore, was now senior partner in Brown Shipley & Co. of Liverpool, merchants and bankers principally in the American trade. The by-election was caused by the death of one of the two Conservative members, the Hon. R. B. Wilbraham.

59 *A Plea for Public Walks* was advertised in the *MG* at 1½d, and published by John Heywood, Deansgate, stationers on a large scale. The *MG*'s first editorial on public walks appeared on 15 May.

60 Another cousin, William Makinson's daughter.

the Monopolists would not listen to Cobden for some time. At last he made himself heard and then he slated them in style. I have been out again this afternoon and evening. On canvassing one of my pledged voters – old Lindsay of Barlow Moor – is turning tail. The screw is on tremendously in Didsbury and Withington and we shall only get a mere handful of votes.[61] However it is to be hoped we may get in. My own notion is that we shall lose by 600.

The 'Plea for Public Walks' has appeared by example in the Guardian twice – twice has that luminary borrowed lustre from the Plea, perhaps more on account of my having sent a copy than because of the merits of the production.[62]

Business has been bad all week and I have very badly attended to it. In fact my mind has been intent upon other matters. I will however when the election is over turn to business with right good will. It will never do to be giving this milk porter attention and to be doing a sort of patchwork – a bit of business – a bit of reading – a bit of learning – a bit of speaking – a bit of public walking – a bit of everything – but no consistent whole – no design – no object – no end. If it will never do Mr Ferguson: je marmment.[63]

Tuesday, 28 May

The Election is over and we are beaten by 3 or 400![64] A hard fight kept up with all possible spirit and energy: a loss unfortunate in every way. However we are better off than many expected and have made way decidedly since the contest in 1835–6. Then the

61 Lindsay not identified. The screw was pressure from landlords or employers.

62 There was a second editorial on 25 May.

63 A variant on a popular saying among young men in the mid-nineteenth century – 'You can't lodge here Mr Ferguson' or 'You mustn't go there Mr Ferguson'. Possibly Watkin intended 'je marmotte' – 'I mutter'.

64 The official result was Entwistle 7,571, Brown 6,973.

majority against us were 1100 to 1800. The whole power of the landocracy has been against us: every devil in the park has been hounding on his serfs to the attack and men who never coerced before have coerced this time. Well we must now set to work to lengthen the register. Put as many names off as possible. Register as many as we can. This latter I think we can do capitally, and we must not forget that the defeat will sharpen our appetite for the means of victory. We must beat the thieves. The chimney against the dung heap – smoke against cow house steam – up with black industry and down with the damned landocracy.

I was up yesterday morning and at Watts by 1/4 to 7. We took what few voters we had to the polls and then I threw myself in to the general struggle like a hyena: this morning I was at it again. Worked all day: by 12 we had polled nearly all our forces and the remainder of the day was spent in hunting after odd votes. Cobden, Bright and others spoke from a carriage opposite the Committee Room this evening to a large crowd. The full return will not be known until tomorrow.

Note! We are beaten but we have gained something, and we are not disheartened, trusting to our own exertions for the future.

Majority for Entwistle 598!!![65]

Saturday, June 1

Wednesday at home, idling away my time.

Thursday brought Borella, Harling and Berlyn over. We had Hedley and his family at dinner. [66]

In the evening H, B and B and I had a sail on the river. On the whole we had a pleasant afternoon.

65 Entwistle was a barrister who lived in Rusholme. He had been defeated in the Manchester election of 1841; he was later chairman of the Manchester and Leeds Railway and a director of the Manchester Chamber of Commerce.

66 The Hedleys were long-standing friends of Absalom's.

Yesterday afternoon dined at Mr John Spencer's a mile or two from Pendleton. My father, Mr Grenon, Mr C. Withington and Mr Atkinson with myself, were the guests – a pleasant party.[67]

Today I shall amuse myself by writing a little address to the working classes on the advantages of registering for the County and for the Boro.

I have done next to nothing this week. Certainly very little has been to be done but I have rather idled away the holiday than improved it. The two election days I was employed very energetically – since when I have I suppose been idling to make up for it.

I will work furiously next week.

Sunday, June 9

Furiously! Again I have been furiously – lazy, when shall I gain that fixedness of purpose which enables men of the humblest capacities to make a figure in the world! Unstable I have been ever and I fear ever shall be. I resolve and do not act – wish and yet will not – desire and I content myself with dreaming. I often think that mine is not the 'temperament of genius'. At least I feel a void, or want, a weakness when anything of moment has to be effected and it is only when warmed by temporary enthusiasm that I can feel myself master of myself and powerful to do something.

Nothing of moment has occurred. The public park requisitioners met on Monday, 25 strong – Potter, Birley, Townend, Wray being of the number.[68] We talked a long while and then formed

67   John Spencer, friend and contemporary of Absalom's who helped refound the Literary Society. Chairman of the Manchester Mechanics' Institute. Manufacturer of dimity and quilting. Lived at Hopefield, Weaste Lane, Pendleton. A. W. Grenon, a merchant in Cannon Street; Charles Withington, a surgeon who lived in Pendleton.

68   Thomas Townend, a merchant, trustee of the Athenaeum, and Treasurer of the Institution. Revd C. D. Wray was a chaplain and fellow of the collegiate church. A canon of Manchester.

a Committee which met on Thursday. I then endeavoured to put the petition in business train and succeeded so that all is now moving on properly. The Mayor I find is remarkable. He is one of those men who feel a conscience of the strength of their own minds that perpetually believes he is leading everybody when if he did but know it he is decidedly led.

I have canvassed a little for Dr Satterthwaite[69] who is a candidate for the office of physician to the Infirmary.

By the way I was at a meeting of Athm directors on Tuesday, a full meeting occupied in discussions about nothing. I, however, managed to have some fun with their petty disputes.

Tuesday evening staid with Edwards.

Wednesday with Geo Wall.

Business moderate. I have not finished it, nor has my father. We shall go to the devil if we do not mend.

Sunday, June 16

Last Monday I dined at Pollocks (the barrister) with Holland, Rafter and Ball – the latter a funny old actor who is lecturing here.[70] Ball kept us in a continual roar of laughter at his tales and jests. After dinner we all adjourned to T.H. Williams where we met R. Cobden, John Bright and others. We had a pleasant evening. I was much interested with R. Cobden's description of life and manners in America. I staid all night at Williams!

---

69   Dr Michael Satterthwaite was on the Committee of the Athenaeum.
70   Joseph Pollock, barrister and member of the Northern Circuit, lived in St James's Square. A member of the Literary Society. William Ball was lecturing on English ballads, ancient and modern, including specimens of comic songs. He was assisted by the Rafters. He assured prospective attenders that they had been received with the highest approbation at the principal literary and scientific institutions of the Metropolis.

Wednesday Geo Wall was here.

Pollock and I have been trying to induce some of the big wigs to unite the Advertiser and Times.

I have published a little pamphlet urging the working classes to get votes.

Business generally speaking has been fair this week. With us however little had been done: a fact to be attributed to the absence of effort. I feel that I am not doing my duty: yet I do not do it. We are really going to the devil for want of work.

I am quite a martyr to that disinclination to calling upon people to solicit them to buy – a defect in my character most disastrous to my interests, most painful to me always. Really it is a constant pain and annoyance to me – at least it is present except on those infrequent occasions when a temporary enthusiasm for business drives it away. I am rocked about by all kinds of changing plans and fluctuating purposes. Good God what life can contain so little of the sweet, so much of the bitter and the sour as mine. How to alter – how to change for the better, I do not know. I keep determining to improve and breaking my determination influenced by a power I cannot withstand. Without faith, hope or charity. I am the sport of chance and shall never I fear do anything worth remembering with pleasure. Surely it must be possible to turn round upon indecision and weakness of character and to assume a boldness and promptness which I do not feel. I see I shall soon be despised by others as much as I despise myself unless I take care. Good Heavens what a fool I am.

Let me see whether for the next week I can do my duty.

Friday evening, June 21

Last Sunday I wrote nearly all day and on Monday, perhaps in consequence, I was extraordinarily low spirited.

In the evening of Monday I went to Geo Wall's and spent evening and night with him. I was better for this and next morning went about my work with a spice of heroism.

On Tuesday evening I went with Borella and Berlyn to a meeting to adopt an address to O'Connell in the Free Trade Hall.[71] The Committee immediately on my entrance, I suppose because they were short of speakers, begged me to move a resolution and as Daniel Lee took the chair and John Brooks and others were there and seemed to wish it, I broke thus my role of non-interference.[72] I spoke in moving the 4th resolution. They tell me I made the best speech of the evening – an easy matter as the shape and manner of them was horrid trash and tho' called upon at the spur of the moment, thanks to our Irish debates in the Lity Socy, made pretty well out. I laid all the blame upon the aristocracy and exculpated the British people, defended the repeal as wise in the absence and declared impossibility of justice, and preached the union of the two people as the only means of doing any real good to both nations.

After I had spoken we left and listened for an hour to Ball's lecture at the Athm. Staid with Borella.

Last night at Mr Makinson's John, Hannah, and Elizabeth,[73] the only stay-at-homes – the rest at Blackpool.

---

71 The address was to express sympathy with O'Connell in his imprisonment and to petition for his release. Following a series of 'monster meetings' in favour of the repeal of the Union, he had been arrested and charged with creating discontent and disaffection and contriving by means of intimidation and demonstration of force to effect changes in the Government, laws and the constitution. His trial began on 15 Jan 1844. He was found guilty and sentenced on 30 May to twelve months' imprisonment.

72 Lee's warehouse was in Cannon Street. Said to be Manchester's only Roman Catholic entrepreneur.

73 Elizabeth was Edward's sister; John and Hannah were the children of William Makinson.

I have minded my business pretty well this week. But for the meeting on Tuesday I might I think have done very well.

We have done well this week. 8500 p sold – tho' many of them have to come in.

Tuesday evening, 25 June

On Saturday afternoon dined at Mr Lascaridi's at Levenshulme with Dilberoglue, C. Lascaridi, G. Lascaridi, Taylor and Milne – a pleasant and jovial afternoon.[74]

On Sunday walked over to Urmston and stood godfather to W.K. Stocks little boy – William Frederick Keating Stock, a Miss Keating was mother. Dined and spent the day at Stocks, visiting in the afternoon Hawthorn Hall, a curious old house of the Time of Elizabeth in the neighbourhood.[75]

74 Antonio Lascaridi (or Laskarides) was a merchant with premises in Dale Street. In 1843 he was a founder member of the Greek community in Manchester. Stauros Dilberoglue was a shipping merchant with Cassavetti, Cavafy & Co. who then lived at 7 Lower Woodlands, Higher Broughton, and was a member of the Literary Society. A contemporary of Watkin's, he had come to Manchester at 14 from Corfu. Cassavetti, Cavafy & Co. had establishments in Cairo, Alexandria, London and Liverpool, buying considerable quantities of Manchester goods for sale in Egypt. The Cavafy brothers were resident there and toured the country with their camel caravans exchanging textiles for bullion. Stanley Chapman, *Merchant Enterprise in Britain from the Industrial Revolution to World War I* (Cambridge: Cambridge University Press, 1992), pp. 156–8.
Taylor may well have been Russell Scott Taylor, who was five years younger than Watkin. The elder son of John Edward Taylor, who had died in January 1844, he had graduated at Manchester New College in 1843 and started work on the *Guardian*. Possibly Milne was the younger Oswald Milne, a solicitor like his father, also Oswald Milne, whose various public offices had made him town clerk in all but name before Manchester's incorporation and who led the Tories against making effective the charter of incorporation.

75 Stocks was a shopkeeper and striped shirt manufacturer at Wilmslow where the Stocks lived – see diary entry for 3 Sep 1844.

Yesterday was laid up with a shocking cold. At home today from the same cause. In town tomorrow.

Sunday, 30 June

Went to a meeting of the directors of the Athenaeum on Wednesday evening and thence to Mr Butler's benefit at Cooke's circus,[76] the present theatre (vice the old one burnt down) – was pleased.

Supped at the Clarence and slept at Berlyn's. On Wednesday morning attended a Public Walk Committee meeting at the Town Hall. The Mayor, T. Townend, Sir T. Potter etc. C. Wray and myself were there.

Friday evening at Geo Wall's.

Yesterday dined at Borella's with the two Moses, Salomans, Berlyn, Harling, Watt. Before and after dinner rowed on the river above the Suspension bridge.[77] Slept at Borella's. Staid there till this afternoon when I left Manchester by the Railway

76 Samuel William Butler, actor and tragedian, latterly resident in Manchester. In 1842 the star at the Theatre Royal, which under John Knowles had enjoyed a revival until it was destroyed by fire in May 1844. Butler died in July 1845, aged 41. Thomas Taplin Cooke established his circus in Mount Street in 1844, the company being mainly drawn from his numerous family. Following the fire at the Theatre Royal the building was converted into a temporary Theatre Royal and was used as such until Knowles opened the new Theatre Royal in Peter Street in September 1845.

77 Presumably two younger member of the Moses family of Moses Levy & Co. and probably Edward Salomans, son of the cotton merchant H. M. Salomans of Plymouth Grove, who spent a short period working in his father's warehouse before embarking on his architectural studies. Later he became an architect of some distinction in Manchester. His work included the Reform Club, and the Spanish and Portuguese Synagogue (now the Manchester Jewish Museum).

The suspension bridge, also known as the little chain bridge, crossed the Irwell at Lower Broughton.

and getting out at Heaton Norris went to service there at Watts' chapel.[78]

Business has been good this week. We have sold a large quantity of goods and some yarn.

Sunday, July 6

Wednesday and Thursday evenings at Lime Place. My uncle and aunt with all the family except Alice at Blackpool.

At meeting of Ath directors on Wednesday evening.

At home yesterday.

Business fair. We did a great deal last week and are in consequence doing less this week, but the market is buoyant and prices are rather on the advance than otherwise.

We are going to have another Grand Soirée in October pro bono Athenaeo. B. Disraeli has offered to take the chair having been invited to attend by Berlyn and myself and several other 'great men' are expected.[79] I have been a good deal occupied with writing and arranging matters concerning the Soirée and have not given that continuous thought to business that I should have done. I really must fix an object before my mind and resolve not only what to do, but what to be and adhere to the object, else I shall make nothing whatsoever out.

Saturday, July 13

Wednesday evening Geo Wall was here.

78 Heaton Norris station was on the line from Manchester to Stockport. Watts's chapel was a Congregational church at Heaton Mersey, a village over a mile from the station. James Watts, the wholesale draper who then lived at nearby Burnage, was the patron of the church.

79 Watkin and Berlyn, as joint secretaries, had written to Disraeli on 4 June. *Benjamin Disraeli Letters*, ed. M. G. Wiebe (8 vols, continuing, Toronto and London: Toronto University Press, 1989–), i. 134.

Thursday was busy in the morning helping Dr Satterthwaite in his election at the Infirmary. He won by 88 of majority.[80]

Friday down in Salford for an hour. The first election under the new charter. 19 Refs, 5 Tories.[81]

I have done something in the way of correspondence for the proposed Soirée, and a little for the Public Walk affairs.

On Tuesday Edwards told me that one of his acquaintances – a large manufacturer, wanted a person to sell his cloth: £300 a year to begin with, the certainty of a speedy improvement. He wanted me to apply for it and said I might get it. I told him I could not leave my father. Since Tuesday the matter has been often in my mind and I have half regretted of not looking after it – and yet how can I? In 5 years I could with such an income save £1,000 – an independence with me! In 5 years, as I am now, I shall not save £50. Really I am in a fix: I see nothing for it but perpetual grinding and no reward worth mentioning.

I have not done much work this week. Today has been my 'best day'.

Saturday, July 20

At home on Monday getting fruit, a pleasant health-giving job.

Thursday morning at the Public Walks committee.

I have written two leaders, at the request of Mr Prentice and Mr Garnett, on the Public Park question which duly appeared in the Times and Guardian this morning.[82] I have devoted some time to Public Walks, the Soirée etc during the week.

80 Satterthwaite was to resign on 1 July 1847.
81 According to the *MG* 17 to 7 for the Reformers (*MG*, 13 and 17 July 1844).
82 Reproduced in the Appendix.

Saturday my memory and other faculties were quite 'obfuscated'. I could neither recollect nor think effectively – I walked home very briskly and by the time I had been at home an hour I was all right again.

Business good. Today I have worked like a devil. I wish I could keep the steam up every day in like manner.

Saturday, July 27

Wednesday afternoon dined with half a dozen (including S. P. Robinson) at the Clarence. Staid all night with Geo Wall.

I have written articles on Public Walks for the Guardian, the Courier and the Times – which have duly appeared.[83]

Thursday morning at the Public Walks Committee.

Last night writing letters on Soirée business with Berlyn till 1 o'clock. Staid with him.

Business good. The only fault has been that we have sold too much.

A good deal occupied during the week with Soirée and Public Walks. Both however will in good time be over.

I am not well. My damn bowels again. I wish I had none!!

Saturday morning, August 3

While waiting for my father to get up I may as well write this.

Wednesday at Mr Jonathan Mellor's, Ridgefield House, Failsworth – the occasion Wm Dean's marriage with Miss

83   The articles from the *Guardian* and the *Times* are reproduced in the Appendix, but not the shorter note in the *Courier*.

Mellor.[84] A large company was assembled, consisting mainly of the Mellor family, (five brothers and four sisters[85]) with aunts, uncles etc.. The two eldest girls were intelligent and one Mary BriggsX, pretty and interesting. Being the only fellow there at all used to 'making himself agreeable', and seeing that there was too much dumbness, I did the main part of the talking to the ladies. Mrs Dean is too good for her husband and the whole family far superior in point of intelligence etc to him.

Thursday evening with Geo Wall who was not very well.

Business continues good.

Soiree and Public Parks again occupied me somewhat.

X has been running in my head a good deal since Wednesday – fine girl.

---

84 Jonathan Mellor, a prosperous tanner and currier of Manchester Street, Oldham, who had recently moved from a house next to his warehouse to the larger Hope House in King Street, and who also had a house and tannery in Failsworth. Ridgefield House was just off the main road from Manchester to Oldham, almost equidistant from each. The Mellors, like Absalom, had been subject to a strong Methodist influence. As a child Jonathan Mellor had been blessed by John Wesley, when he opened Manchester Street Chapel, and he remained a Methodist all his life. He was a JP and had served as a high constable. He was a supporter of free trade and had appeared on the platform when William Brown visited Oldham in the South Lancashire election. Hannah Mellor, his eldest daughter (Sarah had died in 1827, aged 15) was marrying William Dean. William and John Dean were cotton spinners and manufacturers at Broad Holden Mill, Haslingden.

85 Thomas, Edward, William Henry, Jonathan, Hannah, Mary Briggs, Harriet, Hester Ann and John (J. J.). Mary was then 21. She was recorded as having paid a subscription of 5s at an Oldham ACLL meeting in Jan 1844, and was a member of the ACLL Bazaar Committee in May 1845. The Mellors were to have close ties with the Watkins. Hester Ann married Edward's brother Alfred in 1850. W. H. Mellor was a persistent, but unsuccessful, suitor, of his sister Elizabeth, but she never enjoyed good health and died in 1864, aged 46.

On Monday went on an exploration tour through the older part of Manchester that near the Cath. and along Millgate with Prentice. Our object was to find culs de sac and bad ventilation, and easily we found them! I went over the same ground with Ross after 'change. On Tuesday morning I went again and had a look through Thornley Lane or some horrid place with a name like that – up Shude Hill. Little tumbling down-houses, broken windows, squalor, dung heaps before the doors. The people looking as if they had risen out of the dung to life, like maggots! As we passed into these blind courts the old hags and young watchers came to the door to look out in wonder at the intruders. Strange that within 5 minutes walk of the Exchange this should exist!

I have been waiting for the papers again on Public Walks.[86] I don't know how many of my articles have been inserted, not having seen the papers.

I am thinking of preparing a little book to be called 'Manchester': offering it to Chas Knight[87] – nous verrons.

Friday, August 9

Monday evening at Berlyn's writing our Bazaar business. – Monday. Tuesday and Wednesday evenings at Town Hall – Public Park committees.

Thursday the public meeting. Lord F. Egerton moved the 1st Resolution. A good meeting, quite full and the steam up – £7,000 subscribed on the spot. All is right now. I am quite pleased with the result so far. Had a good deal of talk with Lord F. before the meeting about parks, smoke, Athm etc. I had to manage the meeting i.e. to prompt the Mayor and see to the speakers etc. Ross worked with me like a Trojan. He and I have been out today trying to raise some money. We got £300.

86   Reproduced in the Appendix.
87   A Manchester bookseller and publisher. Nothing came of this.

I go tomorrow to Haslingden on a visit to Dean and his wife. Shall return on Monday.

Wednesday, August 14

On Saturday afternoon went to see the Coffin containing the body of Dr Dalton which was laid under a canopy in the Town Hall, darkened and black velveted for the occasion. A rather solemn sight. Crowds of people of all sorts.[88] After this sight went in the coach to Haslingden. Staid there till Tuesday morning. Met at Mr Dean's, Mr Jon. and Mr Thos Mellor and Miss Mellor and Miss Mary Mellor. I had a pleasant day or two with the folk and looked about me. I saw Thos Haywd, Mrs Hawath-Booth etc. With Dean, Thos and J Mellor and the Miss Mellors. On Monday went over to the Grane (John Dean's).[89] Miss Mary Mellor and I, who became my precious, kept one another company. A nice girl. I feel rather fond of her. In the evening went to the top of Cribden.[90] Had a fine prospect and something more exciting still in the way of conversation. Left Haslingden decidedly in a Benedictine humour. Nous verrons – this time. Work! the only way is to work – work – work.

Last night with Berlyn and Capes[91] at the Queen's Theatre. Supped at the Clarence and staid with Berlyn.

This morning at the 1st meeting of the Committee appointed by the Public Meeting (P P) and appointed joint hon Secretary (with Ross). This afternoon was cadging with Sir T. Potter and Kershaw – got £800.

88   John Dalton, chemist and meteorologist. His atomic theory elevated chemistry to a science. President of the Manchester Literary and Philosophical Society from 1817 until his death. Died 27 July, aged 78. 'Manchester bestowed upon Dalton, in death, the honours due to a king' (Lyon Playfair, quoted in Kargon, *Science in Manchester*, pp. 41–2).

89   Haslingden Grane is a township to the west of Haslingden on the road to Blackburn. John Dean lived in the Grane.

90   The prominent hill (1,315 feet) between Haslingden and Rawtenstall.

91   Capes, Dunn & Co. were auctioneers.

Monday, August 19

On Friday evening at Ahgickian's with Borella. Mrs A. and her sister are nice women. We had a pleasant evening and enjoyed much some musical entertainment given by Ahgickian and Miss Thompson (his sister in law).[92]

I left Manchester at 1/2 past 1 with Edwards and went by rail and omnibus to Bradford where we met Sichel, with whom we dined.[93] At 7 left Bradford adding a Mr Hertz[94] to the company, and came to Leeds where we staid all night. In the morning went through Harewood to Harrogate and spent the day there: returning to Leeds in the evening. Came to Manchester by the first train this morning. In Leeds on Saturday everyone had sundry 'larks' – going to the Circus and to the sundry disreputable houses. At Harrogate Hertz and I, very foolishly on my part, took a tour which from certain revelations I fear may leave its effects upon my feeble frame for a week or two. I look with no pleasure upon this journey altho' we had fine weather, a beautiful country to pass through etc. In fact I am disgusted with myself and when I look back a week and remember how much more innocently I was happily engaged I feel humiliated – really never will again go from home knowing that the company with which I am about to enter is loose and disorderly in character. I really must not be exceedingly weak minded or else I should ever so easily be made a fool of.

Was ill last night thanks to drinking Harrogate water without due caution. I have today been very seedy. I walked home as a remedial step and I am rather better.

92　Ahgickian Gosman & Co. were a firm of commission merchants in Bond Street, but this reading of the name is uncertain.

93　Augustus S. Sichel was a member of the ACCL. Sichel Bros were Manchester exporters who also had a warehouse in Bradford.

94　Possibly James Hertz, who like Edwards was later a member of the Baths and Washhouses Committee; see below 4 Apr 1845.

Had a good deal of begging writing etc to do for the Public Walks affair during the week.

Wednesday night, August 28

Tuesday August 20 and Wednesday at business.

Thursday (21st) [sic – for 22nd]– Public Parks Committee meeting at the Town Hall.[95]

Friday (22nd) [sic – for 23rd] dined with James Edwards, – Berlyn, Burton and Armstrong were there.[96]

Saturday went with Berlyn and Borella to Liverpool, at Hodgson's (Sec Liverpool Mechanics).[97] During the afternoon took tea: then to the Theatre. Left Liverpool on Sunday morning at 1/2 p 7, breakfasted at Tantines then went to St Ann's. After service to Failsworth to dine with the Mellors. Mr, Mrs, Edward, W.H. and Jno there with Mary, Harriet and Esther Ann. Spent the afternoon with Mary and staid the night, getting into Manchester at 1/2 past 9 on Monday morning.

Last night (Tuesday August 27) dined again at Edwards with Mr Bateman, 'Bob' Yates, Burton and Armstrong.[98]

95 On 30 August Watkin and Ross wrote on behalf of the Committee to Sir Robert Peel asking for financial assistance from the Government (see Appendix).

96 James Burton junior, later director of the Manchester and County Bank. Acted as secretary to the Athenaeum ball in January 1842. Armstrong has not been identified.

97 William Ballantyne Hodgson, appointed in 1839, aged 23, was the first secretary of the Liverpool Mechanics' Institute. Later principal.

98 Bateman was probably John Frederic Bateman, a young engineer who in 1835 became involved with William Fairbairn in designing and constructing reservoirs for mill-owners. Employed by Fairbairn at his engineering works in Canal Street, Manchester. He designed a medallion embossed with a likeness of Dalton for the 1841 British Association meeting. Married Anne, Fairbairn's daughter. In 1844 was consulted about the supply of water to Manchester. Later became an eminent waterworks engineer and FRS. Robert Yates was a merchant in Faulkner Street who lived in Higher Ardwick.

Dined this afternoon at the Angel with Armstrong, Edwards and Max Walker.[99]

Have done last posting up been very busy with the Public Parks. I have got rather tired and excited – I have been seriously thinking about ——.[100] Whether to speak or not to speak is the question that puzzles and perplexes me. I have nobody to advise with 'little light from within'. Well, must try the impossible of the moment whatever it is! What a beautiful condition I am in!!!

Tuesday morning, September 3 1844

Saturday afternoon and evening at Jonathan Mellor's at Oldham: dined with a number of fellows connected with the mill now worked by young Pattershall[101] and Mellor. Staid up till 1/2 past 1 Sunday morning, left Oldham at 8 to Manchester and then to Wilmslow (with J. Mellor), dined at Stocks and passed a moderately pleasant day. Came to our house in the evening.

Yesterday brought dearest Mrs Dean, Miss Mellor and Mary Mellor, and Mr Henry over to dine at Northen. Old Mellor came with my father after. Went on the water. In the course of the evening an important secret crept out: what will come of it I cannot tell. We shall see what we shall see.

Wednesday evening, Sep 13

Last Tuesday evening but one, Sep 3, Jonathan Mellor[102] and I went down to Liverpool and thence to Dublin in the mail packet. We had a fine passage and reached Kingston by 7 o'clock. From Kingston to Dublin – staying at Greshams' Hotel, Sackville Street. Went to see the old Parliament House – now used by the

---

99   Max Walker not identified.
100   Watkin at this stage of his relationship with Mary Mellor often does not write her name.
101   Not identified.
102   Jonathan Mellor, one of Mary's brothers, was to become a close business associate of Edward Watkin's through their interests in railways.

Bank, Trinity College, the Museum of the College of Surgeons etc. then went down to the Richmond penitentiary to see Dan O'Connell. I will set down an account of the interview when I have more time. At night to the Portobello Gardens.

On Thursday down to see the Atmospheric Railway from Kingston to Dalkey.[103] In the afternoon left Dublin for a three day tour in Wicklow. In the course of Thursday, Friday Saturday afternoon saw Gratton's house Tinnehinch,[104] Glendalough, Vale of Avoca etc.

Saturday afternoon witnessed Dan's triumphal procession from prison.[105]

Sunday at high mass in the Metropolitan Church, Archbishop Murray officiating – all in honour of Dan – at the Methodist chapel and St Patrick's etc.

Monday at the National Schools in Martin Street – at the Conciliation Hall etc. Left Kingston at 1/2 past 6 and ran down the brig Parana, 250 tons, Wilson master, 6 lives lost – a horrible affair.[106]

This affair of ——— is making me very uneasy.

This afternoon went with all the Misses Mellor to see Tom Thumb.[107]

103 In 1843 part of the Dublin and Kingston Railway had been adapted to Clegg and Samuel's atmospheric system.

104 Henry Grattan, the Irish statesman, had died in 1820.

105 On 4 Sep the House of Lords, on appeal, had overruled the Irish court and ordered O'Connell's release.

106 Curiously the *Iron Duke* on which Watkin was sailing ran down a month later a boat from the *Hesperus* in the Mersey with the loss of five lives (*Manchester Times*, 14 Oct 1844).

107 General Tom Thumb, Charles Sherwood Stratton (1838–83), the American Man in Miniature who had visited London and was seen there by 300,000 people in four months, was to be seen in court dress at the Exchange Rooms. He was 25 inches high and weighed 15 pounds (*MG*, 11 Sep 1844). He later grew to 40 inches.

I felt very amorous before but really am getting almost afraid. I find and perceive a want of neatness in her and a vulgarity of ideas which won't suit me at all. On Tuesday afternoon dined at Failsworth with all the family and Mr John Mellor their cousin from Leicester or London, a barrister. After dinner – on I had to go Dean called me out and we went into a room in which Miss Mellor and Mary were standing. After it was arranged how we should go down and Miss Mellor slipped out and shut the door leaving us alone. Now a tete a tete is all very well and the intention of giving us one might be kind enough, but still I was by no means satisfied, and yesterday's affair has further staggered me. I don't know what to do. I hardly can go back either with honour or out of fear of the consequences. My father and I have come to no settlement: business is worse everything looks black and yellow. I fear to take any step, yet fear not to take one. I am really in a dead fix. So much and all in consequence of not marrying M——. My God! How bitterly one false step reacts upon the whole of after life. Well I suppose it will be all the same 10 years hence, but I almost wish now I had gone down in the vessel. God help me.

Sunday, September 16 1844

On Wednesday evening I was waiting at the Railway with ——. She told me she wanted to tell me something: what it was I could not get to know, and in a few minutes the old boy came in quite unexpectedly! I got out of the surprise as well as I could and told —— before they set off to write to me about the matter to be mentioned. On Thursday morning I got a note from her telling me she would feel more happy, comfortable etc if I would come over and speak to her father. Not knowing what to do and not wishing to go over to Oldham on Saturday afternoon, I wrote to the old man telling him how the affair stood and asking his permission 'to pay my addresses' etc. I wrote to —— to tell her what I had done. I wrote again on Friday night. Hitherto I have got no answer in any way. Whether they expect me to come over or not I don't know. I was upon the point of doing so, but I spoke to my father, who was greatly surprised, and he advised me to leave the matter until old ——— returned from a journey he is about to take. I wish I had never stirred in the matter and tried to conquer the feeling which has been pushing me on. However it may be all right – still I doubt, and feel ill too again, weak, spiritless and easily fatigued. The continued messiness and anxiety with which I am surrounded kills one. I did hope for consolation and motive from this new affair, but it seems to have been a vain hope. Well I must try to work and do my duty and leave all the rest to providence.

Business is not good and several unpleasantnesses have arisen since I returned home. Perhaps it would have been better for my happiness if I had sunk in the vessel.[108] The first page of this book contains the cause of nearly all my errors and misfortunes.[109]

Saturday, September 22

On Monday morning I had a letter from old M. telling me that the matter had better be named at once to my father and that if he had no objection he (M.) would not stand in the way. I have had a correspondence with ——— during the week and feel much better pleased and satisfied. Unless I am deceived she is a warm hearted, frank girl – and heart is what I want. I fear I am too suspicious. Tomorrow I go over to Failsworth to see her.

This evening I have been talking with my father and have asked his consideration of three propositions, which I am to know about on Monday. I have worked on the whole well during the week. Certainly I have been successful: for I have sold a good quantity of cloth.

---

108 Watkin refers to the brig *Parana* with which the mail packet collided – entry for 13 Sep.

109 Presumably in that part of the review of 1843 which is missing.

I feel much assured about ——— what a damned suspicious temperament mine is! The slightest thing upsets my faith in any one. Will this folly harshness of unbelief beset me always? For once I have attended well to public business and my own too; the Public Parks have been well worked this week. £2,700 additional. I shall have to address a public meeting in Salford on Wednesday night. Must prepare my speech as I walk to town tomorrow.

Friday Sep 27 1844

On Sunday morning I walked over to Failsworth and spent the day and till Monday morning there, going to Chapel in the morning and evening. I was very much pleased with what I saw and said and did and am (or rather was for I am a changeable rascal) quite satisfied with my choice.

I saw ——— on Tuesday in town and met her on Wednesday with her sister.

On Wednesday night I went with Ross to the Public Park meeting in Salford. We both spoke. Staid at Geo Wall's. Next morning (yesterday) his marriage to Alice took place. I acted as one of the managing men in the arrangement of the proceedings. The breakfast was at our house and was really beautifully done. At 1, Mr and Mrs Wall left for Matlock and I went to town.

This afternoon waited on Lord F. Egerton at the Royal Institution.

I shall be in town tomorrow night and Friday.

On Monday night Berlyn and I dine with Disraeli at Atherton's;[110] on Tuesday I dine there again. On Wednesday I have a Public Park meeting to attend and on Thursday the

---

110   James Atherton lived at Swinton House, Swinton Park, Swinton. On 3 Aug he had invited the Disraelis to stay at Swinton Park.

Soirée takes place. So I have work enough on my hands. I wish it was over as I must bundle to with a vengeance for if I am to be married at all I must get the money.

The Public Parks go on well.

Friday night, October 4

On Sunday (and Saturday afternoon) Berlyn and I were hard at work upon the Soirée.

On Monday evening I went with Berlyn and Charles Swain to the Atherton's at Swinton to dine with Disraeli. We met Rev. Bradbury and James Crossley.[111] Disraeli was very polite: his wife being fatigued, or ill, left table before dinner had proceeded beyond the soup. We had a very pleasant evening. Disraeli threw off restraint – told us some spicy stories, some very silly. His manner is elegant and to my mind intensely yet quietly affected. His face is a singular one – a little Jewish – eyes fine dark and languishing, a clear pale face and at times destitute of all recognisable expression. His face is one of those which make you doubt. He has the art of concealing what he feels and you look in vain to his face for anything which can prove to you that he is influenced in reality by what you say to him. His morality – in minor matters at least is lax. Speaking of a tilt with Hume about the Shrewsbury magistrates he said 'that you know that was a sacred subject with me – to be sure Hume was quite right, but I was bound by every duty to prove to the contrary.' And again on Wednesday when we were scheming to present reports

111   Charles Swain (1803–74) was apprenticed in his early years to his uncle's dye works, then a lithographer and bookseller – Swain & Dewhurst. He was a poet, author of *The Mind and Other Poems* (London: Simkin & Marshall, 1831), which he dedicated to Southey. A fourth edition was published in 1844. FRSL. Hon. professor of poetry at the Mechanics' Institute. Locally known as Manchester's Tennyson. Politically Conservative.
        Revd Samuel Bradbury was minister of Cannon Street Independent Chapel.

going to the *Herald* and *Post*, in order to try him I said we must offer the man (Grant), who perhaps will furnish a report of half a column, payment for a column if he wont send anything at all. 'Yes' he added at once, 'that's the way, we must hocus him. Lord why you can't get on at all in England without it.'[112]

All this made me set him down as an artful but clever dodger well read and trading with the stories of learning accumulated during the enthusiasms of youth and the heartless use of men learnt in mature years amid the villainies of profligate political and literary circles.

Cooke and Taylor, however, say there is more heart and good nature about Ben than people think but that he is eaten up by vanity.

On Tuesday I went again to Atherton's to dine. I went up with Cobden. We had Disraeli and his wife, the Mayor, Cobden, Canon Clifton, Col. Bunbury, Birley, Gladstone, Wood Gibson, Crossley, W. R. Wood[113] and one or two more. Mrs Ben gave us most flaming accounts of her husband – how Louis Philippe had read Coningsby, as much as John Russell, Peel etc. How Peel could eat more beef steaks than any man in the house and how the Queen read nothing and got up early that she might not get too fat etc. How Disraeli had never been happy as a boy (or) youth and said he was only just becoming so. How his father had considered him as a dunce during his boyhood and multitudes of other things.

On Wednesday at noon I went to 'Change with Atherton and Disraeli and assisted in the introductions going on. In the

112 Disraeli was then MP for Shrewsbury. Mrs Disraeli had much admired the ornate ticket for the soirée, a proof of which Watkin and Berlyn had sent to Disraeli. *Disraeli Letters*, p. 143.

113 Col. Bunbury was Lt-Col. 67th Foot, 1835–46. Robert Gladstone was a Manchester merchant who lived at Withington Hall. Wood Gibson was a merchant who lived in the Crescent, Salford. Also a director of the Manchester and Salford Bank. W. Rayner Wood was the son of George W. Wood MP who had died in 1843.

evening with Garnett and Berlyn to Athertons' again. Met Lord John Manners[114] and a party of Manchestrians. Lord John is a decent – well sympathyed spooney, though a well informed spooney. I stuck 'his old nobility' into him.

On Thursday (yesterday) the Soirée took place, near 3000 persons were there – everything brilliant, fine, grand, effective. I was introduced to C. Hall, Smythe, Rowland Hill and a great many more.[115] After the speaking which was fine and in which great and new admissions were made by the speakers, a vote of thanks was proposed by Rowland Hill and seconded by Torrens McCullagh[116] to Berlyn and myself and after a eulogium from Disraeli carried by nem dis. I briefly responded – they say well.

On Thursday we had a morning meeting of deputies from the Institutions in the county. Atherton in the chair. I spoke, sadly too often.

114 Lord John Manners, prominent member of the Young England Group. Son of the duke of Rutland. Cobden criticised Watkin for inviting the Young Englanders as he regarded them as political humbugs. He deplored the idea of Manchester throwing itself at the landed aristocracy (Cobden to Watkin, 9 July 1844, MCL 219/3).

115 Charles Hall, a Manchester lawyer who succeeded to the practice of Duval, the conveyancer, in 1844. Smythe, Conservative MP for Canterbury, a free trader and member of the Young England Group. Rowland Hill, inventor of penny postage, then chairman of the London, Brighton and South Coast Railway. Later secretary to the Post Office.
Absalom considered that Disraeli gave a good address, but there was no good *speaking*, and none of the speakers knew what to do with their hands (*AWJ*, p. 3, Oct 1844). Cobden in his speech said that the conjunction of Lord John Manners on one side of him and Smythe on the other would prevent the possibility of the Athenaeum ever being thought of as a party institution (Watkin, *Cobden*, p. 135). Disraeli told Lord Londonderry that he, Manners and Smythe had met the largest assembly ever collected within four walls (letter of 4 Oct, *Disraeli Letters*, i. 145–6).

116 Torrens McCullagh, assistant commissioner on Irish Poor Relief. Joined ACCL. Later introduced Watkin to the Liberals in Great Yarmouth where he fought two elections.

This affair is now over and I feel astonished at our success. It convinces me that I have a forte in getting up and organising Institutionist meetings. I have had all sorts of congratulations etc today, and certainly the meeting will have a great and most useful effect in the country. Well done us. We have committed Young England to self-supporting self-governing Institutions. I have made them denounce intolerance and all sorts of exclusiveness and illiberality.

——— and her brother and sisters were at the Soirée. I did not quite like all associating with big rascals and rascality makes a fellow of my fickle temperament somewhat fastidious. Well! We shall see. By the way I danced with Miss Emily Atherton.

And now business – business – business.

Sunday, Oct 6

I was busy yesterday getting in the Soirée accounts and making a number of little matters right.

Today at last I have had a day of quiet inactivity. I have read a little and dreamed. Wasted the day away. Lots of compliments about the meeting. A note from Revd R. B. Aspland[117] this morning full of praises and declaring that Cobden very warmly sang my praises on Friday at Ashton.

I am changed about again in the favourable vein and am rather fiery again about ——— what a flat I am! Well! nous verrons.

Saturday night, Oct. 12

Monday night at the Essay and discussion meeting. Spoke briefly on a question of Greaves' about the spirituality of the 18th Century.[118] Stayed with Berlyn.

117 Revd Brook Aspland, from 1837 Unitarian minister at Dukinfield. One of the secretaries of New College, Manchester and editor of the *Christian Reformer*, the Unitarian monthly. Active in free trade circles and pressed for the Dissenting Chapels Bill.

118 John Greaves, long-standing member of the Literary Society. A banker.

Thursday at Kemble's readings.[119]

Met —— on Thursday afternoon and saw her off by the omnibus.

Public Parks – busy about.

Business brisk and we have had our share.

Yesterday we had a dinner party here. Edwards, James Burton, Berlyn, Dilberg and Harling here.[120]

I have had invitations to attend Soirées at Rochdale and Bury. The Rochdale one took place last night and I could not go. I think I shall go to Bury.

Friday night, Oct. 18

On Monday night we had a little party – the Alcocks, Sumners and Mordacques here.[121]

On Tuesday evening went to Kemble readings – Henry 8th, with Thos Mellor, Mary and Mrs Dean.

Wednesday night with Berlyn at a party at Mrs Leresche's house in Broughton. A most snobbish lot present including the Kearsleys and a bitch called Prescott who writes poetry under the signature of Hypatia, and who talks all sorts of shallow sentimentality.[122]

Last night (Thursday) went with James Edwards over to Bury to attend a meeting (tea party) of the Mechanics Institute. The

119 Charles Kemble, the actor, now nearly 70, was giving Shakespeare readings – *Much Ado about Nothing* on 10 Oct.
120 Dilberg may be an abbreviation of Dilberoglue.
121 All neighbours of the Watkins. Joseph Sumner lived on Sharston Green.
122 Mrs Leresche lived at Mount Pleasant, Bury New Road. Although it is possible that William Kearsley, merchant of Dale Street who had a house in Lower Broughton is referred to, the MS is unclear. Turner Prescott was a Manchester solicitor.

affair took place in the Brunswick school rooms – 500 people. Grundy in the chair.[123] A good meeting. I spoke – pretty ack [text unclear] and we got them out of debt by a little arrangement.

This afternoon I went up to the Golf club which meets on Kersall Moor at the invitation of Mr Atherton, dined with them at their house – Barbour, de Castro, A Wright, Barge, the two Burts, Ross and myself there.[124] Pleasant speechifying and singing, eating and drinking. We broke up at 5 minutes past 8.

Tomorrow I go to Failsworth for Sunday.

The Ath Soirée continues to be the topic of discussion with the press. The French papers had several articles about it. It has really had a great effect and I don't think it has injured me at all with the nobs – oh! how I wish I had the cheek necessary for taking advantage of the acquaintances and respect I have made. But nature denies it.

Monday night, Oct. 21

On Saturday night I went to Failsworth and spent yesterday there coming back to business this morning. ⸺ and I became very familiar and I feel all the more confirmed in my opinion of her – whether right remains to be seen. At all costs she has no over estimate of herself and rather an over one of me. I think she will be a good manager and retain a warm heart and enthusiasm.

---

123   George Grundy of Grundy & Beard.

124   J. H. de Castro was a merchant. George Freeland Barbour was a trustee of the Athenaeum and the brother in Robert Barbour & Brother. Robert built Bolesworth Castle near Chester. John and Robert Barge were calico printers in Broughton. James Burt had been borough reeve at the time of the Reform Bill. Thomas Burt was later an MP. Watkin later wrote, 'the Manchester Golf Club … were wont to play on Kersal Moor on Friday afternoons in red coats and mostly decked in tartan bonnets' (Watkin, *Cobden*, p. 115).

Friday night, October 25

On Tuesday night at the dinner of the Athm directors at the Albion.[125] About 22 sat down. Potter in the chair. Ross in the Fire Chair. A pleasant evening. Plenty of good eatables and drinkables. I spoke. Thos Mellor went with me as my guest.

Staid the night with Mr and Mrs Wall.

Wednesday evening went over to Failsworth to see old Mellor and be present at a party of young folks, friends and school companions of Esther Ann.

Thursday (yesterday) dined at Charles Swain's with Berlyn, Lockett and Mrs Swain. Mr Marsden coming after dinner.[126]

Much pleased particularly with Swain's account of his first public appearance as an author. Was shewn some letters from Southey and some presentation copies of books etc.

In the week have been pretty active and industrious. Business rather worse.

My father and I have had two or three flare-ups. I am now waiting to have a talk with him. Nous verrons. It is high time I knew my position and did something to improve it.

Sunday morning, October 27

Saturday morning my father and I talked matters over in going to town. The upshot is that he will see old Mellor and that the arrangement as to business is

125 The Albion Hotel was in Piccadilly.

126 William Lockett, silk manufacturer and merchant, a member of the provisional committee of the Manchester Anti-Corn Law Association and first mayor of Salford, 1844–45. Mr Marsden, possibly George Marsden, a solicitor, one of the earliest members of the Chetham Society and the Manchester Law Society, or Henry Marsden of Marsden & Chapel, Cannon Street, father of William Marsden of the half-holiday campaign.

the income from property to go to him;

the business to bear the charges of business, interest of mortgage and the maintenance and clothing of the family;

the rest – to be divided into ninths – 5 for me, 2 for Alfred and the rest for my father.

If we do more business this will do well enough, but if it is to be of any use to me I must make it so by more hard work than I have yet got through. It will – on reflection – I think come to this that in a year or two the whole weight of the business, with the whole maintenance of the family, falls upon my shoulders. Well I must e'en do my best. I was pleased with the arrangement at first, but on reflection I fear it will not do me much service. However, one thing is certain, that I can make a bad arrangement good by working it.

I saw Mary yesterday with her mother – my sister, she and Mrs Dean, go over to Haslingden for a few days on Thursday.

Friday November 1 (night)

As I go to Haslingden tomorrow I post up tonight.

Wednesday at a Ath. directors meeting – staid with Berlyn. Thursday as usual at the Public Park committee meeting.

Today helping to return Geo Wilson for St Michael's Ward: by dint of personations he sails in by a majority of 7! Thus shall popular services be rewarded.[127]

127 George Wilson, chairman of the ACCL, in which cause he attended 1,961 meetings. One reason why there was such a close contest was that many voters declined to support him on account of his 'seldom attendance' at council meetings, but the high esteem in which he was held and the knowledge that when absent he was engaged on even more important public business prevailed. St Michael's was one of only three

Saw Mary on Tuesday – a little put out of the way by an ill-tempered note of mine. All right now.

Public Parks have taken up much of my time this week – it is a sad bore to have a constant object of this kind interfering with business and breaking up that occasional enthusiasm which a few fortunate passes create and which is the best stimulus and creative of effort and success. Well – one must do something for posterity.

This is my question at the Literary Society on Tuesday 'Young Englandism – a progress or a regression.'[128] I have hardly anything yet prepared: I am almost afraid that my journey tomorrow will effectively prevent my proper consideration of the matter.

Tuesday evening, November 5

Went on Saturday afternoon at 4 with Thos Mellor to Haslingden. Did a little business and then gave myself up to enjoying myself as much as possible. I did not however quite relish all. I must be hard to please indeed.

Yesterday my sister, Mary, Thos M and I went over to the Grane to see Mr John Dean – a very pleasant walk. In the evening we had a party at Deans – Rev Mr Gray, Hale etc and a sentimental Miss Hoyle.[129]

wards where there was a contest in Nov 1844. The Conservatives had 3 seats out of 16 (*Manchester Times*, 2 Nov 1844). 'Personations' is presumably used in the sense of proxies as there is no suggestion of impersonation in the press report.

Wilson was engaged in the corn trade and starch and flour manufacture. Later director and deputy chairman of the Manchester & Leeds Railway (Lancashire and Yorkshire), 1848–67, where he became chairman 1867. President of Lancashire Reform Union 1858 and chairman of National Reform Union 1864.

128 By 6 to 1 it was decided that Young England was retrogressive.

129 Revd William Gray was perpetual curate at Haslingden. The Hoyles owned a woollen mill at Haslingden.

Came to Manchester this morning with W. Dean in his gig: a wet ride.

This evening opened the question at the Lity Society in a fair speech. We had a slender house but a spirited and constrained discussion.

Friday, Nov 8

On Wednesday evening attended a meeting of the workmen at Sharp Bros & Co.[130] John Sharp in the chair. Ross and I and Watts addressed them soliciting their aid to the public parks.

Stayed the night with Borella who accompanied me to the meeting.

Last night at the meeting of the auxiliary committee at the Town Hall!.

Mary Mellor came home with me today by the one o'clock omnibus. She is staying a day or two.[131]

Friday, very busy Public Parks, my own business and lots besides.

Sunday morning, Nov 10

Mary Mellor still here. I have passed some very happy hours, but somehow the recollection of business will intrude and at times the contrast with present moments of pleasure and the certainty of lots of difficulties to be encountered is annoying.

---

130 Until 1843 Sharp had been a partner in Sharp, Roberts & Co., manufacturers of textile machinery and locomotives formed in 1826 by amalgamation. Sharp had retained the Atlas works, Roberts the Globe works, both by the Rochdale Canal.

131 'It being understood that in due time they will marry' (*AWJ*, 8 Nov 1844).

I must strive with all my soul to labour hard for myself and others. I want more solitude and must have it if I am to make anything of it.

Thursday, Nov 21

Last Friday (Miss Mellor having left here on the morning of that day) I went with Ross and Watts to attend a meeting of the hands at Whitworth & Co Chorlton St.[132] – our purpose to induce their subscription to the Public Walks. We met in the Smithy, a large high, black-looking room. They appointed one of their own number Chairman and then I spoke to them, about a quarter of an hour, and was followed by Watts and Ross. I left as soon as Watts had done speaking and went in a coach containing Mr Mellor, Jn and Thomas to Mr William Mayson's Victoria Park. We met there William, his wife, the Maysons and a number of people I knew only by sight – the evening was rather dark. Talk music. Supper broke the dull routine and after supper we had a little speechifying in which I was made to take a part, acquitting myself pretty well.[133] Went to Failsworth.

Spent Saturday night and Sunday at Failsworth.

Yesterday afternoon (Wednesday) took M. M. to Baileys. We had one development taken. Mary's was good with the exception of one or two things. Mine, as I expected, bad. Went up to Failsworth.

Mr Aspland wants me to write an essay on Public Parks for a magazine of his. I think I shall.

I am invited to dine with the Mayor on the 5th Dec. I have invitations to the Conversationes at the Royal Institution.

132 Joseph Whitworth had set up at 44 Chorlton Street in 1833. By 1844 the establishment had a workforce of about 170, specialising in machine tools. Norman Atkinson, *Sir Joseph Whitworth: 'The World's Best Mechanician'* (Stroud: Sutton, 1996), p. 139.

133 William Mayson, merchant of J. Mayson & Co.

Saturday night, Nov 23

I have been working pretty briskly since Thursday and have little to report either good bad or indifferent.

I have written and been written to by Mary.

Last night I went up to the W. Makinsons and had a regular roasting from them in a friendly way about getting married.

I have today and tonight to write for Aspland and also to try to prepare for my intensive grand effort about 'Manchester'.

Sunday, Dec 1

Last Monday with Mary Mellor and Wm Henry at a Conversatione at the Royal Institution – the subject the improvement of Public taste. I spoke – a dull discussion.

On Wednesday evening at Geo Walls.

Thursday evening at a party of Mr Alcock's – dull, got sallied about getting married: mother Sumner heading the van in the fun.

Yesterday morning brought Mary over here, and left for Manchester at 5 to go to the adjourned conversatione held at the Ath. Cobden in the chair. A good meeting and spirited discussion. Spoke – pretty well.

M.M. here of course.

Next week I go Monday dine at Buile Hill.[134] Tuesday two Public Park meetings – Wednesday dine at Ridgefield.[135] Thursday at the Mayor's.

---

134 Sir Thomas Potter's house in Pendleton, built by Barry, 1825–27. Now a Salford museum.
135 Jonathan Mellor senior's house at Failsworth.

Tuesday, Dec 10

Last Monday at Buile Hill to dinner. Cobden, Brotherton, Robt Gardner, Atherton. Geo. Wilson and others were there. A pleasant evening.

Staid all night at Marsden's Hotel.

Tuesday at Leise St. No meeting – at the Lit Socy.[136]

Wednesday at Mr Mellor's dinner party – a pleasant party.

On Thursday morning found a letter from John begging me to go over immediately to see him as he was in such a state that he could neither work nor do anything.

Immediately left town. Went by Birmingham and Cheltenham to Oxford where I got about 1/2 past 3 on Friday morning.[137] Found John done up over work, made him better and brought him back. Reached town again at 11 on Saturday morning.

Knocked up – a cold – miserable nasty journey.

Last night (Monday) at Failsworth. Poor Polly[138] has been ill.

Have been made Hon Sec to the Pottinger Testimonial Committee – have been rather busy with it.[139]

---

136 The question, proposed by T. E. Williams, was: 'Ought the state to furnish funds for ecclesiastical objects?' It was affirmed by 6 to 5.

137 The direct line between Oxford and Birmingham was not yet open.

138 i.e. Mary.

139 Sir George Pottinger had been made plenipotentiary to China and superintendent of British Trade in 1841. Captured Amoy, signed the Treaty of Nanking in which Hong Kong was ceded to Britain. Governor and commander-in-chief Hong Kong, 1843–44. A banquet was held on 20 Dec in Manchester in his honour because he had opened up the China trade.

Wednesday morning, Dec 18

Monday Dec 9 at Failsworth.

Wednesday do.

Friday Miss Mellor came here with me and staid till yesterday morning.

Monday evening, Dec 23

On Tuesday Dec 17 at the Lity Socy – spoke on Duval's question on the French Revolution.[140]

Wednesday night at Failsworth.

Thursday and Friday very much occupied with the Pottinger dinner; it came off on Friday evening in the Town Hall which was fitted up for the occasion. The Mayor was in the chair.

Previous to the meeting an address was presented in the Mayor's parlour.

Pottinger is about 5 ft 10 or 11. Stout, fuzzy dirt coloured hair, dark brown face, arched eyebrows, aquiline nose, moustaches, and a certain immobility of expressions. Like Ben Disraeli he is non-understanderable. The dinner was splendid and luxurious, the speaking bad.

A good deal of wine was drunk at the dinner and Edwards and I did not reach home till 1/2 past 3: being rather groggy.[141]

---

140   'Have the benefits resulting from the French Revolution in 1789 compensated for its miseries and crimes?' The debate was adjourned until 14 Jan.

141   Cobden was otherwise engaged and could not attend the dinner. He told Watkin that he was sorry to have been prevented from sitting down with those monopolist humbugs who were ready to hurrah for free trade in China, and vote against it in England. He asked whether

On Saturday afternoon a grand Soirée took place in the F.T. Hall to celebrate the half-holiday anniversary. The Mayor presided and Sir H. Pottinger came to the meeting with Col. Malcolm, Lady Pottinger, Miss Pottinger etc.[142] A vote of thanks was acclaimed to Pottinger and the old fellow returned thanks in a good and useful speech. He said that tho' born of an aristocratic (good) family himself he had had to make his way in the world by his own exertion. He had been away from England for 40 years and could tell all young men that the path to distinction was open to all if they but depended on themselves.

Yesterday at Failsworth.

Friday, Dec 27

M. M. came with me here on Friday evening and has been with us ever since.

Wednesday was but a sorry Xmas day to me as I was ill and uncomfortable. Have been ill since but now am rather better.

Mr Atherton wrote me to become a member of the Chamber of Commerce – he says he takes a great interest in my welfare.

Business is good.

Today perhaps because I have been low-spirited, I have almost wished that I had not resolved to enter upon the doubly blessed

---

Watkin was aware that the very same creatures who gave money to Pottinger in Preston signed the petition in favour of the present Corn Law which was presented with so much effect by Lord Stanley last Session on the very evening of Villiers' motion – Charles Villiers moved annually a motion to repeal the Corn Laws (Cobden to Watkin, 7 Dec 1844, Watkin, *Cobden*, pp. 98–100).

142 Col. Malcolm of the 3rd Light Dragoons. Watkin seconded a resolution thanking carriers and railway companies for endeavouring to assist in the establishment of the half-holiday. Disraeli and Carlyle sent messages to the Soirée.

path of life. Money – money. By the way mon beau pere [...] espere devenir pere.[143] This is going ahead with a vengeance!! Shall I make similar progress? Heaven help me if I do.

CHAPTER 5

The diary for 1845

Friday, Jan 3 1845

Much better than I was. The Christmas has not been a happy one. New Years day (Wednesday) I spent in stocktaking at the Warehouse.

M.M. left yesterday morning; and I went to Failsworth in the evening staying until this morning.

Business good.

My annual resumé is on the other side.

Jany 3 1845 (for January 1)

In my little summary for the year 1843 in the beginning of this book I say I will 'make no resolves', but I evidently wish to improve in morals, mind and usefulness. Alas I fear, nay I feel, that my morality has deteriorated and that my mind has been damaged by the loss of that freshness which moral sentiments give to it – and as to my usefulness – alas! alas!!

During the year I have been working at a great scheme and at many little ones. The Public Walks and Parks have consumed a great deal of my time but fortunately the object is in a forward and satisfactory state. I have had a noble coadjutor in Malcolm Ross and he and I, I believe, shall be of still further use in this community.

The little goes have been Irish affairs, South Lancashire election, the alteration of the management of the Advertiser (failure), the Athenaeum Soirée (a brilliant and useful affair) etc.

During the year I have made 11 speeches at public meetings, dinners and in workshops (Public Parks), 4 at the Athenaeum, and 6 at the Lity Socy. A fair allowance of gab! I have written about half a dozen leading articles, two pamphlets and a little matter or so besides.

In business I have been moderately industrious and I do think that my business ability is improved: nonetheless I am sadly behind.

The great event in my history is my attachment to Miss Mellor, an event to me altogether unanticipated, as I had previously serious thoughts of a perpetual batchelorship. I have, in consequence, to work so as be able to maintain a wife, and at present this seems a distant and difficult task. My father and I do not hit it and I am sure that banking gives him far more practical interest than my love affairs. Like Richard 'I am myself alone' and must fight without assistance or sympathy. Had I a moral groundwork on which to rest this would matter little, but alas, I have no sound morality and I am seemingly given over to a chaos of religious opinions and to the guidance of the misfortunes of my own 'reason', a light brisk or dim with the weather or with the chance of the day.

I want fixed principles. I ought to have reflected and acted better than I have in consequence. I had a solemn warning when that frightful accident in the Channel took place, within a little of death, and with the alarm and danger of knowing that 6 fellow creatures had been sent in a moment to their long account. Upon me, I ought to have come out of the ordeal a new creature – alas! alas! Shall I ever improve? Shall I ever act as if I knew that the eye of the almighty was ever upon me and that every thought and wish and idlest word would have to be accountable for? I fear greatly I am surrounded too by circumstances quite antagonistic to personal improvement. I allude to disagreements and irregularity at home, to the want of direction and mind at the head of our family affairs, to the influence of the old habits and remembrances and to a naturally weak and vacillating will – a curse most noxious in its consequences. Well, nothing, no difficulty is too strong for the power I have at my disposal. I can mend if I will – why therefore do I not?

I have lost (at present) the habit of reading and I am certain I am not intellectually as strong as I was.

I have now a new incentive to work and to improve, 12 months more must make a great difference in me, one way or another. I may be made or I may be married. God help me by helping me to help myself.

If I have improved in morality, consolidated my opinions, increased my stock of knowledge and my power of economy, improved my habits of industry and saved £150 by next January, I shall be satisfied.

Let me try – manfully – worthily – I will.

Monday evening, January 6

On Saturday afternoon I went up to Failsworth and accompanied W.H. and Mary to Mr Walmsley's (a mill owner and manuf) where a tea party of female operatives was taking place.[1] I staid a short time and then left with W.H. for Oldham to attend a Free Trade meeting in the Town Hall there. The meeting was good both as to numbers and spirit. Jonathan was in the chair (as one of the High Constables) Mr Cobden, John Brooks, Mr Knott, I, Rev Mr Shepherd, Dronsfield, Mills and others spoke.[2] The object was to increase the number of Free Traders on the county

1   The Firs, Failsworth. T. & H. Walmsley ran Firs Mill, Failsworth.
2   Jonathan Melllor senior. William Knott was an Oldham hat manufacturer. Revd Shepherd was the Wesleyan Association minister at Oldham; Daniel Dronsfield a cotton spinner and fustian manufacturer at Werneth and Moorside Mills; James Mills a manufacturer of Waterhead Mill, Oldham.

register. I was called upon unexpectedly but spoke pretty well. After the meeting a number of us went to Fletchers'[3] and had supper and as soon as Mr Cobden's and Mr Brooks' health had been drunk, W.H. and I left in Brooks' carriage with Mr C. and Mr B. and were set down at Walmsleys. I danced a little at this place and made a short speech which seemed to please the folk, and Mary and I left.

I was at Failsworth yesterday, coming away this morning.

Business is fair.

Monday evening, Jany 13

Last Tuesday evening (Jan 7) at a lecture of Horncastle's and then to Borella's with Berlyn.

Wednesday evening at a dinner at Mr Penny's.[4]

Thursday evening at home trying to make my sister (who was distracted with Tic doloreux [sic][5]), a little better.

Friday morning brought my sister to town to see Helsby – no use.[6]

Friday evening at a feed given by Edward, Thomas and Jonathan Mellor at Failsworth. Some of the principal younger men of Oldham etc were there (22). I had to speak and tell tales and

---

3   Probably Richard Fletcher, a cotton spinner, who lived at Greenacres Moor, near Oldham.

4   Derick W. Horncastle, one of the Gentlemen of the Chapel Royal, was giving the first of six lectures, three on Irish music and three on English melody. 'Richard Penny was known among us as "Struggle" to commemorate the emphasis with which he declared we were engaged in one' (Watkin, *Cobden*, p. 114).

5   Severe facial neuralgia with twitching of the facial muscles.

6   Probably Richard Helsby, surgeon dentist of George Street and Baguley Lodge, Northenden.

had my health proposed in an eulogistic speech by Nathan Worthington, one of the Constables.[7]

Yesterday afternoon went up to Failsworth and staid till this morning.

My sister is a little better.

Business not quite so good.

Thursday evening, January 16

Tuesday night at the Lity Society – a stupid discussion on the Adjournment of Duval's paper. I opened on the spur of the moment.[8] (at Geo Wall's).

Wednesday evening with Mary to the Soirée of the essay and discussion Society at the Athenaeum. Dull debate. Danced twice then came away in a cab, going to Failsworth where still this morning.

My sister is still exceedingly ill. I don't know what we should do. It is really miserable to see her in this state without having the power of alleviating her sufferings. God help us!

Business is rather quieter.

On taking stock it appears that we are behind. We have made £900 in commission and the rents will make it £1,000 yet we have not saved a rap!!! John's expenses £200 !! account for part of the mischief, but bad account keeping (no cash account) and the absence of any presiding mind in our affairs are the main reasons. With all this there is a mighty pretty prospect for me! We can hardly hope in normal times to get more than a gross income of £1,000 and if we must be always behind,

7   Cotton spinner (J. Worthington & Son) who lived at Hollinwood.
8   The question (see diary entry for 23 Dec 1844) was affirmed by 5 to 4.

where the devil shall we stop. We want some decisive step either in economising or enlarging our income, but we have not the means of taking it. My father has no energy left for his own affairs and is in bad health. He will try to keep the books and the purse. I can perhaps increase the income, but cui bono? will ever and anon strike in. Of what use when all, all is spent, frittered away and all is imbecility? Well I am rightly punished for my sins! I am in the mill and I suppose must go on like my old, battered, blind horse hopelessly until some change of fortune arrives. I can truly say that I am myself alone. I have to do all for myself surrounded with many hindrances and with much that weakens and wounds the spirit. I am not respected at home and am considered, I imagine, too much as the family drudge who has no right to do anything but slave for the rest with quietness and contentment.

Trust in God! I say sometimes. Alas I don't know what such a trust is! and I cannot trust entirely in myself. Well, well, heaven help me. Sister ill, father ill. John perpetually depressed, Alfred not well and discontented, mother old and myself weak enough and imbecile enough, at the same time a wish to get married and no power of carrying my wish into effect, thanks to the imbecility and practical (tho' not intentional) selfishness of others in good part.

Here is a picture 'most hideous to behold'. I am ill too. My constitution seems to have had a shock and I suffer from those everlasting disorders of the bowels which are the only 'hereditaments' I ever perhaps shall inherit from my ancestors. Well my boy, we shall see.[9]

---

9   On 13 Jan Absalom noted that 'Elizabeth is still suffering from the Tic [douloureux]. Mrs Watkin brawling, untidy and slatternly – the house not clean – yet a considerable expense. Edward grossly insolent.' On the following day he wrote, 'Elizabeth worse. Edward's insolent madness has caused a relapse' (Goffin, p. 244).

Tuesday afternoon, January 21

On Friday night (Jan 17) at the Oldham assembly held in the Town hall, with Mary, Jon'n, Thos Mellor and Miss Fletcher. I was very ill to start with, but the excitement and the heat improved me.

Saturday afternoon and Sunday at Failsworth.

Monday night (last night) with Mr Cobden and John Brooks to Bury to attend a Free Trade tea party. 600. Spoke.

I am ill.

Mary and I have just walked over here (Northen).

Monday evening, January 27 1845

Wednesday night at the Ath directors' meeting, and thence to Failsworth.

Thursday night at home.

Friday do.

Saturday afternoon to Failsworth – came back this morning.

I am ill. For two or three weeks I have been ailing and now am much thinner and weaker. I don't make any progress and can hardly tell what to do or what to think about it. Heaven help me!

Business is pretty good. I find however that the annual stocktaking leaves me £5 better! and the general account about £130 worse!!!

Here is great encouragement for entering upon the 'rosy path' of matrimony. Perhaps this nasty fact makes me prone to regret the step I have taken. It would perhaps have been better if I had never known ———. I almost think that in my present mood and circumstances I should be disposed to back out could it be done honourably and easily. I am in a strange position and a strange temper. Unhappy enough.

My sister is better and John is improving.

Sunday Feb 2

On Tuesday evening Mary came over here with me.

On Wednesday evening to the annual meeting of the members of the Athm, a capital meeting. My father made a good speech. I said half a dozen words.

Thursday and Friday at home courting.

Saturday very busy in town.

Business is pretty good.

I have the largest number of votes at the Ath. this year again (227) Berlyn next (210) – the lowest 127.[10]

I feel happier and better by far today.

Tuesday Feb 11

Last Monday but one at Geo Wall's (The Lity directors' meeting)

Wednesday at Failsworth.

Friday evening and night at James Edwards with Berlyn.

---

10   A year later Berlyn resigned from the Athenaeum 'regretting the circumstances which had led to his severances from the institutions which conveyed no blame to him individually except in following a system in which others were deeply engaged with him' (*MG*, 31 Jan 1846).

Saturday afternoon and Sunday at Failsworth.

Last night at Geo Wall's

Have been lazy this last 8 days. It won't do. I must work harder. It is true I have been ill but I ought to have strength of mind enough to conquer ill-health and natural cowardice.

Business not good, but fair.

I expect to go with John Brooks to an Anti Corn Law tea party on Wednesday (tomorrow).

Tuesday Feb 18

Last Wednesday I went to Preston with John Brooks. We had a cold ride in the R.M.[11] A fair meeting and a cosy hour or so after at Crofts Hotel. Old Johnny told me all about his flax mill and his other affairs. He says he lost £70,000 by claim Lees and £80,000 by his flax mill, that he has £180,000 on the water and abroad and wishes he could reduce his affairs into a tolerable compact and look after North Lancashire.[12]

On Thursday night at Failsworth.

---

11 Presumably the Royal Mail coach.
12 W. E. A. Axon states that the £70,000 was lost because his creditor failed, having falsely assured him when taking the loan that the property was unencumbered. Presumably the creditor was Lees (*The Annals of Manchester: A Chronological Record from the Earliest Times to the End of 1885* (Manchester: John Heywood, 1886), pp. 251–2). Brooks in 1834 had a fortune of over £300,000, much of it in his calico-printing business. He overextended his trade overseas particularly in South America and in May 1838 had debts on his books of £259,000 due from export houses and agents abroad. By 1846 his capital was from £150,000 to £200,000 and he decided to retire from business. S. D. Chapman, 'Financial constraints on the growth of firms in the Lancashire cotton industry', *Econ HR*, 2nd ser., XXXII (1979), 5–69, at p. 63.

On Friday night at the Ath, (a special board to see to the mortgage) and at a lecture on mesmerism and phrenology by a Mr Craig: he examined my head afterwards.[13]

Saturday afternoon and Sunday at Failsworth

Last night at Failsworth.

Mary and I came over here this afternoon.

Business bad.

The essay I wrote on 'Recreations for the Operative Classes' appeared in the Feb number of the Christian Reformer. Mr Aspland has been full in his thanks to me and I believe the paper has been favourably noticed by the Sheffield Iris.

I have written a short article for tomorrow's Guardian on the Manchester movement for Public Parks etc.

Feb 22

On Thursday night to a party at Mr Alcocks with Mary.

Business fairish.

Nothing new except the old state of weakness and imbecility which makes wish to do everything and to do nothing.

Busy with the Public Parks, Athm etc.

13 Two lectures were given by Edward T. Craig on 'Mesmerism, Heads and Characters with public manipulations of the audience and mesmeric illustrations showing the powerful influence of music on the human frame'. George Wilson was president of the Manchester Phrenological Society, of which Cobden, who had his head examined, was also a member. Phrenology was then seen as an attempt to construct a science of the mind and to study human personality which could be improved by exercise, discipline, education and social reform, and this made it attractive to reformers.

On Wednesday went with Chas Walker to see some land out at Bradford and dined with a Mr Porter. Saw Townley Parker about it on Friday with Ross, Walker and Porter.[14]

Sunday, March 2

Mary here still. She has been ill but is now better.

Nothing new. I have been an imbecile and idle as ever this past week. On Thursday was at home and I came home at noon on Friday, a practice which I find will not promote my business ability or increase my industry. Business has been flat, stale and unprofitable.

I must work harder and be more constant in my efforts or I shall never do anything.

During the last month or so have not done much good and I see plainly that on my present expenditure saving to any extent is impossible. Thus I find myself in the 'pleasant' situation of not knowing what to do. I want to marry. I am keeping a woman that I love indefinitely waiting and I cannot tell when or how I must manage to furnish my house or keep my wife and myself after I am married! I can hardly imagine a more unpleasant situation. If there were any outlet the matter would be different but there is at present no light. Perhaps however some little glimmer may break upon the gloom as suddenly as changes often take place.

---

14 Charles Walker was the son of Thomas Walker, and a Manchester alderman. Robert Townley Parker of Cuerden, near Preston, was MP for Preston, 1837–41 and 1851–57, and had been sheriff of Lancashire in 1817. His father's widow, the daughter and heiress of Peter Brooke of Astley, had married Sir Henry Philip Hoghton of Hoghton Tower near Blackburn, who had died in 1835, and it was her estate at Bradford which Watkin was seeing.

March 8

On Monday night at Failsworth.

Tuesday evening at a meeting of members of the Ath to consider about the Mortgage. A good meeting. I spoke.

Wednesday evening with Mary and W.H. to the F.T. Hall to hear Fox.[15]

Thursday evening at Failsworth.

Friday (last night) at a Committee meeting of the members of the Athm Mortgage. £1,000 raised already.

Yesterday afternoon out in a coach with Ross and the Mayor, also Campbell from the Botanical Gardens looking at different sites offered for Public Parks.

Went to Gorton, Bradford, Newton and Harpur Hey. When we returned I went and dined with the Mayor at his house in John St.[16]

During the week I have been very busy parking, Athenaeuming and courting and I have not attended to my interest as I should have done.

Tonight a Soirée takes place at the Ath (Mortgage). I expect I shall have to speak.

Monday, Mar. 11

On Saturday night the Soirée took place – a dull affair – my speech the dullest thing of all.

15   A meeting of the ACLL. W. J. Fox, former Unitarian minister, political writer and lecturer, one of the ACLL's most effective speakers and on the ACLL staff from 1843. Author of *Letters of a Norwich Weaver Boy* in the ACLL newspaper. MP for Oldham 1847–52 and 1857–62.

16   Alexander Kay lived at 19 John Street. Nothing came of the visits to Gorton and Newton.

On Monday (last) night Ross and I had a dozen fellows to dinner at the Palatine to get up the steam for a ball in aid of Public Baths – a lushy night.[17]

Monday, Mar 17

Wednesday evening at Failsworth.

Thursday evening do.

Friday afternoon with the Mayor and Ross looking at sites for Public Parks. Staid at Temperance Hotel. Directors meeting at Athm

Saturday afternoon at Failsworth. Staid till this morning.

Business bad – very bad.

The weather is most unaccountable. The frost is exceedingly intense. The river was frozen over this morning at the Boat.[18] Not a leaf is yet to be seen and every out door operation is at a stand. Printing cloths suffers in consequence.

I have been busy with Public Parks with the Athm and with the Washhouse Ball[19] and with a project for a new newspaper.

Regarding the latter since Garnett so sillily backed Mr Birley in the Chamber of Commerce affair, the desire for a new paper has been much increased. Tom Potter has once or twice asked me to 'go into it' and I seem to be thought of by some as the likely man to manage it. Ballantyne, at the Guardian office (the sub editor) – with whom I have once or twice spoken on the matter, called upon me last Monday and gave me some particulars and we met by appointment at the Athm on Wednesday evening

17   'lushy', slang for drunken.
18   The inn on the Mersey at Northenden.
19   The proposed grand Fancy Dress Ball in aid of Public Baths and Washhouses.

and there discussed a statement of the probable progress of a newspaper and an estimate of the profits of the Guardian. B. wished me to go into it. I told him how I was situated and that it would not do for one to leave a certainty for the chance of success. He tells me [he] had £200 a year and now has £250 from the Guardian. He seems rather sanguine about success provided I undertake the thing. I shall see. I feel half inclined to venture should the party be disposed to do it and disposed to desire me to do so. There never was a better time for it. I fear nevertheless that to sell calicos will be the highest office I shall fulfil in this life.

Monday, March 24

Last Tuesday evening came home.

Wednesday evening at Failsworth.

Thursday do.

Friday (Good Friday) In the afternoon Mary and I went to Oldham and had tea in Manchester St. We afterwards went with Mr Mellor, Edward, H. A.[20] and Harriet to the Lyceum exhibition. Good. Saw John Hibbert, Dimcroft and Tipping of the District Bank.[21] Walked back to Failsworth in the wet.

Saturday afternoon at Failsworth. Yesterday too – a tolerable allowance of courting for a young one!!

Business bad. Cash account I find unkept, and my prospects bad, bad, bad.

The paper affair I think over for the present.

---

20   Hester Ann.
21   Tipping was later manager of the head office of the District Bank. Dimcroft not identified.

Friday, Mar 28

Tuesday evening at the Lit Socy a paper of Molineux's.[22]

Wednesday at Failsworth.

Yesterday at do.

Yesterday morning at the Funeral of poor old Sir Thos Potter. Went in a carriage with Ross, Edwards and Syddall, a procession a mile and a quarter. About 100 carriages. The morning turned out wet and one got drenched about the legs. Poor old Tom. He died last Thursday but one morning at 4.[23]

During the week we have been public parking. We have bought Lark Hill for £4,500. They wanted £5,000 and we got it for £500 less. The house cost £10,000. We have got the press to work to land the purchases. I wrote a stiff leader for the Advertiser for tomorrow.[24]

Business bad, very bad. Not sold a yard this week.

I have advertised for a house (to buy).

Tuesday, April 1

On Saturday afternoon to Failsworth. On Sunday morning went with Thos Mellor to Cross St Chapel – to hear Robberds

---

22 'Was the religious movement in the 16th century, conventionally known as the Reformation, sound in principle and have its results proved to be conducive to the happiness of mankind?' The discussion was adjourned until 8 Apr when Watkin was in London. It was then affirmed by 10 to 1. William Molineux was a member of the Literary Society and collector to Manchester Infirmary.

23 Benjamin Syddall and Sons were silk manufacturers. The interment was at Ardwick Cemetery. The public funeral was at the request of the corporations of Manchester and Salford.

24 It has not been possible to trace a copy of this issue of the *Advertiser*.

preach the Funeral sermon for Sir Thos Potter.[25] An oration – excellent.

Had one or two disagreements with Mary.

Yesterday afternoon with John at Failsworth.

Friday, April 4th

On Wednesday afternoon at Failsworth.

Last night at a dinner party at the house of the Mayor, 19 John St. About 24 people there including Mr William Barlow and bride.[26]

On Wednesday morning saw John off by the 1/2 p 6 train – then walked thro' Cheetwood by Fairy Hill to Broughton. Breakfasted with Borella after looking at some houses.

On Thursday morning Mary and I walked across country from Failsworth to Broughton.

Business has been miserable. We hope that the weather, now so lovely, will lead to better demand.

Public Parks – the Ball for Baths – busy with both.[27]

---

25 Revd John Gooch Robberds, the senior minister at the Unitarian Cross Street Chapel where the Potters and many other leading Mancunians were members, and where Revd William Gaskell (Mrs Gaskell's husband) was also a minister. His paean of praise to Sir Thomas, entitled 'The Value of Energy in Union with Benevolence', has been described as a realisation of the Christian ideal of the duty of public service. John Seed, 'Unitarianism, political economy and the antinomies of liberal culture in Manchester, 1830–50', *Social History*, 7 (1982), 1–25, at p. 5.

26 Cotton merchant and dealer, lived in Ardwick.

27 James Burton junior, James Dunn and F. W. Holland were the secretaries of the Grand Fancy Ball in aid of Public Baths and Washhouses. Holland was a mill manager but later owned his own cotton spinning mill in Salford.

I have to go to Liverpool with Ross tomorrow for Tuesday night we journey together to London to see Sir Robt Peel. I have this evening to draw up a case for our guidance.

Sunday, 6 April

Yesterday afternoon with Ross to Liverpool to see Mr Earle, the steward of the Railway.[28] Our interview was favourable. In the evening returned and went to Failsworth.

This morning came with Mary here.

A most beautiful day – the sky as clear as glass.

On Friday night I go to London – we shall see with what success.

I wish the Public Park matter were ended – I want to throw myself more vigorously into business.

Monday April 14

On Tuesday evening (1/4 to 9) went with Ross to London where we were joined by the Mayor (Wednesday morning) and set about our interview with Peel. Egerton who ought to have gone with us was taken ill of gout. Entwistle, Gibson and Brotherton went with us, during the interval Wyse joined us.[29] We mustered in a sort of Library at Downing St. and when ready were shown into a large room where Peel sat behind a table with a desk surrounded by books and papers. When we entered he rose and requested us to be seated. We opened our case – had a talk of 40 minutes. I spoke three or four times and

28 Presumably Hardman Earle, formerly a director of the Liverpool & Manchester Railway, who was now on the board of the Grand Junction. Earlestown, near Warrington where the two railways met, was named after him. Possibly some business connected with the parks necessitated the meeting as Ross was there.

29 All local ACLL MPs representing South Lancashire, Manchester and Salford, respectively. Thomas Wyse was MP for Waterford, 1835–47.

got £3,000 offered! We wanted £80,000!! So much for our first rebuff. After leaving Peel we went down to the House and saw a number of MPs with the wish of getting up a feeling in favour of our case. We saw Hutt, Bucknall Escott [*sic*], Archbold Hastie, E. Buckley and others.[30] On Thursday Ross, Edwards and I (E joined us on Wednesday night) called on Macaulay, Lord Jno Manners, Lord John Russell and others.

Friday with John Macgregor.[31]

At the League meeting on Wednesday night and after at the Haymarket Theatre.

At Kelly's place on Thursday night.[32]

Left London at 5 on Friday for Oxford. Staid there, seeing John, till Saturday at 3, then left for Manchester coming by Cheltenham and Birmingham.

Went to Failsworth soon after my arrival in Manchester yesterday morning.

Business damnable.

Thursday evening, April 17

On Tuesday night and last night at Failsworth.

Business most miserable – cloth coming down – no sales to be effected and expenses not covered or near it by receipts.

---

30 Sir William Hutt, Liberal MP for Gateshead; T. G. Bucknall Estcourt, Conservative MP for Oxford University, a free trader; Edmund Buckley, ironmaster and coal owner from Ashton-under-Lyne, Conservative free trader, MP for Newcastle-under-Lyme; Archbold Hastie was Liberal MP for Paisley.

31 Statistician and historian. Joint Secretary to the Board of Trade, 1839–47. MP for Glasgow, 1847–57.

32 Watkin wrote Keely, but possibly John Kelly, an Irish-born printer who became secretary of the National Anti-Bread Tax Association in 1841.

The little capital will soon be locked up and we shall be fast. Business may mend, however, and then we shall go on again.

Atherton in his usual implying and feeling and suggesting way offered me the Secretaryship of the New Chamber of Commerce yesterday. Salary £100 or £130 a year and other chances. Of course I could not bite.

I do hope trade may mend. I am again in very low spirits. There appears to be no opening in the clouds.

We make no way, and my position becomes everyday a more painful and perplexing one. Well! Something may very likely turn up.

The dissenters and evangelicals generally are making a dreadful kick up about Sir Robert Peel's grant to Maynooth. They threaten all sorts of things against Gibson, Brotherton, and Cobden even, for their conduct in voting for the Bill. Alas that the Anti-Catholic spirit should again be worked in all its furor.[33]

Tuesday, April 22

Friday afternoon went with Mary to Failsworth – staid till Monday morning I enjoyed myself very much indeed.

Yesterday Mary came over here.

Business is rascally – not a transaction today! All bad and all black. Everything I have in hand is going bad or seeming to do. I want fortitude much.

33 Maynooth was a Roman Catholic college in Ireland in a state of disrepair to which Peel's government proposed to give a much increased grant against the wishes of the Evangelicals and Dissenters. Cobden, then MP for Stockport, and other radicals along with the Whigs supported Peel, enabling him to push the bill through. Gladstone resigned in protest from the presidency of the Board of Trade. Several protest meetings had been held earlier that week in Manchester.

Friday night, April 25

On Wednesday afternoon up to Failsworth. Looked thro', with a view to taking, a house belonging to Mr Heywood.[34]

Thursday evening to Failsworth again. Walked with Mary up to Oldham where we staid the night. Got wet going up.

On Wednesday I was foolish enough to join Burton and Borella in buying 100 shares in the 'Direct Northern'. I may lose and I may gain. In either case I think this is the last time.

Business still rascally.

Thursday night, April 30

Saturday and Sunday at Failsworth – took the house I had before looked at for £24 per annum certain etc on Saturday.

Monday night at Failsworth.

Last night at the fancy ball with Mary with Mr and Jon'n M. and Dimcroft.[35] A brilliant spectacle – everything bright and beautiful. Staid till 1/2 p 3.

This morning dull and spiritless.

34 Mr John Heywood lived at Failsworth Lodge and had 'the reputation of being immensely rich but lived at the rate of about twenty pounds a year, with one old woman by way of a domestic servant'. H. J. Crofton, *A History of Newton Chapelry*, 2, pt 2, Chetham Society, new ser., 54 (Manchester: Chetham Society, 1905), p. 231. Absalom said he had never seen a large and well-arranged garden in such a state of neglect (*AWJ*, 3 Sep 1845).

35 The baths and washhouses ball. In 1846 Sir George Grey, then MP for Devonport, introduced a bill for promoting the voluntary establishment of public baths and washhouses in boroughs and parishes of England and Wales. It enabled local authorities to obtain the initial cost of building out of the poor rate and to borrow for this purpose. Royal Assent was given on 26 Aug 1846 (Public Baths and Washhouses Act, 1846 c. lxxiv).

My shares are down to £2 per share!!!

I am in for a loss of £60. So much for my folly.

Business rather better. Sold 15,000 ps.

Friday evening, May 9

Wednesday (May 1) at home. Thursday morning my Father went with my sister to London.

Thursday night to Failsworth.

Friday night at home.

Saturday at Failsworth till Monday morning.

Monday afternoon (May 5) drove Mary over here in the sociable.

Tuesday night at Failsworth.

Wednesday evening directors' meeting, Athm. Failsworth again. Last night do.

On Monday night I wrote an article on the case of Manchester (Public Parks) which appeared in the Guardian of last Wednesday.

Busy Parking and fiddling about in new newspaper – we shall see.

Business fair.

News from America rather bellicose.[36]

36   The dispute between the USA and Britain over Oregon. The matter was not settled until 1846 when the present boundary between the USA and Canada was established.

A Mr Grainger has been with me (London) today.[37] Took him to the Mayor.

Monday evening, May 12

On Saturday to Failsworth, where I spent yesterday. The Public Park business has engaged me much in the last few days. I have now in hand two or three matters of weight and Ross is away.

Business fair – done pretty well.

Tuesday evening, May 20

At Northen Monday evening, at Failsworth on Tuesday and Wednesday.

Mary came with me on Thursday. Mr Shuttleworth and John here to dinner.

Friday at Failsworth.

Saturday aft. do.

My father and sister came by the express train on Saturday evening and I met them. At Northen till 11 o'clock on Monday when left for Failsworth and staid there till yesterday morning. There last night.

During last week I bought for the Public Parks committee Lady Hoghton's land. 31 acres at £200 an acre and 23 acres of Fitzgerald's at £250 deducting £350. The remaining 20 acres to be under offer to us for 3 years.[38]

37   R. D. Grainger was lecturer in physiology at St Thomas' Hospital London – see note to entry for May 27.

38   Lady Hoghton's land at Bradford: see entry for 22 Feb above and n. 14. Fitzgerald's land was at Walness Vale and was added to that purchased from William Garnett to form Peel Park. The Fitzgeralds, who had acquired the Walness estate by marriage in the eighteenth century, continued to own part of the estate, including Pendleton Colliery and the site where Manchester races were held from 1847 to 1868 when they refused to renew the lease on moral grounds.

Business this week flat – flat – flat.

Tuesday evening, May 27

Wednesday night at Failsworth.

Thursday walked there to dinner.

Friday went at noon with Thomas and Mary to the Altrincham flower show, thence to Northen.

Saturday at Failsworth – and Sunday.

Last night at a lecture which I had almost to get up on the causes of insalubrity by Mr Grainger – moved the chairman and at the end proposed a vote of thanks.[39]

Business bad. Spirit of times miserable, pluck low, energy nil. What the devil to do. Am I a fool?

Bowels rather better.

Mary, poor good little girl, unwell.

Friday, May 30

Wednesday afternoon to Oldham with Alfred. A looks thro' P Sims mill.[40] Went from Oldham to Failsworth in a coach. Staid till Thursday morning.

Last night at Failsworth.

---

39   Watkin is referring to the organisation of the lecture. Grainger spoke to a large audience at the Athenaeum on the Causes of Insalubrity of Towns and the Means of their Removal with particular reference to Manchester. Robert H. Kargon, *Science in Victorian Manchester: Enterprise and Expertise* (Manchester: Manchester University Press, 1977), p. 114.

40   Possibly Simister of Church Lane Mill is intended.

Business bad.

My spirits this week have been very poor indeed. I have been shorn of all my little energy and left at times in perfect prostration of purpose. This is really miserable.

I wish my Public Parking was over that I might settle with all my soul to business. I must, I will conquer this absurd qualmish, useless nonsensical dependence on nerves, bowels, east winds and rain. It won't do Edward at all. Gird up thy loins for the fight with thyself which must be waged.

Tuesday, June 1

On Saturday to Failsworth where I spent Sunday and went last night. On Sunday Mr Daniel Mellor of Leicester was at Ridgefield. We had a kind of 'flare up': too much laughing and frolicking for Sunday.

Mary and I have had a few little sessions – disturbing, but like all such things the clouds are gone.

Business bad.

I have worked ill – indeed I feel myself diseased. My brain might be made of pulp – no string and bands in them.

I wish I had finished my Public Parks and other engagements and could then try to get right. Perhaps however the present excitement may be needful to keep me going at all.

John in a poor way.

Tuesday, June 8 1845

On Tuesday evening to Failsworth.

Thursday   do.   do.

Friday with Mr Mellor and Mary looking after furniture.

Yesterday at home. Mary here a pleasant example in the morning. In the afternoon old Mr Makinson came with his daughter Hannah – this damaged our enjoyment.

Business fair.

My spirits have been rather better in the last day or two: my bowels thank God are more regular than they were. I have been trying suppers of porridge – that seems to do well.

We have printed the announcement of the directed issue of £8,000 for Public Parks.

Sunday, June 15 1845

My beloved Polly has been here all the week and therefore I have no misfortunes or unhappiness to record. She is an excellent little girl and I always feel happy when I am privileged with her presence.

Business moderate

Langton is come back from Madeira and looks well.

Sunday, June 22

Mary is still here.

The painting etc of my house at Failsworth is nearly finished and as I see no present obstacle I intend to be married on the 3rd of September next. Then will commence my serious duties and an amount of responsibility, which I at times almost shrink from, will devolve upon me. I must work as I have never yet worked and evolve new faculties of all kinds.

Business just moderate.

I have been furniture ordering lately. Mr Mellor is going to furnish my dining room at a cost of near £100 and I expect the rest will cost me £300 at least. It is expensive work, a deal of trouble and partly folly, for many of the things public fashion compels us to have are of no use at all. But I cannot expose my wife to Mrs Grundy however I may be disposed to set her at defiance myself.

Sunday, June 29

Mary still here.

Business fair

Mr and Mrs Mellor dined here on Wednesday last.

Sunday, July 6

Northen

Mary here. We have been to town and last night went to Baguley Hall to see Mary's old school fellow Ann Marsland.[41]

Business is fair. I have sold an old stock of delaines and liberated about £700 sunk foolishly in advances on this stock.

I have canvassed for the Athm mortgage a little, but have met with some rebuff and as the members and directors shew a great carelessness in effecting the object, I think there is little or nothing more to be done with it.

Public Parks progress slowly. The lawyers now find hindrances.

I am lazy and I feel quite quite sure it wont do. I must and will try to become as industrious as anyone else. I have no chance but this industry of doing anything and therefore all hope or ambition.

41   The hall, near Northenden, belonged to T. W. Tatton, but was let to William Marsland, the cotton manufacturer.

Sunday, July 8

Today an evenement. Last night (I came home at 1 with Mary who had been ill of toothache and had been with me to Helsby's) my father told me Mr Spencer had been to the Warehouse to tell him that Smith late manager of the Bank of Manchester, a man of great power and energy, who is getting up railways and improved cultivation company in Jamaica (his native place) wanted a Secretary to go out with him on the 1st Aug.[42] Someone to make himself master of the whole detail and then come home and represent the two institutions in London, and he had spoken of me. The salary was for the Jamaica year £800 or upward and all expenses paid, and afterwards 5, 6 or 700£ a year.

My father of course left me to myself. The result is that I have today been with Spencer and Smith and as I will not consent to postpone my marriage and as Mary cannot go out with me (although she says she would) I have thrown up the chance. It was and is a fine opening, but I cannot, I cannot, I cannot.

What a fix I am in.

Monday, July 15

I have been working (I am the Hon Sec) in aid of the sufferers of the late fire at Quebec.[43]

42 William Smith had met Absalom on the train returning from London some six weeks previously and had told him he was returning to Jamaica. He said he was the largest shareholder on the Jamaica Railway (*AWJ*, 17 May 1845). Smith was later described as the projector and resident director (*Railway Times*, 27 Dec 1845, based on the *Jamaican Despatch* of 22 Nov).

43 A public meeting had been held on 10 July with the mayor in the chair to respond to the mayor of Quebec's appeal for aid for the victims of the fire in which damage of £1 million was done to property and 1,650 dwellings destroyed depriving 19,000 persons of food clothing and shelter. Before the meeting £1,000 had been promised with a further £1,700 at the meeting (*MG* and *The Times*, 11 July 1845).

Mary left on Saturday and I went with her up to Oldham where I staid until this morning.

Business flat.

Monday, July 21

Tuesday and Wednesday evenings at Oldham.

Thursday, Friday, Saturday and yesterday at Failsworth. Very busy furnishing (an intolerable business), Quebecking and seeking trade which is not as satisfactory as it should be. I am making no real way.

Monday, July 28 (3 o'clock)

Have just come home with Mary and I found Hannah Makinson and Davis here – devil take them.[44]

Have been pretty much at Failsworth during the week.

I have bought 50 Great Northern of France and 50 Ormskirk[45] scrip at 5¾, and 4 and 4⅜. The former up by £1 and the latter a little. I hope (from the information and advice I have had) to make 200 pounds.[46] If I do I shall be down right happy at my wedding and shall be sure of a year's keep besides all I can make during it.

Business but moderate.

---

44   They married on 12 Aug.

45   The Liverpool, Ormskirk & Preston Railway.

46   The Manchester correspondent of the *Railway Times* commented on 24 July: 'Prices this week have been preposterously forced up, and we have no doubt we shall ere long see a frightful reaction, which will draw into a vortex of ruin many of those who without resources or means should never have entered into desperate and wild speculation.' It seems that the Great Northern of France shares were bought at 5¾ and the Ormskirks in two lots at 4 and 4⅜.

Tuesday evening, August 5

On Tuesday at Failsworth.

Wednesday ill – came home with Mary by the omnibus. It rained dreadfully and we had to take a phaeton from Cheadle to come all the way home. Mr Smith and James Whitelegg here when we arrived.[47]

Ill till Thursday night. Polly nursed me very kindly lovingly and patiently.

Saturday to Failsworth.

Sunday at do

Last night do.

I have sold my shares and shall make £110.[48]

Business flattish.

Tomorrow will be a little star in my existence. I have (with Ross) to present to the Town Council the trusts of the Public Parks, Lark Hill and Hensham Hall.

Failsworth, Friday night

Since my last entry I have been nearly every evening here.

Ross and I presented the deeds to the Town Council with much eclat. We were plentifully praised by the mayor and Nield and loudly applauded by the rest. The paper had a full account.

---

47 Smith of Hill End, a neighbour and family friend. James Whitelegg was a friend of Alfred's. Absalom wrote on 15 June 1845, 'He and Alfred drink too much' (Goffin, p. 246).

48 On 31 July Ormskirks and Great Northern of France both reached £6½.

I have sold my shares and shall make £110. A good business. God knows I need it. I have bought a few more which came down 10s and are now rising, I hope for a profit.

Business has been just bearable, but I really have not been able to mind it.

I have nearly finished furnishing. The expense is infernal and in consequence the irritation it produces is annoying. I have taken a great step – we shall see whether I can maintain it.

We are to be married on Wednesday Sept 3. The house here is sufficiently turned upside down.

I have to see John Bright tomorrow about a newspaper.

August 30

Business has been tolerably good during the week.

On Wednesday next I shall be married. I have everything in apple pie order and hope to be happy.

Events have happened –

The Railway Mania is at its height.

1st I bought 40 Sheffield and Lincoln Junction at 3½. They are now worth about 8.[49]

2nd Mr Atherton sent for me on Wednesday and talked long about the advantages of my connecting myself with Railways. He said I was just the man, that men like me could not be got, that any price could be had for them, that there was an opening and I could have the matter. I promised to think and see him again when I returned from my wedding trip.

49   Coincidentally a constituent company of the Manchester, Sheffield & Lincolnshire Railway of which Watkin was to become general manager in 1854 and chairman from 1864 to 1894.

On Thursday morning however Atherton again sent for me and said that Messrs Newbery and Tootal[50] wanted me to take the Secretaryship of the Trent Valley, Midlands and Grand Junction Railway, that I could have my own price etc etc. At 1/2 p 1 I saw these two, was introduced by Atherton, promised to look after a dinner to Tootal,[51] and to see to the intended public meeting in favour of a direct connection with South'n,[52] and had the appointment offered. To cut the matter short I have undertaken it and shall begin in a fortnight. Tootal says he 'will make my fortune'. Nous verrons. As an earnest he informs me I have shares allotted in two railways, both at a good premium – a sop for Cerberus.[53]

50 Newbery of Seedley Bank, Manchester, who had been prominent in the movement for municipal reform, was another manufacturer active in the promotion of railways. Director of the Manchester and Birmingham, like the Trent Valley Railway (TVR) and the Grand Junction a constituent of the LNWR. Captain C. E. Cleather had been appointed secretary to the provisional company in April 1844. It is not clear why the TVR wished to replace him. In 1841 he had been replaced by Mark Huish as outdoor superintendent and secretary of the Grand Junction.

51 The TVR shareholders gave a sumptuous dinner to Tootal at the Albion Hotel at which 200 were present. He was presented with a plate service worth 1,800 guineas (*Railway Times*, 27 Sep 1845).

52 A reference to the proposed, but abortive, Oxford, Newbury, Andover, Manchester and Southampton Railway, in which Tootal had an interest and of which Absalom became a director (*AWJ*, 15 Sep 1845; Goffin, p. 249).

53 Watkin here mentions two different but associated railways. The TVR, authorised earlier in 1845, was to run from Rugby to Stafford directly and Watkin, as later entries show, was to be an active and virtually full-time secretary of the company. The Trent Valley, Midlands & Grand Junction Railway (TVMGJR) was conceived as a line from Wychnor, south of Burton-on-Trent on Midland Railway's line from Birmingham to Derby, to Lichfield where it would link with the TVR, and on to Rushall between Walsall and Wolverhampton and so provide links to Stourbridge, Stourport and Hereford. The South Staffordshire Railway was planned with a similar route and as early as 6 Sep 1845 the provisional committee of the TVMGJR told the South Staffs that they were willing to amalgamate, but the former had given an income guarantee to the Birmingham Canal and its demand for equality of

Sunday, 24 Sep

I remember readily a passage in Germes diary – 'owing to my marriage unable to maintain this regularly'.[54] I thought then it was strange such a cause should prevent regularity, but I find my marriage (which took place in good fine weather and under all sorts of favourable circumstances on Wednesday morning Sep 3) does prevent many practices I had wont to have recourse to.

To cut all matter short I am now regularly installed in office as Secretary of the Trent Valley Co (act got) and to the Trent Valley Midlands and Grand Junction Railway.[55]

I have been awfully busy and my nerves from trying to load my memory too heavily have once or twice failed me. I must take care not to harass matters.

September 28

I have been very busy all week with my Railway work.

I have managed to push Tootal and others into a new line from Manchester to Oldham with a branch or extension to Saddleworth. I hope to make a good thing out of it.

---

capital in the amalgamated concern ruled this out until both proposals were entering the parliamentary stage in Feb 1846 when they came to an agreement. The two companies amalgamated as the South Staffordshire in Oct 1846, and in 1867 became part of the LNWR.

Watkin had 1,000 £20 shares in the TVMGJR (probably never paid up), but there are no surviving records of the company's meetings or of its committees. Watkin briefly replaced Captain Cleather as secretary, but does not seem to have been very active in that capacity and by early 1846 Foss was the secretary. The only reference to this role in this diary is in the penultimate paragraph of the entry for 24 Sep 1845 (TNA, RAIL 638/1 and 1160/32; *Railway Times*, 20 Sep 1845).

54 The reading is doubtful and the quotation has not been traced.

55 The Act authorising the Trent Valley Railway had been given Royal Assent on 21 July. The office was in Marsden Street, Manchester.

Friday evening, October 17

I have had a busy stirring and anxious time since I last made an entry.

I have got together what should have realised 800 to 1,000£ had I not been fool enough to buy the shares at too high a Prem and should now have been comfortable. As it is I have no ready money and been very anxiously watching every cloud having a drop of rain. Today the Bank have raised the rate of Discount and I fear we shall have to pay for it? If I lose my winnings what a fool I shall think myself.

I have been energetic and industrious of late and I have got up some really good moves.

The Oldham Rail will be good. My father-in-law and brother in law are on it, the former deputy chairman – my doing.[56]

I want them to buy the Rochdale Canal[57] and have had all the trouble and thought of the matter – imagination – working everything. If this move succeeds I shall make my reputation as a Railway man. If I fail, why I have done my best.

This is quite a new life to me, and I think I hit. The field is wide and rich and if I am not wanting in myself I shall derive some of the benefit which now flows almost entirely to others.

Mary, poor lass, has had a most miserable attack of Tic and I have been very anxious about her. She is now better and I am in better spirits about her.

56   On 14 Oct the promoters agreed to proceed to Parliament.
57   The Rochdale Canal ran from the Calder Navigation at Sowerby Bridge to Piccadilly and Castlefield, Manchester, where it joined the Bridgewater Canal. The Oldham did not succeed in purchasing the Canal, and in 1847 the Manchester & Leeds Railway, despite some initial success, failed to obtain powers to purchase the canal. In 1855, however, it was leased to a consortium of four railways, including the Manchester, Sheffield & Lincolnshire of which Watkin was then the general manager.

What I want now is to sell my shares and realise, and then with 4 years maintenance in my pocket for our times – in a house at £24, I cannot fear the reckoning which must come upon all of us.

The men I am working with are many of them sad rascals. Tootal 'my Governor', is a damned scamp, a selfish fellow who 'makes use' of all men unscrupulously and seeks his own ends without caring for any man. I don't like him.

If I had money and could but launch out, I should be in my element. But I am but a Secretary.

The game is getting dangerous. Robert Gardner called today, said he was afraid, was very sorry to have allowed his name to appear on the Manchester and Milford Haven Railway – told me that Tootal had asked him to pass his name for £2,000 for it with the District bank. They had refused unless he had given that in writing. He had a little difference with Tootal in consequence etc etc. Damn Tootal.

Oldham District Railways

Oldham Oct. 18

Sir,

I beg respectfully to call your attention to a placard issued by the three High Constables, calling a Meeting of the Inhabitants for the purpose of obtaining an expression of public opinion in favour of the Oldham, Manchester, Liverpool and Birkenhead Junction Railway of which two of the constables are promoters. It appears to me that such a proceeding on the part of the authorities of the town is to say the least of it very imprudent and must create a feeling that the official duties are in this instance made subservient to private interest.

To counteract as far as possible any attempt which may be made to prejudice the public mind against the district Railway at the proposed meeting I beg earnestly to request that you will make a point of attending the Meeting at the Town Hall on Monday next at 8 o'clock and get as many of your friends as you can to attend also.

I am Sir

Your humble servant

Kay Clegg[58]

Meeting on Monday night – splendid – licked the Oldham District people in style. 1200 people.

October 24, Friday evening

After two or three weeks of fear and doubt I have sold my shares. I am cleared out. So much for my fortunes. I am not a ruined, but a 'temporarily done up' man and I am, at least I was, proportionately miserable.

Polly, however, has raised my spirits and her kind courage and beautiful cheering expressions, not a word of complaint tho' I have lost £1,000, makes me almost ashamed of having given way to despair for a few moments.[59]

Well I must try to get the money back again. It is a hard blow, however, a bitter blow.

Sunday, October 26

Happy at home[60] with my wife after a very hard week's work and a host of annoyances and troubles. Would to God that I

---

58   Kay Clegg was an attorney and town clerk, King Street, Oldham. Jonathan Mellor senior was one of the High Constables whom Clegg accused of abusing his position.

59   Presumably this included some previous gains.

60   'Spacious and well-furnished', commented his father (*AWJ*, 3 Sep 1845).

had just as much as would keep me snugly and that I could read, think and be quietly active. But it is denied me. Perhaps I may attain it. But alas how dead I am to anything but money and comfort and present happiness – oh 'that something after death.'

Thursday night was the Soirée. Talfourd in the chair – splendid meeting.[61]

Nov 16, Sunday

A happy day at home with my wife.

An eventful week.

Last Monday evening I attended a Meeting of the inhabitants of Failsworth and Newton in support of the Oldham, Manchester, Liverpool and Birkenhead line. A fair Meeting. Lancashire opposed. I used him up.

Tuesday night after a hard day went off to Birmingham where I staid all night and next morning went on to Tamworth to see to the arrangements for the 'sod cutting' of the Trent Valley line. I looked after everything I could and made matters pretty right. I found Brassey and John Stephenson, two of the contractors for the works, very decent fellows.[62]

In the afternoon Tootal and others came. Went on to Sir Robert Peel's, or Edmund Peel's or to the Hotels.[63]

---

61   Sergeant, later Mr Justice Talfourd. An Athenaeum Soirée at the Free Trade Hall.

Macaulay had earlier declined an invitation to take the chair (Cobden to Watkin, 21 Apr 1845, MCL M219/3).

62   Thomas Brassey and John Stephenson (not related to George and Robert Stephenson) were both civil engineers and contractors. In August the tender for the construction of the Trent Valley Railway had been let to Mackenzie, Stephenson and Brassey.

63   Sir Robert Peel lived at Drayton Manor and his brother Edmund at Bonehill House, both near Tamworth. Edmund was chairman of the Trent Valley Railway.

Dined at Edmund Peel's in the evening – for Robert Peel. Geo Hudson MP, Col. Anson, MP, H Ricardo MP, Hon Captain Carnegie, MP, E and H Tootal, Watkins, the new Mayor of Manchester, Brassey, myself and many others were there.[64] After Mrs Peel had retired we had the usual toasting. In the course of the evening Sir Robert Peel proposed the health of Mr Hudson and, speaking of his practical talents, probity, influence and elevation from a comparatively humble to an elevated office, said 'This is not the house in which such men should be forgotten and ours is not the family which should ever forget to pay that respect and honour to which such talents, so successful, entitle the possessor.'

This was said in better words and more fully, but it clearly conveyed the idea that Peel was looking back to old days and old ties, remembering the struggle that his family had had to make with the etiquette and the humbug of the aristocracy, and yearning in spirit after that honesty of mind and manners to which the class in which he now moves are strangers.

Later on Mr John Peel (Robt P's brother) replied to the toast of his health and in doing so said – in the picture gallery of Drayton Manor may be seen two portraits of two brothers, both of whom raised themselves by their own personal merits and exertions to the highest legal eminences and opposite these portraits are to be found two others – those of a father and

---

64   George Hudson, Conservative MP for Sunderland, the Railway King, had no interest in the TVR itself, but the Midland crossed the TVR at Tamworth and their High Level station was above the TVR's. Col. George Anson was then MP for Staffordshire South. Later a director and briefly chairman of the LNWR, before going out to India where he became commander-in-chief of the Army. Ricardo was chairman of the neighbouring North Staffordshire Railway and Liberal MP for Stoke on Trent. Captain Carnegie was Conservative MP for Stafford 1841–47 and a supporter of free trade. Later a director of the LNWR. Henry Tootal was Edward's brother. He took up several railway directorships but remained in textiles. Alderman W. B. Watkins had succeeded Kay as mayor.

son who likewise raised themselves to a high and honourable position which a Briton can occupy, 'that father, Gentleman, was my honoured parent and that son is my right honourable relative near me.' This was received like the other discourses most cordially.

Next day Thursday was the sod cutting. I breakfasted at Edmund Peel's in the morning. At 1/2 p 12 we had a Trent Valley board, and I was appointed formally as Secy, at 1 o'clock a lunch in the Town Hall, Tootal in the Chair, and at 3 we moved off in procession to the ground near Tamworth and the ceremony took place,

At night we all dined at Sir Robert Peel's – a high honour no doubt.

Sunday, November 23

This week, following on the heels of the last, in which sod cutting and dining with the premier were so prominent, has not been quite eventless.

There is still little to record.

When I entered upon Railway business it was with the most favourable appearances. All was life and animation. Now all is flatness and disappointment. Then everything was at a premium, now discount instead of premium stands on the share list in many cases. Then all was smiling and hopeful. Now everyone wears a long face, and looks miserable. Then men begged and prayed and acted with mean servility to get shares. Now they do all this and more to get rid of them. Every day I see some dirtiness and blackness performed – an incontinent haste to 'get out'.

I have lost near £1,000 made during the harvest time. Oh, that I had acted on my own determinations and not speculated, but the thing is done.

I have now a place of £500 a year – I will try to keep that and to make it bring me something more.

I am unwell today. I fear I am knocking up thro' over work and anxiety.

I have embarked in the 'Newspaper line' – John Bright £1,000, McKerrow £1,000, Ballantyne £500 and Edward Watkin £250 – title Manchester Examiner to come out as soon as possible. I do not know what the upshot may be but the present appearance is favourable. This is a great step. It may ruin or make me.

I believe my dear little wife is in a fair way to becoming a mother. I have a good deal of pleasure in the prospect of a little one: tho' I am anxious as to the safety of herself. Much anxiety I must have about it.

Sunday, Dec 13

Since I last made an entry I have been ill and desperately anxious. I am overworked and cannot keep up my spirits under the load of engagements and cares I have to endure.

My Newspaper has been delayed by Ballantyne's illness and I begin to fear that if it is to answer I must make it do so and that I cannot give the necessary time for the purpose.

My Oldham line is in peril. The Chairman wants to resign and a small set of sneak premium hunters want to abandon the line. A Meeting of the Shareholders is to take place on Wednesday and we shall see whether the report I have drawn up, if adopted by the directors, will set the shareholders right or not. Lots of difficulties beside. Cooke[65] and Tootal want to wash their hands of the thing – meanly and villainly.

---

65   Thomas Cooke, Gorse Field, Pendleton, merchant and cotton spinner, was a director of the London and Birmingham Railway.

Trent matters go badly. Tootal bullying and tiresome. I am hesitating and deliberating whether or not to give up my situation and take my chance with the paper. I am sick of the rogues, and their mean roguery. My mind is wearied and I feel disgusted. I get home at 9, 10, 11 o'clock at night, going at 1/2 past 8 in the morning and cannot so far get ahead of my work.

Why should I kill myself, make myself imbecile for a good salary? Yet what must I do?[66]

Dec 19

Things look a little better today.

Yesterday our Oldham meeting took place, and we completely chewed up our opponents, carried everything by acclamation, resolution of confidence etc etc. Cooke eats his own words and we nailed him regularly to the matter.[67]

This is good.

The newspaper is getting more into shape.

Pretty good.

Tootal last night wrote in my Memm book his advice to me to attend only to Trent matters in the Trent offices etc etc. This made me write him a very decided letter offering to resign. This

---

66 Despite these worries Watkin found time to attend the Literary Society on 9 Dec when the question 'Is it impossible or inexpedient or too late to lay down British railways on a system, and would not such a system for Ireland be the best possible system?' was debated. The first part of the question was affirmed by 7 to 3, and the second part negatived by 4 to 1. Cooke was present as a visitor.

67 The report of the provisional directors was received. George Arnott, seconded by Watkin, moved that the directors be empowered to proceed with every possible spirit in the progress of the work committed with every confidence to their hands.

morning we have had all matters out and I have got the weather gage of him.

Good again. I made a really good speech at the Oldham meeting and it had its effect.

I feel rather better today. Mary and I, with Jon, Thomas and Miss Mellor went last night to Mr William Brierlow's – a large party given for us.[68] Came away at 12 and slept in Manchester Street.

68   Brielow not identified.

CHAPTER 6

The diary for 1846

Jan 4

I am getting better. I have in some measure got Tootal under and I am daily growing more and more au fait in Railway matters. The paper so far goes on well. I fear however (always something) Ballantyne's want of business habits.

I have taken a house in Broughton – Woodland[s] Cottage and go on Saturday next if possible. £45 a year. This is dreadful, but am most hopeful to make up for it in some way.

Polly, as ladies wish to be, everything that I could wish – in all ways.

Sunday, Jan 11, Woodlands' Cottage Broughton

Poor Harriet M dangerously ill!

My sister ill of horrid tic dolereux [*sic*] for weeks and must go to Ilkley to try the cold water cure.

Polly not well, as ladies in her situation usually are. Poor little girl. Just removed from Failsworth and got into my comfortable little house. Built by old Tuer for himself and his old wife.[1] Rent horrid £45 per annum. We must screw dreadfully to keep 'all right'.

---

1   William Tuer, a Broughton resident, who probably invested in property at the same time as Absalom built on Frog Place, Broughton, as they went to Broughton Old Hall together to see about the gravel (*AWJ*, 6 Dec 1823). The entry for 11 January below makes clear that this was not the house which Absalom had built, also called Woodlands Cottage.

The newspaper (Manchester Examiner) appeared for the first time yesterday. The sale was tremendous and the advertisements, canvassed for weeks, good. The profit will be £33 on this publication. Hopeful the rest may be as good.

John Bright called yesterday to beg that I would leave the Railway business and go smack into the paper (I would think).

Bazley says we should publish 3 times a week.[2] All right down well – after such trouble at last.

Saturday, Jan 17

A very busy week. Very much work and very much anxiety. Oldham line almost done for by a report from Bidder on Tuesday.[3] Much anxiety in consequence.

Poor Harriet Mellor ill of a fever and not expected to recover! Poor Polly not well.

Today with Burt to Houldsworth to try to make a cover for our defeat (Oldham).[4]

In the middle of the morning, before this, the people came in a great hurry to say that the press had broken down!!! A full stop to our progress!!!! The sale being very brisk, and the pains and expense of getting up our report very considerable. (We had Selkirk (Newcastle) Hewitt, Liverpool and Actis our own man.)

2 The *Examiner* promised free trade without sham, mistake or compromise, and attention to railways, perhaps an indication of Watkin's influence. 'To a great practical subject, the railway system, the Examiner will be found devoting its careful attention, supporting all that is safe and advantageous to the public, yet exposing the delinquencies of sordid speculation' (*Manchester Times*, 9 Dec 1845).

3 George Parker Bidder, civil engineer and mathematician (known as the calculating boy). Engineer to the Oldham as well as, with Robert Stephenson and Thomas Gooch, the Trent Valley Railway.

4 Houldsworth, cotton spinner of Ardwick Green, was chairman of the Manchester and Leeds and of the rival Oldham District.

This was dreadful. Ultimately we got leave to go on the Guardian for machines, and actually worked off our remaining impressions on their premises. Very kind of them.

Paper really taking. John Bright and I kept Ballantyne company at the offices till 1/2 p 12 last night, writing and correcting.

Tuesday, Jan 20

My poor sister in law Harriet died last night! Alas poor girl. Lively good natured and kind hearted – she is gone. Another little link snapped asunder. What loosening we take before we fall. Poor Polly greatly grieved and all sorrow.

Another hitch about the Oldham line – the lawyers this time.

Friday, Feb 27

I am becoming irregular. I hardly know how many things have taken place since I last wrote.

Peel pushes on – a division after a three weeks' debate expected tonight. The protectionists fight hard, damn them.

I went up to London (Oldham and Trent) on Friday and staid till Tuesday last.

Mary in London now.

My sister returned from the cold water place worse.[5]

Examiner in circulation all that could be expected (avg 5,700). Advts mending.

We have bought the premises in Market Street and Cross St. for £2,950. We should do better as soon as we get into them.[6]

---

5   Elizabeth had been to Dr McLeod's fashionable hydropathic establishment at Ben Rhydding, near Otley, Yorkshire (Goffin, p. 251).

6   The *Examiner* remained on this site.

The Trent line sold on the 13th to the London & Birmingham £23 premium! We shall have done therefore soon.[7]

Friday night, Mar 13 1846

Stirring events since my last entry.

Last Monday morning our Trent Meeting took place – all right – unanimous – vote of thanks to the Secy – at 1 o'clock lunch – at 7 in the evening dinner at Tootal's – a pleasant party made so by the presence of Naysmith, Fairbairn and Lillie and a discussion between them about the new crossing of the Menai, Stephenson's, steel rails, a new steam coast defender etc.[8]

On Wednesday morning I went up to Stafford to help Capt Carnegie with whom I had scraped an acquaintance at his election. Carnegie is one of the Lords of the Treasury.[9] I got to Stafford about 2 and visited all sides and all sorts, so that I might scrape together a complete idea of the Electorate of Stafford. I found it almost all bribery and corruption, rotten everywhere. In the evening I went with Carnegie, Hawkes and others to visit the Burgesses in their houses of ale. We visited about 30 of these places and went thro' Hogarth's Election all over! Drink, dirt, tobacco smoke and grin familiarity. Hawkes a fine young fellow and a protectionist under the name of Dawson, alias Mr Moonshine, followed us and left 10/- or £1 to be spent on drink at each place.

7   It had been intended from the start to place the TVR 'under the care and control of one or other of the great companies with which its successful working must necessarily be identified'. The London & Birmingham Railway (soon to amalgamate with the Grand Junction and the Manchester & Birmingham Railways to form the London & North Western) paid £28 for each £20 share on which only £5 had been paid up, making a total profit of £478,000.

8   James Nasmyth built up the Bridgewater Foundry, Patricroft. Famous for his steam hammer, but his firm built locomotives. William Fairbairn set up his engineering works in Manchester with John Lillie in 1817. Had bought out Lillie in 1832.

9   Carnegie had to resign his seat on being appointed one of the Lords of the Treasury, an office of profit under the Crown as were all ministerial appointments until the early twentieth century.

Yesterday morning Robinson and Lees came over and as we discovered that Heyworth had retired and that Sleigh was come to contest the place, it was decided that I should be nominated as third candidate in order to demolish Sleigh and vindicate total repeal.[10]

In a few words we made Carnegie pledge for total and immediate repeal. I quashed Sleigh and was elected on the shew of hands by a tremendous majority! I was told over and over again that I was sure to be elected if I would go to the poll. However this was impossible both in point of honour and prudence and I sent out an address stating why I could not proceed to the Poll and calling upon electors to support Carnegie in preference to Sleigh, and then came away.[11]

I have this afternoon received a very handsome letter from Carnegie in which he hopes I may become a bona fide candidate at the next Election and expresses his deep obligations.

He wins by many hundreds.

This is a triumph for me.

I am somewhat exhausted by overwork and excitement.

Sunday, April 6

Last Monday but one I was up on a deputation with Turner, Bazley, Stewart[12] and Tootal to Sir Robert Peel, to present a petition, which I had had the getting up of, praying for the

10   Samuel Lees, like Robinson, was a leading member of the ACLL in Manchester. Laurence Heyworth was from Liverpool. He had been invited by the Stafford Liberals to contest the seat, but, a teetotaller, retired on finding the extent of the alcoholic treating expected in Stafford. Later MP for Derby.

11   Carnegie won an overwhelming victory, polling 738 votes to Sleigh's 25. He lost the seat at the 1847 general election.

12   Probably not Stewart, but Robert Stuart, cotton spinner and founder member of the Manchester and Salford Banking Co., who was closely

immediate enactment of the Free Trade measures introduced by Government. We had a very courteous interview and walked away considering we had done the state some service whether they knew it or not.

I have been busy preparing for handing over the Trent (of which I am to continue Secretary, I believe) and in sundry other matters.

Examiner going on well, about 5700 per week. Premises in Market Street now being pulled down to prepare for the building up. When we put all right here I think we shall do.

I am in quite a new life, one of action only. No time to think read or reflect – at least I do not manage to make time.

Polly moving towards the trying time. I hope it will be a little lad!

Sunday April 12

Very busy drawing all Trent matters to a close: night and day work almost.

We shall finish I expect on the 13th or 16th. I believe it is decided that I should retain the Secretaryship of the Trent Co. under the new masters. I have had a hint of the desirability of making me agent in Manchester for the amalgamated companies. I do not know yet what will finally be done. I have had no definite proposition laid before me, but shall act in the safest manner when the time comes.

At Oldham on Friday (Good Friday).

---

involved with the ACLL. The petition received 1,222 signatures in 24 hours and was signed by all the bankers in Manchester, by 55 members of the town council and by manufacturers representing £30 million of capital and employing 120,000 people, so Peel told the House of Commons (*The Times*, 25 Mar 1846).

John Bright is urgent with me to leave all and follow the Examiner. Nous verrons.

Work, continued and unvarying is the only way by which I can achieve anything, and why should any man achieve without it. The world would sooner get into a poverty stricken case, if we all could shine and be praised and popular without a stroke.

I am again trying to arrange with Houldsworth for the Oldham line, the bill for which has been read a first time. I hope I may this time manage it.

At the interview between myself Mr H. and Robert Gill a curious scene took place.[13] They forgot themselves and let out their individual policy and difference, Gill declaring that the M & L had pursued a policy which placed them even in greater difficulties than ever; H. that had Gill been Chairman, the shares would have been worth £30 less than they were! Funny, with two long headed men, great railway men too.

Woodland[s] Cottage, Sunday evening, May 31 1846

– a most glorious evening, stratus sky, warmth, clearness of atmosphere, delicious quiet.

Since my last entry (April 12) at which date I was in the midst of my business and my projects, a full or almost a full stop has been put to my proceedings by an illness more distressing and more depressing than I could have expected to experience.

Busy with preparations for handing over the Trent to the London and Birmingham Company and paying all our Shareholders on the 15th and no later, not helped in the office by any head, as we have there but hands, having in fact to crowd the work

13   Robert Gill of Adlington Hall, builder. Constructed the Palatine Hotel and Buildings in 1842 in advance of the station at Hunt's Bank (Victoria).

of a week into two days, I was extremely busy. The work, and the necessity of examining almost every figure in the numerous accounts made me sufficiently excited. I staid late on Monday night, all night on Tuesday and worked on until 1/2 past 2 on Wednesday afternoon, when as I was drawing a cheque for Mr Houldsworth's money, my head went, and I was taken in Mr Tootal's carriage, half fainting to Mr Smith the surgeon in Mosley St. Shortly after I was taken home where I remained till the following Saturday – ill, but positively working at home. On Saturday I returned to town, was taken ill again and had on Monday (April 19) to go to Fleetwood. Here Polly and I staid till Friday (April 24) (going to Blackpool and verily upset in a car on the way on Tuesday) when we came back and went to Northen.

At Northen we staid till Friday May 1 then out to Oldham and staid till Monday 4th.

On Tuesday 5th I went to London to attend a L. & B. committee meeting.[14] I was duly appointed Scy. On the 6th was desperately ill again and came home on Friday 8th.

Staid at home till Monday 11 when we went for the day to Northen. On Tuesday 12th went to Oldham and staid till Saturday 16th.

Staid at home (Mr and Mrs Mellor being here for a day or two) till last Saturday but one, when we went to Oldham and staid till yesterday.

All this interspersed with occasional visits to the office, and to the doctor, and repeated fits of illness, indisposition and depression in which I would have died if not daily, at least periodically.

14　The Trent Valley Committee of the London & Birmingham Railway.

I have learnt a lesson. May it not be forgotten. God grant that its remembrance may check future sins and follies.

I am still incapable and cannot write more tonight, except to mark down the kindness of my relatives and the noble affection of my dear wife during this long, painful and weary trial.

Sunday morning, June 14

I am decidedly better and think that the crisis of my illness is past.

On Tuesday (June 2) Mary and I went to Northen where we staid till Saturday.

On Saturday I was at the office for about an hour, Monday till noon, Tuesday till noon, Wednesday till 1/2 p 6 in the evening, Thursday till noon when my father came home to dinner with me. Friday at home and yesterday (Saturday) at the office till 1/2 past 2.

I am getting once more into business and if I am careful I think I should do.

Thursday was the day for our Committee meeting in London. I did not go and sent to Benson a letter to the Committee tendering my resignation. This I understand they did not accept.[15]

I am always fearful that the good resolutions at the time of sorrow are weakened. God grant that the lesson may not be lost. If it is how miserably shall I act!

15 Robert Benson junior had taken his father's place on the board of the Liverpool & Manchester Railway and was a director of the London & Birmingham Railway. Though a heavy investor in railways he was now a partner in the cotton spinning firm of Worthington & Benson. Following his father's death he moved to London in 1847 to set up Robert Benson & Co.'s bank.

Some notion of making Wilson's school into a house.

Polly drawing nigh. Waiting anxiously.

Examiner not doing so well.

Sunday, July 12

During the night of the 16th June Polly was ill and I fancied it was 'the event'. I sent a cab off post haste for the nurse who came at 2 in the morning, when we had discovered that we had made a false alarm. The nurse has been here with some short intervals ever since.

Polly, considering all things has been uncommonly well and goes about as lightly as possible though she carries evident signs of the new approach of our son and heir.

Since my last entries matters of interest have arisen. The district railways bill has been thrown out. The Oldham & Birkenhead, our line, preamble proved and a fair prospect of getting thro' the Lords in spite of the threatened most strenuous opposition of the Leeds Company who have got a heavy blow and great discouragement from this defeat. Jonathan has had to bear the burden of the matter – I have been at home quite unable to help in fight before Committee. Mr Mellor has stood it nobly with that firm purpose which characterises him and is pleased with the result.

Last Saturday night but one, Sunday and Monday night we were at Northen. Mary standing the journey very well.

On Wednesday afternoon July 8 I went up to London by the Express with Cooke and Tootal to attend our Trent Committee. On Thursday morning I called upon some railway people and then went up the River from Westminster Bridge to Chelsea, after which I attended our meeting, where an understanding was come to that I should remove the Trent business to London in September. I thus have a little time for relaxation after which it is expected that I should relocate in London. I shall in September have to decide on this, and really it presents so many difficulties I hardly know what to say or do. However something will no doubt turn up as an alternative and when the time comes I shall be able to decide.[16]

I should note down as it really is an event the dissolution of the League.

Peel's Corn Bill and Customs Bill received the Royal Assent on the 27 June. Peel resigned on the 30th. The meeting to dissolve the League took place in the Town Hall here on Thurs. July [2]. A full meeting. All the old faces. Cobden and Bright both there, Wilson in the chair, effected the dissolution. In the afternoon at the same place a meeting to originate a national tribute to Cobden took place – £18,000 raised in the room.

There is dissatisfaction at the oneness of the testimonial. Some people think that Bright is neglected. There has been some Whig jockeyship in the matter. Bright naturally feels hurt at the almost utter forgetfulness of his name.

Bright tells me that last September as he was journeying in Scotland he received a letter from Cobden saying that his affairs were in such a position that he should be compelled to resign his seat and give up the agitation. He exhorted Bright to burn the letter (a beautiful one, says B.). Bright immediately wrote off to Cobden to take no step till he saw him, gave up his journey, came hurrying back, with others raised £10,000 which he lent to Cobden and the stop prevented!!! There is a little of the private history. Two months more and Peel sealed the doom of protection. It is virtually no more. What an exaltation, what a falling back, if Cobden had been driven poverty stricken

16 The office was moved to London in Sept 1846, but despite his work being mainly in London Edward and Mary only moved house to London in 1848.

from the field. How Buckingham and Richmond would have gloried, how the cause would have languished for the time!

Peel's conduct thro' the whole of this business has been noble. Poor Haydon who has committed suicide says in a journal, which has come to light, putting down the fact that Peel gave him in his necessity £50 while Disraeli was hunting him – 'And this is the man who they say has no heart.' After all old Peel with all thy faults thou proved thy origin from brave old Lancashire.

Elihu Burritt, the learned American blacksmith, was here on the 2nd July to dinner, a simple, plodding, learned, strong-minded man.[17]

I am better, not well but better, occasionally very nervous and open to sudden irruptions of low spirits and alarms and all sorts of fancies. I am not yet able to do more than half a day's business, but even this is a great improvement.

I have suffered much, but oh! how grateful I should be for the lessons. God grant that it may be in remembrance as long as I live and that my whole life may shew its influence.

17 A peace advocate then visiting England. Formed the League of Universal Brotherhood, and instrumental in organising the Brussels Peace Conference, 1848

CHAPTER 7

Conclusion

In his last entry in his diary for 12 July 1846 Edward Watkin recorded that 'he was better, not well but better'. He went to Fleetwood in August with his father for rest and relaxation. Two days after their return Mary gave birth to a son, Alfred Mellor, and in 1850 a daughter, Harriette Sayer, was born.[1]

Despite his doubts Edward did retain the secretaryship of the Trent Valley Railway (TVR) under the new masters. Though not fully recovered and working under some difficulty, described in his *Recollections*, his railway career had begun in earnest. He was appointed secretary to committees by the LNWR and also acted as secretary to a number of subsidiary companies and committees responsible for building branch lines, though a further breakdown in 1851 led to a visit to the United States and Canada to recuperate. On his appointment as general manager of the Manchester, Sheffield & Lincolnshire Railway (MSLR) in 1854, he and Mary and their children moved back to the Manchester area. When Absalom was failing before his death in 1861 they moved to Rose Hill, Northenden, which continued to be Edward's main residence until his own death. The headquarters of the MSLR, of which he was chairman from 1864 to 1894, were in Manchester but he had extensive interests elsewhere, particularly with the Grand Trunk Railway of Canada of which he was president from 1862 to 1868, the South Eastern Railway (SER), chairman 1865–94, and the Metropolitan Railway, chairman 1872–94. His interest in the SER led him to put forward a scheme for the Channel Tunnel which proved abortive after much controversy. He was knighted in 1868 and became a baronet in 1880.[2]

1   Sayer was the maiden name of Absalom's mother. Harriette married Henry Worsley-Taylor in 1871. It was their granddaughter, Dorothea, who discovered the diary, which has now been placed in Chetham's Library, Manchester.

2   The baronetcy became extinct on Alfred's death in 1914.

Neither he nor Bright continued long with the *Examiner*. Bright resigned following his election as MP for Manchester in 1847, by which time Watkin had also left. The *Examiner* had been founded to a considerable extent to be the voice of the Free Trade party in Manchester as Prentice's *Times* was increasingly not fulfilling this role. This was so much the case that in late 1847 George Wilson and Henry Rawson bought the *Times* from Prentice and installed A. W. Paulton as editor, and in 1848 they bought up the *Examiner* and amalgamated it with the *Times*.

In the decade following the Stafford by-election Watkin was less politically active than at any other time in his adult life and took little part in the Manchester life which had so occupied him before his marriage and employment on the TVR. He resigned his membership of the Literary Society in 1847.[3] Later he entered national politics. He was briefly MP for Great Yarmouth in 1857, losing the seat on petition, and was defeated there in 1859. He was a Manchester City councillor 1859–62, was Liberal MP for Stockport 1864–68, and following defeats at by-elections elsewhere was MP for Hythe in Kent 1874–95, first as a Liberal, but, becoming increasingly right-wing on foreign affairs in Gladstone's second government, then as a Liberal Unionist.

Mary Watkin died in 1888 after 43 years of marriage to Edward, who died in 1901, having been married to Ann, the widow of Herbert Ingram, the founder of the *London Illustrated News*, from 1892 until her death in 1896. Both Alfred and Harriette survived their parents.

---

3   His father announced Edward's resignation at the Society's meeting on 28 Sep 1847 when it was resolved that Edward be requested to pay the subscription (14s) due for the session 1845–46 and 6s for fines incurred for absence after which he had ceased to be a member agreeably to the 13th rule.

Appendix

Public parks

Contents

Articles by Edward Watkin

Related correspondence

Unfortunately no copy survives of Watkin's pamphlet *A Plea for Public Walks* which was published on 18 May 1844. He did, however, write a number of articles for the Manchester newspapers. They were unsigned, but it is clear from Watkin's diary entries that those published on 6 April, 20 and 27 July and 3 August 1844, and 19 February and 7 May 1845 were requested by the editors and written by him. He also states that the *Guardian* borrowed lustre from his pamphlet on two occasions, so it seems likely that the article on 25 May was largely an extract from the pamphlet. The short article of 15 May antedates the pamphlet's publication and he states that the pamphlet was only written in the week before it was published but by then he had completed the draft of the requisition to the mayor and he may well have provided the text of the article or a draft of it. It is in any case included as an introduction to the series appearing in the *Guardian*.

Manchester Times, Saturday, 6 April 1844

Public walks and promenades

Manchester and Salford contain a population of about 300,000 souls, the major part of whom are engaged actively during the work-days of the week in tiresome occupations. Perhaps there is no town in the world where a greater proportion of the population is in constant employment. In Manchester the great majority of those who are able to work do work; there are no idlers among the "working classes". Whether fortunately or unfortunately, it is the fact that *we cannot afford to be idle*. The man works, the woman works, and the child works. If ever there was a busy hive of industry, it is to be found beneath the celebrated smoke of Manchester. The number of houses in Manchester and Salford is about 50,000. Perhaps not one in fifty of these has a garden or ground attached to it. The wealthy class almost exclusively possess a luxury, at once simple, innocent and refining. The operatives, as a body, have no garden, no flower beds – nothing in summer to remind themselves of the green fields and flowery roots, amidst which the boyish days of many of them were joyously spent. It may be said 'Oh, but they have the country open to their walks.' Alas the bare mention of *the country open to the poor* calls up in our minds horrible visions of 'steel traps and spring guns', of boards with 'trespassers prosecuted with the utmost vigour of the law,' inscribed in great characters upon them, of dusty highways and low pot-houses. The people have no right to walk in the country, except upon the Queen's highway and upon country roads. What a blessing the Earl of Stamford's park at Dunham has been to thousands![1] There can be no pleasure greater than that derived from seeing the throng of town's people which, in all sorts of vehicles, donkey carts, dog-carts, milk carts, and all sorts of carts, pours itself on fine summer holidays into the park – in the delirium of an intoxication caused by smooth lawns, the shade of huge trees, and the real live swans and stags. But how painful it is to reflect, amidst the mirth and glee with which the avenues re-echo, that thousands and thousands cannot afford to take a trip so far, and must content themselves with trudging along the great way-sides, happy if they can by stealth smell the perfume of a rose bush or a bed of pinks, through the narrow openings in an iron palisade! It is no use calling upon Jove, unless at the same time we set our shoulders to the wheel. We believe a very general and increasing desire for the establishment of some public grounds, open to all by right, exists in the town; and we have heard of the preliminary steps being taken to call a meeting to embody this desire in some tangible plan. This is the proper way to proceed. If a project is good it will succeed; and we are sure that a well-digested plan for endowing the people with a garden or a park of their own will meet with the cordial approval and support even of the Nonconformists who, like ourselves "like not endowments."[2]

1   Dunham Massey, three miles south-west of Altrincham, was one of the principal seats of the earls of Stamford. Mrs Gaskell recorded that for years Dunham Park had been one of the favourite resorts of the Manchester workpeople. Quoted in T. A. Coward, *Picturesque Cheshire* (2nd edn, London: Methuen, 1926), p. 13.

2   This seems a far-fetched comparison. There is no reason to suppose that because Nonconformists objected to the endowments of the established Church of England, they would not favour parks open to the people and belonging to the town.

The Guardian, Manchester, Wednesday, 15 May 1844

Public walks

It will be seen, from a paragraph among our Stockport news, that active measures are being taken for providing public walks for the use of the inhabitants of that town. A committee has been appointed by the Town Council and from communications which have passed between the gentlemen composing it and Lord VERNON'S agent, there is good reason for supposing that his lordship will give a most eligible plot of land for the purpose. Application is to be forthwith made to the government for a grant from the sum voted by parliament, in aid of local subscriptions for the establishment of public walks.[3] A few weeks ago we noticed that £1,000 had been allotted out of the same grant, for the furtherance of a similar object at Oldham.[4]

We hail these proceedings as symptoms of a decided improvement in the condition of the working classes. If means of rational recreation be afforded to the operative, the ale-house and the gin-palace will lose their attractions; and his wages, instead of being worse than wasted, will be employed in providing him with increased comforts. Our own town, however, seems to us disgracefully backward in making due provision for the great want which has so long existed. Will the wealthy inhabitants of Manchester, who have been so long celebrated for the readiness with which they have come

---

3   Lord Vernon offered Springer's Field for public use in 1844, and though accepted, it could not be transferred until 1851, when his son became of age, and, because of a lack of money on the part of the corporation, the park of 8.5 acres was not opened as Vernon Park until 1858. Henry Heginbotham, *Stockport, Ancient and Modern* (2 vols, London: Sampson Low, Marston, Searle and Rivington, 1892), ii. 413–15.

4   The Commissioner of Forests and Works had in fact offered £1,000 to Oldham subject to an equal sum being raised by the town. Although there was a public meeting in the Town Hall and John Fielden subscribed £100, and Hibbert and Platt £80, the money was not raised. The proposal was therefore held in abeyance until the Lancashire Cotton Famine when in 1863 the Government offered loans for public works. Hartley Bateson, *A Centenary History of Oldham* (Oldham: Oldham Borough Council, 1947), p. 149.

forward to support every institution intended for the benefit of their poorer neighbours, look quietly and supinely on, while comparatively small places such as Oldham and Stockport, establish public walks? – a proceeding which, we unhesitatingly affirm, will have an infinitely more powerful effect on the moral condition of their inhabitants, than any that it has ever fallen to our lot to advocate. If the opulent inhabitants of Manchester take this course (which, however, we cannot for an instant believe), they will afford considerable justification to the tory press, when the latter taunt them with hard-hearted indifference to the condition of their workpeople. Let them, then be up and doing in a cause in which neglect is a positive crime. Let Manchester apply for a portion of the government grant before it is too late.

The Guardian, Manchester, Saturday, 25 May 1844

Want of public walks in Manchester

This great city of 300,000 souls; of incomparable importance; of untold wealth – does not boast of a single yard of park ground upon which the foot of the poor may, by right, be planted – does not possess a single tree or bush, set apart to refresh the gaze, and revive the heart, of the weary prisoner of the town. Hardly a village on the continent is destitute of a piece of ground, bordered by avenues of stately trees, adorned with flower beds, and abounding with shady resting places, *the property of the community*. Here on fine summer evenings, the whole population – the rich and the poor, the master and the workman, each attended by his family – the grey-headed grandfather and the prattling child, may be seen in delightful company; a pleasant contrast to the opposite want of sociality and common sense at home! In France, the public resorts have greatly improved the dress and demeanour of the poorer classes, and have led to the extension, to the very lowest grades of society, of that admirable politeness, peculiarly French. Rouen, the Manchester of France, is in summer, green with foliage; trees line its streets, and shade its courts; and its principal thoroughfare possesses two rows of noble elms, limes and chestnuts, worthy of the royal parks.[5] With us the shade and verdure are forbidden by the smoke; but surely we can plant and water beyond the influence of small chimneys, – *A Plea for Public Walks etc.*

The Guardian, Manchester, Saturday, 20 July 1844

Public parks, promenade and playgrounds

England is by no means remarkable for the public provision of those opportunities for open-air recreation and exercise which our continental neighbours so wisely secure in the immediate vicinity of all their larger towns. Indeed, it would seem that the energy with which we pursue industrial undertakings absorbs all regard for everything but mere *production*, and prevents us from remembering that we should *enjoy*, as well as produce, the materials for enjoyment. To get a living – rather than to *live* – this is the vice of our superior industry and commercial enterprise.

Scantily as the large towns of this country are supplied with places for public recreation, Manchester stands forth in the unenviable notoriety of being the only town of importance in the kingdom entirely destitute of parks, promenades, or grounds of any kind, for the free use of its population. London has its magnificent parks,[6] Derby its arboretum, the magnificent gift

5   The comparison with Rouen was also made by Mark Philips at the meeting on 8 Aug 1844 when he referred to the town being surrounded by picturesque walks and gardens formed on the ground occupied in ancient times by the ramparts (*Manchester Times*, 10 Aug 1844).

6   The royal parks in London were formed in the seventeenth century. James I had formal gardens laid out to form St James's Park. Hyde Park, some 340 acres, was opened to the public by Charles I. Charles II made Green Park a Royal Park. By 1841 the greater part of Regent's Park, created after the Napoleonic Wars, was open to the public. A closer parallel to the proposals for Manchester was that of Victoria Park, Hackney, probably first suggested by Joseph Hume to bring amenities to the East End. The Government acquired about 290 acres paid for in part by the sale of a lease of York House (now Lancaster House), St James's. Laid out by James Pennethorne, it was opened to the public in 1845. Christopher Hibbert and Ben Weinreb (eds), *The London Encyclopaedia* (2nd edn, London: Papermac, 1987), pp. 333, 400, 644, 718–19; George F. Chadwick, *The Park and Town: Public Landscape in the 19th and 20th Centuries* (London: Architectural Press, 1966), pp. 37, 111–12, 121–4.

of the late Mr STRUTT,[7] Liverpool its parade,[8] Glasgow its Green,[9] stretching for nearly a mile along the banks of its river; yet our Manchester, needing such public places more than any other town in the world, offers its toiling inhabitants nothing better than the dirt and dust of streets and highways. This apparent absence of regard for anything but mere work, strikes every observer from a distance with the greatest force. The stranger sees, and wonders at, our almost living machinery, and admires, the perseverance and devotion of our people. Imagine his surprise when he hears, that this people, the makers and workers of this machinery, the rearers-up of an industry which has astonished the world, leave themselves and their children, from year to year, without a yard of ground upon which they can be merry and happy in common! We remember the following passage in a letter from THOMAS CARLYLE, published last year in the *Guardian*:–

> *"I have regretted much in looking at your great Manchester, and its thousand-fold industries and conquests, that I could not find in some quarter of it, a hundred acres of green ground*

7   Joseph Strutt, the first mayor of Derby after the passing of the Municipal Reform Act, had given 11 acres for an arboretum, laid out at his expense by J. C. Loudon. It was opened in 1840. For a contemporary illustrated description see Stephen Glover, *The History and Directory of the Borough of Derby* (Derby: Henry Mozley and Sons, 1843), pp. 60–5.

8   In Liverpool the Parade, about 600 yards long, had been created in 1821 along the river wall alongside Prince's Dock by the dock estate and corporation as a result of the development of docks. Prince's Park was laid out from 1842 by Joseph Paxton and James Pennethorne at the initiative of Richard Vaughan Yates, iron merchant and philanthropist who lived in nearby Aigburth Road. It was a park with private suburb, but there was some public access. Joseph Sharples, *Liverpool* (New Haven and London: Yale University Press, 2004), pp. 95, 121, 267.

9   Glasgow Green had been common land purchased parcel by parcel and laid down to grass. In 1730 extended to 59 acres. Serpentine walks and shubberies were added in 1756 and by 1810 the Green had doubled in size. In 1813 it was extended again. By 1827 road tolls and an entrance charge were introduced leaving only the Low Green free to the public until 1857. Elizabeth Williamson, Anne Riches and Malcolm Higgs, *Glasgow* (London: Penguin Books, 1990), p. 456.

with trees on it, for the summer holidays and evenings of your all-conquering industrous men; and for winter season and bad weather, quite another sort of social meeting place than the gin-shops offered! May all this, and much else be amended."

And disgraced we shall be if it not be amended!

In looking over the 'report upon the sanitary condition of towns' in the chapter upon Manchester, it will be found that, while the deaths in Broughton, which has a garden to every house, are 1 in 63, and Cheetham and Crumpsall 1 in 53, the deaths in Manchester are 1 in 28! And also, that, while the average length of life of professional men, gentry, and their families is 38 years, – that of mechanics, labourers and their families, is but 17 years![10] These great and lamentable disparities arise, no doubt, from a multitude of causes; not the least of which is the absence of all medical knowledge amongst the lower classes. Nevertheless, it is evident that the want of proper places for games, sports, and recreation of different kinds, both for children and adults, must have a fatal influence upon public health; particularly as this want inevitably leads to an even worse evil – the loss of the regular habit of taking exercise.

The confining nature of many of the occupations of the people renders out-door exercise of paramount importance to almost all. It must be borne in mind too, that every day the difficulty of amply providing for the necessities of the population increases. A constantly enlarging circle, or belt, of building is every year added to the town; and the few footpaths and lanes once accessible are now almost obliterated. The formation of public walks has been too long delayed. Now that the attention of the public is directed to the greater importance of the subject, we do hope that the wealth and spirit of Manchester will be dissatisfied with any thing but such an effort as will place us in the front rank, instead of where we now are – in the rear; and will set so bright an example of regard for public health, and the

10 First Report of the Commissioners of Inquiry into the State of Large Towns and Populous Districts, PP, 1844, XVII.

innocent enjoyments of the people, as to excite the emulation and imitation of every town and city in the realm.

No petty interests or narrow views are involved in this question. The health of 300,000 persons in good measure depends upon the settlement of it. The manners of the humble and the poor, and the endurance and improvement of those friendly feelings which should exist between the higher and lower classes, are deeply affected by it. We hope that the establishment of public places, the property of, open to, and frequented by, the whole population – by people of every grade – may be the beginning of a general system of amendment, in which class feelings and prejudices (still to too great an extent remaining), and that spirit of exclusiveness which keeps men of one class from men of another in all things but mere labouring, will be entirely swept away.

Manchester Times, Saturday, 20 July 1844

Public walk and parks

We once again address our readers upon the importance of freeing the town of Manchester from the disgrace entailed upon it by the want of those opportunities for exercise and recreation in the open air so vitally necessary to the health and happiness of our population. Upon no class would the benefit of the measures we advocate fall so opportunely and so blessedly as upon the operatives of our busy town; we propose therefore to say a few words upon the question as affecting the interests of the masses.

In Manchester there are about 40,000 houses, most of which are occupied by people of the humbler classes. By far the greater number of these houses are small in size and inconvenient in construction; they are *cluttered* together with more regard for the saving of ground rent than for the comfort and health of their inhabitants. In many districts, particularly in those inhabited by factory operatives and loom weavers, the crowding of houses into narrow, dark, ill-drained and ill-ventilated alleys and lanes; and the cramming of persons into miserable dwellings is frightful to contemplate; 20,000 men, women, and children, too, live in cellars, deep below the ground. We do not hesitate to say that the paupers in our workhouses, and the prisoners in our best conducted gaols live in a more healthful atmosphere, and have a greater space assigned to them to move about in and sleep in than the many, many thousands of our hardest working people. The habitual ill-health, the consumption, rheumatisms, fevers caused by the utter want of attention to the sanitary state of our towns, are dreadful to think upon. We should start with horror could we summon up before us the prematurely old-aged, and the emaciated, stooping forms, sinking under the presence of diseases, fed and propagated in the pestilential atmosphere of that which should be a *home*, but is a *grave*.

Perhaps out of the 40,000 houses in Manchester, 600 have gardens attached to them, and these are the dwellings of the rich, not of the poor. The poor man has no little patch of green ground adorned with flowers, or shaded by trees, wherein he might, in the long summer evenings, and on Sundays, gather his family about him, and put aside the remembrance of his daily toil. Under present circumstances such pleasure he cannot have. Roused betimes, the working man hurries to his task, and that accomplished, he returns to the comfortless cabin from which the morning saw him depart; squalor and darkness overshadow his dwelling; the sweet sound HOME to *him* brings few pleasant recollections and many bitter ones; perchance, in a dark corner the wife of his bosom or the child of his love lies in helpless suffering; his home is more noisome, more comfortless than the factory or shop in which he works. Alas! the lot of 'these our brethren' is hard indeed; but it is of little use bemoaning it, unless we are prepared to do something to soften and improve it. We propose, then that ample opportunities be afforded to escape to fresh air and pleasant scenes. We demand for the working classes, on whose untiring labour we all so greatly depend some little participation in those advantages which wealth enjoys, and which hard work entitles every man to possess. We point to the shortened lives of the working classes, and we trace their premature deaths, in great measure, to their almost universal imprisonment in mills throughout the day, and foul unventilated courts and alleys throughout the night. The Improvement Committee[11] may find some remedy for the latter evil, but as regards access to the green fields and the reviving face of nature, we say that the rich are guilty unless they make all provision in their power for the physical enjoyment, the bodily health, and the mental advancement of the poor.

We every now and then hear it lamented that there should be 'so much atheism and infidelity amongst *the lower orders*'. We are not prepared to admit that the poor are less religious than the rich; but we would ask those who complain of this asserted want of belief in sacred truths, is it not wonderful that the dwellers in the darkness of cellars *believe as much as they do*? The suffering poor see the wants of man hemming them in on all sides; they fancy that warehouses and mills, nay even the stones in the street, are more esteemed than they are. The providence they recognise as immediately affecting their happiness is the self-interest of man disregarding or oppressing them. All is of the 'earth, earthy'; man they feel as a master, and, alas, some of them cease to seek for or behold GOD as a FATHER. They see huge mills, filled with almost living machinery, the work of MAN; they see houses, and mansions, and carriages, constructed by the skill of MAN; they find all these things regulated, improved, constantly cared for, and they feel themselves, God's creatures, as they are told, they are, destitute of sympathy from the great, of happiness, and often of hope. Where is the wonder, then, if misery scars over that inscription of heaven's own writing upon the human heart, which tells us that there is a GOD of justice and of love for all men? No! Before we contemn the feelings of the poor we must give them a chance for improvement. Let us cut the bonds which bind them in darkness; let us not only give their labour full scope, but send them forth into fields and

11 The Improvement Committee of Manchester Corporation was set up in 1843 when the Police Commissioners finally relinquished their powers. Arthur Redford and Ina Stafford Russell, *The History of Local Government in Manchester* (3 vols, London: Longmans, 1939–40), II: *Borough and City*, p. 76.

flower gardens, and under the shades of trees; let them at times escape from the world of man to the world of man's Maker, and we may be assured that the voices which speak of GOD, in the sighing of the breeze, in the rustling of the leaves, in the notes of the wild bird, and in the cheerful purling of the stream, will sound gladly and hopefully to the sighs of many, made wiser and better by teachings till then removed far from them.

The public meeting on the 8th of next month will test the sympathy of the wealthy with the sufferings of the poor.[12] We have always maintained that the sympathy was deep and active, and we trust it will, on the occasion referred to appear in all its freshness and virility. We believe that at no former period was it felt, by the affluent merchants and manufacturers of our town, so strong and universal a desire to improve the condition of the working classes, as at present. It is now generally understood that by improving the temporal and moral resources of our humbler fellow-creatures, we are adding to our own comforts and advancing our own happiness. Let us picture to ourselves the moral pestilence that pervades a community from a low-minded, uneducated, coarse and sensual population; and on the other hand the blessings and charms, and enchantments that spread their brightness over the land, where virtue, industry, order, contentment and happiness reign. In crowded cities occupations of vice abound, but the evil is sadly aggravated where the humble classes are deprived of all outdoor enjoyment, unless they pace along the dusty and dirty public road, or repair to the village ale-house garden, and there mix with their love of the country deep potations of beer. To raise the standard of virtue and self-denial among working-people we must rescue them from the riot of the drunkard and provide for and attach them to quiet sylvan scenes sacred to pure and innocent enjoyments. Thus we shall have some powerful means of diffusing happiness among our toiling thousands and enjoy the gradual satisfaction that we have contributed in a slight degree, to elevate and improve the social and moral condition of our fellow men.

12   The meeting is described in the Diary entry for 9 Aug 1844.

In drawing attention to the forthcoming public meeting on this subject we trust that all classes of our townsmen, throwing aside for so praiseworthy an object, all party or peculiar opinions, will assemble together on that occasion, and use their best exertions to accomplish the excellent objective which all must have in view. By energy and judgment very much may be effected, we believe that the inhabitants generally are vitally alive to the importance of the design, and have no doubt that when the opportunity offers, they will certainly aid it by their purse and personal efforts.

The Guardian, Manchester, Saturday, 27 July 1844

Public parks, promenades and playgrounds

We have before said, that the utmost possible facilities for exercise and recreation in the open air, are imperatively demanded by a regard for the health and vigour of our industrious population. Without health there can be little happiness or usefulness, without the *spring* supplied by pleasant relaxation, there can be no steady and continued effort. Intense occupation wears away the forces both of the body and the mind; and exercise and healthful recreation, in new scenes, and amid objects suggestive of new ideas and more pleasant thoughts, can alone effectually restore the waning strength of the weary worker, and arm him with the renewed energy for further struggles with difficulties and obstacles, so plentifully strewn in the paths of all men. Public grounds of easy access from the town, would, we are therefore convinced, have the happiest effect on the health and pleasures of all classes.

In a town, inhabited as ours is, by people from all parts of the kingdom, – people the most opposite in taste, education, and condition, – the neighbour like unitedness of feeling and purpose, existing in communities where the individuals are reared up from infancy together, can have but partial place. In every class unless a corrective can be found, coteries, cliques, and parties must grow up, under laws, tacitly obeyed of the most exclusive character. By frequent meetings together for some common object, little asperities are smoothed away; misunderstandings and misappreciations are set right; and men, concreted by the first chances of their position into little knots, unite harmoniously together in one great band, all the better, perhaps for having undergone the process. Without these necessary preliminaries to union, *cliqueism*, with all its evils must be perpetuated, – sections must remain adverse to, or ignorant of each other, – and a dangerous and unnatural absorption of individuals into social parties and factions, and isolation of parties and factions within themselves, must go on.

Though we have still sadly too much social exclusiveness in Manchester, we would believe that it is rapidly on the wane. One of the most gratifying features of the times is the greater disposition evinced by the rich to bring themselves into friendly contact with the poor. Broad-cloth is ceasing to despise fustian; and by judicious management, fustian will learn to esteem broad-cloth all the more in consequence.[13]

We would ask our townsmen, if the frequent meeting together of different classes, and of the sections and individuals belonging to them, on terms of equality, – in public resorts, where families may meet families without shame, or the affected mannerism of exclusive circles; where the master may meet the men, and the man the master; where all assemble on common and neutral ground of an innocent love for the free, fresh air and the beauties of nature, – is not certain to lead to more friendly feelings and a more united spirit, among the various portions of the community.

Such meetings would greatly benefit the male, but they would be of more service still to the female population. Men

13 The cloths refer to the dress of the middle and working classes. Chartists referred to themselves as 'the fustian jackets'. The term had originated in Manchester and Feargus O'Connor dressed in a suit of fustian when he spoke in Stevenson Square following his release from York gaol. He referred to it as the 'emblem of your order'. Cobden took care that the ACLL could present its audiences with several speakers in fustian coats. Paul A. Pickering, *Chartism and the Chartists in Manchester and Salford* (Basingstoke: Macmillan, 1995), pp. 168, 170 (Cobden to Sturge, 4 Mar 1839, BL Add. MS 50,131, f. 506).

meet much more frequently in the world than women. Classes of men cannot be kept wholly apart; but classes of women are castes, in the sternest sense of the word. What does the wife of the operative cotton-spinner see or know of the wife of the millowner? And what does the latter know of the habits, and thoughts, and manners of the former? Women readily discover excellencies of behaviour and deportment, and are prone to imitate what they admire; they have more sympathy with their sex, than men have with theirs; they have more heart, and a more subtle knowledge of the finer and more minute traits of character; and they are sure to find benefit, as well as pleasure, from the observations which assemblages of different ranks of people will enable them to make.

With a well-founded prospect of adding to the health and comfort of the lower classes, and at the same time, of drawing them away from the debasing temptations now surrounding them; with the hope of drawing closer the bonds of respect and esteem which should bind all classes together; with the certainty of breaking down the wall which shuts out the light from thousands, and of letting in a new and genial influence, to do its work of reformation amongst the people, – there is ample incitement to perseverance in struggling for the consummation we desire. The good to be effected by it cannot be estimated in money; and mere pecuniary considerations therefore sink into insignificance. But, surely, a few thousand pounds will not be judged by the now-flourishing merchant and manufacturers of Manchester, when not merely great interests are at stake, but when the credit of the town has to be redeemed from the just imputation of previous apathy and culpable inattention

Manchester Times, Saturday, 27 July 1844

Public parks, gardens and playgrounds

The fine summer skies with which we have, during the past week, been favoured and the beautiful aspect of the country, as seen in the lucid atmosphere accompanying them, will very likely have had the same effect upon our readers as upon ourselves, and have made them think frequently of the grievous injustice of excluding any of God's creatures from influences as exhilarating and so improving; and of the manifold and weighty reasons drawn not only from justice but from charity and mercy, for immediately throwing open the fair museum and magazine of nature to the toil worn population of this great coal-furnace of industry. Indeed the barbarism which has induced us to remain passive as a town under deficiencies of so vital a character as those of which we have so frequently complained can only be explained away by the fact that, the struggle with monopoly and oppression of various sorts, has absorbed the entire attention of the active minds, and left them for many years neither time nor energy to spare from the great conflict for existence. Now that a temporary lull in the intensity of political excitement has taken place – a sort of phase to gird up the loins for that approaching and last rally in which aristocratic oppression will be made to bite the dust – we may fill up the breathing time with some valuable social reform. The one we advocate is worthy of the aid of all true lovers of the species.

The parks have been named the 'lungs of London'; they have saved thousands of lives, and sweetened the lot and poetised the existence of all the dwellers on Cockaigne.[14] Dusky, smoky, toiling Manchester has no lungs. The rich and influential are asked to extend to the hard-handed and honest operative the boon of breathing fresh air, uncharged with dust and smoke, a few times a week. Surely this will never be denied. We take the matter, if not a *fait accompli*, at least as one of those things effected in the judgment and resolved upon by the will of the public, and only requiring the necessary working out on the part of the industrious few who may superintend the practical arrangements.

We particularly hope that in the public provision for open air exercise and recreation which will be made, everything will be done to secure the efficiency of the ground appropriated to

14   Cockaigne is defined in Brewer's *Dictionary of Phrase and Fable* as an imaginary land of idleness and luxury, famous in medieval story. It may mean the land of cakes. London was so called with punning reference to Cockney (London: Cassell, 1981 edn, p. 253).

sports and manly games. The young require something more exciting – we almost said boisterous – than mere walking about. Quoits, cricket, golf, skittles, and a variety of other games adapted to every degree of strength and proficiency with a well-ordered gymnasium, ought especially to be provided, since vigorous, buoyant health requires it. On the Green at Glasgow, on the Bruntisfield Links in Edinburgh,[15] the 'weaver lads' with a good sprinkling of well-dressed youths, may be seen every fine summer evening deep in the enjoyment of sports so useful because so destructive of that morbid, brooding misanthropic spirit, engendered by the monotony of every-day occupation. Men who play at cricket three or four evenings a week will not commit suicide. The fine evenings make them taste the luxury of *health*, and men do not feel ever anxious to quit the world when any door of relief and means of exhilaration is open to them. Sir Walter Scott said – 'Take exercise and fortify your constitution, for there is no courage without health, and without courage there can be no truth – no virtue'. We rejoice in the awakening of public feeling upon the sanitary condition, mental and moral, of the great mass of our fellow citizens, and that there is prospect, in addition to what may be done by the voluntary efforts and contributions of the wealthy, of an Improvements Fund at the disposal of the Town Council being applied to the opening of courts and alleys, so as to allow that thorough ventilation which is requisite to the preservation of health.

The Guardian, Manchester, Saturday, 3 August 1844

Public parks, etc. – Public baths

Having in previous articles spoken of some of the reasons for the provision of places for public recreation, it may be as well to add

15   Open land used for golf from the early eighteenth century. In the depression after the Napoleonic Wars the unemployed cleared it of whins and quarries, and subsequently the House of Commons, against the wishes of Edinburgh Corporation, inserted a clause in an Edinburgh Improvement Bill which forbade building on Bruntisland Links and the Meadows. A. J. Youngson, *The Making of Classical Edinburgh, 1750–1840* (Edinburgh: Edinburgh University Press, 1966), pp. 181, 255–6.

a few words upon the more practical parts of the subject. We take it for granted that public parks, playgrounds, gardens, and promenades, will be established; and that no niggard economy, nor paltry meanness of design, will disfigure a public effort, of which the community and especially the humbler portions of it, are naturally entertaining so hopeful an opinion. We say again 'Let the effort be worthy of Manchester.'

Manchester covers so large a surface, that the *distance* from opposite extremities of it, would, we believe, present a serious obstacle to the efficiency of any *single* public resort, however near to the confines of the town it might be placed. The people of Hulme, for example, would receive little advantage from a park within a tree-growing distance from Ancoats. Readiness of access is so important, that we are convinced of the necessity of having one public place on *each* of the four sides of the borough. With *four* public resorts, a delightful variety might be introduced; we might have a public promenade and park, an arboretum, a garden, and a park and playground; and thus avoid any disagreeable sameness of arrangement.

Extent is a matter of great importance. By all means, let us not be miserly of the ground: let us have room enough. The parks and public grounds of London and Edinburgh cover some thousands of acres; the Green at Glasgow, 105 acres; the Phoenix Park, Dublin, 1,500;[16] the arboretum at Derby, 11 acres; the Jardin des Plantes, at Paris, 70 acres.[17] In all these cases, as much has been done as possible; in many of them, – that of Glasgow, for instance, – a small plot has been gradually augmented by systematic extension. Manchester should not begin with less than 80 to 100 acres. With such an area, properly divided and allotted, we should commence satisfactorily, leaving it to future

16   Phoenix Park was created from 1662 as a royal deer park by the first duke of Ormond from the former lands of St John's Priory of Kilmainham. Planted by the fifth earl of Chesterfield in 1747 when Viceroy of Ireland, and the greater part thrown open to the public. Decimus Burton made improvements in the 1830s. Christine Conway, *Dublin* (New Haven and London: Yale University Press, 2005), pp. 287–91.

17   The Jardin des Plantes was opened to the public in 1651.

public spirit to enlarge and multiply with the increase of the wants of our population.

We have no idea, however, that the whole of the public ground required would have to be purchased. We think, and shall continue to do so until experience shall determine to the contrary, that the spirited landowners, by whose estates we are surrounded – the WILTONS, and the EGERTONS, and CLOWES'S, and DUCIES and STAMFORDS[18] – will liberally aid us with donations of land; particularly as it must be evident, that, by judicious arrangement, the value of many a somewhat obscure plot may be increased by such acts of liberality.

Government aid, may, to a limited extent, be obtained. We do hope, however, that the independent merchants and manufacturers of Manchester will depend mainly upon their own exertions, and rather regard Government assistance as a means of *enlarging* their design, than as an absolute necessity to its working. Government, like a higher power in the old adage, 'helps those who help themselves.' Let the people of this vast emporium of industry aim high enough. We have heard £50,000 named as the sum which ought to be raised by private subscription. This, we think, is too much; while £20,000 is too little. Suppose then we try to obtain £30,000. Let not the largeness of this sum startle any one. The whole of the money cannot be wanted all at once. Three or four years would be required to form the public places: therefore a contribution of £400 will be but about £100 a year for four years. The sum we name is but 6d per head per annum. Surely, we shall not refuse to pay this paltry sum to redeem a portion of the still redeemable health and happiness of poor industrious people!

All the public grounds in Germany have 'cafés' attached to them; and on the 'Platforms' of Switzerland, houses are open for the sale of various refreshing beverages.[19] We may, with great propriety, imitate much of this; and, at the same time, avoid the danger consequent upon the sale of intoxicating liquors. Commodious apartments for the sale of refreshments

18   See p. 51 and note 135 to Chapter 1.
19   Mark Philips had also praised the open space at Frankfurt-am-Main.

of different kinds – strictly excluding temptation to inebriety – would be a great and useful addition to the plan, and would further aid in leading the humbler classes to forsake the noise and debasing influences of the tavern and beer-shop.

Before closing this article, we would express a hope that attention may be given to the propriety of establishing PUBLIC BATHS, open to all on a very small payment, if not in connection, at least simultaneously, with public parks and grounds. Next to additional means of exercise, more aids to cleanliness are wanted. The working man may take distracting exercise in our crowded thoroughfares; but he cannot obtain even a scanty supply of water without great annoyance. Baths may be erected at small expense; our canals would supply plenty of water; and a charge of one penny per head has been in other places more than sufficient to defray all charges.[20]

We have all along been presuming, that the public would come forward with the needful funds for these many and great changes for the better. That the spirit which has led Manchester to the van, in almost all the great national efforts for national good, will nobly appear now that the well-being of her own sons and daughters requires its ministering aid. The public meeting now at hand will test this, and, we think, show that we rightly estimate the philanthropy of our townsmen – that Manchester is not tainted with that doubtful universality of benevolence which would weep over the woes of Esquimaux at the poles, and at the same time leave poverty and misery unheeded to perish within its own streets.

Manchester Times, Saturday, 3 August 1844

Public walks, parks, gardens and playgrounds

The more we think upon this question, so frequently brought before the notice of our readers, the more anxious we feel that at

---

20   Public baths had been established near the Infirmary in 1781, but there was a general lack of such facilities in Manchester and elsewhere. In Manchester in Mar 1849 a further ball was held in the Exchange in aid of public baths and washhouses; in 1856 baths were opened in Miller Street, Manchester.

the public meeting next Thursday, Manchester should vindicate its character for that true benevolence, which, while it forgets not the the claims of distant distress, amply solaces the wants and woes of the suffering at home.

Exercise and recreation in the open air have been proved, by the most indisputable evidence, to be of the absolute necessity to the health and lives of the humble classes. By repeated arguments we have shown that not merely the physical, but the mental and moral health of the community greatly suffer by compulsory imprisonment, amid bricks and mortar, and that the adequate provision of places of public resort, freely open to every man, woman and child in the town, would confer benefits of a permanently improving tendency upon the whole mass of our population.

One argument in favour of the measures we advocate has not yet been mentioned; we allude to the want of public resorts for the sake of invalids, and of persons recovering from lingering ill-health. Those who have been laid upon the bed of sickness in the centre of a busy and noisy town, for weeks and weeks, can alone appreciate the misery of being obliged, for lack of some pleasant vicinage, to sit out the time of slow recovery, surrounded by darkness and din, and drab walls. The poor sufferer, prostrated by the disease which has just left him – feeble, languid and sensitive – literally yearns for a seat under some shady old tree, where he might remain in peace, undisturbed by the rude noises which now assail his distracted ears, and able, without exertion, to enjoy the sights and sounds presented by the fair face of nature, with the rapture of the prisoner released. While confinement to the house in town is sure to delay recovery, and disturb and distress the convalescent, the opportunity of betaking himself, in the warmth of the mid-day sun, to some near retreat, and of there quietly recruiting his strength and spirits, most rapidly and pleasantly restores him to health.

The poor operative, who has left his distant home beyond the Tweed, or across the Channel,[21] to seek employment with us,

---

21   Probably the Irish Sea, rather than the English Channel, is meant.

and who, in the midst of his sojourn falls sick amongst strangers who care little for him, and whose careless tendance aggravates the miseries and discomforts of their crowded lodging-house – would be blessed indeed could he at the distance of half-a-mile or a mile from his weary abode, find a park filled with fine trees, and finished with seats and grassy resting-places, where his weariness might be removed in quiet repose, and his heart be strengthened with his strengthening body, as he called to mind the dales, and groves, and honest friends, about his former home.

We do not hesitate to assert that two-thirds of the population of Manchester are debarred, by the culpable negligence we wish to have atoned for, from the peculiar advantage, so needful in a crowded town, of which we have spoken; and we are sure that the loss of life and the loss of valuable labour – besides a good deal of individual suffering – must be the result.

At the meeting on Thursday a great deal has to be done. In the first place, the great principle must be, as we hope it will be, enthusiastically confirmed – that the humblest classes have a moral right to such public provision as may be required by their health and well-being. Thus the extent of the public feeling of duty must be tested. 'Friend' said a worthy Quaker to a sighing exclaimer about some sad catastrophe, 'I am sorry – very sorry – *I am sorry TEN POUNDS – pray how much art thou sorry?*' Money, not mere speeches will be wanted. Let us make a demand for the people of Manchester – we demand then the sum of £50,000. Surely the 2,800 spinners, manufacturers, and merchants who frequent the Exchange, and who profit by the strength and health of the people, will not grudge a voluntary subscription as life insurance of that by which they live.

In conclusion, we exhort our friends to crowd to the meeting, and thus testify their regard for the poor and the miserable, – their desire to mingle a few sweet elements in the bitter cup of want, – their wish to raise up the lowly and the suffering, – their high appreciation of the truth of that heaven-born declaration – 'One is your Master, even Christ, and all ye are brethren.'

The Guardian, Manchester, 19 February 1845[22]

Public walks, parks and playgrounds – Proceedings and progress of the committee – Public baths and washhouses

The subscriptions to the fund for establishing public places for exercise and recreation, for our industrous population, now amount to the sum which, at the commencement of the movement, we considered it possible to obtain, viz. £30,000: one stage in the progress of this spirited effort is reached, and we can look back from it upon what has been done with advantage to the success of the future.

This attempt to supply some of the more urgent physical wants of the operative classes by a wise and liberal provision of aids to the improvement of health, and of opportunities of renewing the wasted forces of the body and of the mind by that pleasant relaxation – the best restorer of the exhausted frame – commenced in an awakened and educated desire to perform efficiently those sacred duties which the rich and prosperous owe to the poor and the unfortunate. It took hold on the public mind, because, appealing to this high sentiment of duty, it appeared to be enlarged in design, and practical in its operation; and the support given to it has exceeded the full measure of spirit and liberality for which Manchester is distinguished. In six months, the contributions of nearly 3,000 persons have been handed in; and that contribution of *opinion*, of vital necessity to the success of such a great undertaking, has been equally decided. Three large public meetings have been held, one of them (in the Free-trade Hall) attended by 6,000 persons; and unanimous votes of approval and support have been recorded. The contributions to the fund are of every possible amount from sixpence to £1,000; and the contributors comprise some of the poorest members of our working population, and some of the richest of our local gentry. All professions, all creeds, all

22 The article which appeared in the *Manchester Times* on 19 Feb 1845 was virtually identical with this article in the *Manchester Guardian* of the same day. It contained no significant differences and so is not reproduced here.

classes, and we may say, all countries (for the foreign residents have been honourably distinguished as subscribers), have lent themselves to the assistance of this movement. When we review the whole course of proceedings, we find ample cause for satisfaction at the progress already made, and new evidence of the enterprise and right feeling of this great hive of industry. There is hardly a parallel in the success of the effort.

The committee have had a great work to conduct. They have spared no pains in the discharge of their onerous duties; and now that the magnitude of the fund justifies an application to parliament for a handsome grant, we feel assured they will be supported by the voice of the whole community. We may mention, that nearly the whole of the amount subscribed has been obtained by the gratuitous exertions of the committee and their auxiliaries.

So soon as the support of parliament and the government has been obtained, the committee will select, from the offers of land made to them, sites for the public places. We have no doubt, that the wisdom and energy which have marked their previous proceedings will attend them in this, the most important and most delicate part of their duties.

The subscriptions have been obtained for "public parks, walks and playgrounds". Baths and washhouses were not at first included in the scheme. We believe that an appropriation of some portion of the fund to the establishment of baths, &c. would meet with the cordial approval of the subscribers; but, as a great deal has to be effected with the money, it would be better, we think, to originate some special movement for the creation of a special fund. A fancy dress ball, on a grand scale, has been suggested as the means of raising a sum sufficient for the purpose. Without offering any decided opinion on this suggestion, we may observe, that such a ball under proper patronage, would be well supported; and certainly it would be better that the profits should be thus devoted, than that they should be the reward of mere private enterprise.

The community have yet to do much. More money will be wanted. Large as is the amount subscribed, it shrinks into littleness compared with the wealth and population of Manchester. A population of unparalleled industry has to be served: and surely their best interests will meet with far other than a niggard assistance.

The Guardian, Manchester, 7 May 1845

The government grant in aid of public parks and walks – The case of Manchester

When Sir Robert Peel's offer of £3,000 was announced to the public, we expressed our conviction that it was altogether disproportionate to the wants of the community, and to the great and peculiar claims of Manchester upon the common purse; but we then took occasion to declare our sincere belief that the premier, however mistaken in his estimate of the just demands of this town, was actuated by the best and kindest motives; and we would again remind our fellow-townsmen, that his munificent donation of *one thousand pounds*, and the memorable declaration which accompanied it, are recorded proofs that one of the best and warmest supporters of the great plan for placing the means of rational and healthful exercise and recreation at the command of our hardworking population, is SIR ROBERT PEEL.

Time has now been given for the re-examination of the case; and, whether the discussion lead to a more liberal offer or not, it will be well to re-state it, with the additions to its force elicited in an investigation in some measure forced upon us by the disappointment of our expectations.

We must observe, at the outset, that we admire the principles of self-assistance in all public, as well as in all private, undertakings; and we are as much alive to the danger of making spiritless towns depend upon *government* for aid, instead of upon *their own resources*, as the most watchful chancellor of a bare exchequer could be. But the practice of stimulating the public spirit of the country by holding out the hope that, when individual effort has done its utmost, the *empire* will come to its assistance has long been recognised, and is perpetually adopted.

In the case between Manchester and the government, then there needs no discussion of the *principle* of making grants – the practice is that of the government, not that of Manchester. Especially was this recognised in the vote of parliament in 1841: the £10,000 then voted as a beginning, 'being to enable her majesty to issue *money in aid of local subscriptions*, towards the expenses of public walks &c. in the neighbourhood of large towns." Indeed the movement for popular recreation and exercise commenced within the walls of the house of commons – and, after groping its way for some time most sluggishly, it was at length taken in hand with vigour out of doors.[23]

It seems to us that the government which failed to provide, during the course of its existence, with systematic regularity, those aids to popular progress which are at once the fruitful sources of national greatness, and the best securities for an enlightened love of liberty and public order – would leave unexecuted one of the most important of its positive functions. To adorn the empire and illustrate its social history by some enduring monument of national philanthropy, is the work of the statesman whose ambition leads him to look beyond the mere routine and formality of administration. In any great work of this kind it is of the first moment to excite the enthusiasm of the public: when once this is roused, it should be fostered and emulated. A "very few drops of cold water will condense much steam." The statesman, who by an-ill-timed and ill-judged economy discourages the exertions of the people themselves, is guilty of the waste of a power and of a spirit, the course of which might have been most glorious.

23 The Government was slow to accede to requests for grants from the fund. 'A Return of the Manner in which £10,000 voted for Public Walks in 1840 was expended', dated 11 Apr 1843, showed that only £500 had been granted – £300 to Dundee and £200 to Arbroath. (No such vote has been traced for 1840, and 1841 was probably intended.) Lincoln's memorandum to Peel of 6 Apr 1844 states that since the return of 1843 the only grants approved were £750 to Sunderland which had not yet been paid and the conditional one to Oldham referred to above. PP, 1843 (187), XXX, 727; BL Add. MS 40,563, f. 306.

These most useful, because most needed, efforts on behalf of which we speak, are of no mere local moment. We again insist upon the fact, that the physical and moral health of our town populations is involved in that complete provision of opportunities for innocent relaxation which is their aim and end; we assert that the want of public resorts of this kind is a crying and enormous evil, for the continuance of which the whole community, both directly and indirectly injured, is responsible. What are our manufacturing towns but refuges and homes for the surplus population of the whole kingdom? Manchester has within its boundaries a resident population brought from every town and county in the united empire, and a continual stream of bread-seekers flows to it, as a head-quarters of employment, and passes onwards to all the neighbouring residences of mechanical industry. Anything then, which mitigates the evils incidental to town-life – any object which promotes the health and happiness of the people, by birth or adoption, of Manchester, is a matter of interest – taking the term in its narrowest sense – to the realm at large. Better than monuments to the Duke of York, raised at a public cost of TWENTY THOUSAND POUNDS; better even than Trafalgar Squares, good though they may be – are those works of local or national benevolence, which throw open the fair expanse of nature to a toil-worn and worthy population.[24]

Manchester contributes a vast sum to the national revenue. There are no complete returns published; but a very moderate reckoning of the *concentration* of taxation here apparent will show that if the general taxation amounts to £2 per head, Manchester will pay at least £4 per head upon its population. This alone is a strong ground of claim for a drawback, now and then, in aid of its public works. Yet, in looking over the printed list of 'services' from 1825, to January 1844, we find that, while London, Dublin, Edinburgh, Bristol, Belfast, Glasgow,

---

24 A memorial to Frederick, second son of George III, was erected in the 1830s. Its cost of £25,000 was largely met by stopping one day's pay of every soldier in the army of which the duke had been commander-in-chief. Trafalgar Square was laid out by Barry in 1840 and Nelson's column erected in 1839–42.

Dundee, Kingston, even Lyme Regis, are recorded as recipients from the national purse, the name of Manchester is not, in one single instance, to be found![25]

While £109,886 has been paid since 1825, for improving and keeping up the Caledonian Canal, Manchester has, without aid, made and worked its own canals. While the Liffey and the Shannon have been improved at the national expense, and roads in various parts of Ireland made, the Irwell and the Mersey have been deepened and widened by local enterprise; and for our roads, we have been indebted to ourselves alone. £36,000 were voted from 1825 to 1832, for building the College of Edinburgh; £5,000 for building the College of Surgeons, Edinburgh; £14,568 have been paid since 1840 to London University; £6,936 have been given for building "a hall for the general assembly of Scotland, in Edinburgh". Above £20,000 have been voted for Trafalgar Square, London. Glasgow has had £14,800 for a new customs house, and £8,000 for a new post office, since 1838. £5,000 have been given to complete the general prison at Perth; and these are but a few of the instances.[26] In addition to this, London, Dublin, Edinburgh and other places, have been provided with public grounds, or had them improved, out of the proceeds of crown lands and properties: Dublin, for instance, with its Phoenix Park of 1,500 acres, and London with its circle of parks; and some of these places have had their streets widened, and their squares enlarged out of this really national revenue. Now, Manchester contributes to, or loses by, all this. It has done its own work in all things, and has at the same time paid its quota to every

25   The document is probably 'The return of Sums of Money, by way of loans or grants on public works in England and Scotland', PP, 1843 (124), XXXVIII, 455.

26   Several of the items in the list are not valid comparisons with the case of the Manchester parks. The Caledonian Canal, unlike the canals in Manchester, was thought to have a strategic value for the movement of troops. Customs houses and post offices were the responsibility of central government. As Lord Lincoln made clear to Peel, the Government had spent very little on parks; the £3,000 agreed for Manchester was by far the largest grant from the fund.

public work in the kingdom. Surely, then, it should now claim a larger discount returnable from its contributions than £30,000.

We do not complain of grants to other places. Let a wholesome stimulus be equally distributed in grants throughout the realm; but let not our industry, our wealth, and our liberality, be made the reason for a denial of our just demands. Our case may be summed up in a few words: We greatly need the execution of certain public works; and, having done our utmost, we require assistance to complete our effort: other towns have received frequent and large grants (to which we have had to contribute), while we have not received a shilling; now therefore we claim the extension of a recognised practise to us – failing which we shall be fully entitled to protest against its one-sided continuance.

Related correspondence

1 Malcolm Ross and Edward Watkin to Sir Robert Peel, 30 August 1844

Public walks, Parks gardens and Playgrounds[27]
Town Hall Manchester, 30 August 1844

Sir

We take the liberty of enclosing you a Report of a Public Meeting held here on the 8th of August and the address of the Committee appointed to carry out the general desire for the immediate establishment of Parks, Walks and Playgrounds in this neighbourhood and of soliciting at this early stage of the proceedings, your financial assistance toward an object which we are assured will meet with your cordial approbation.

The liberality of Lord Francis Egerton, and other non-residents who are interested in the prosperity of this community, encourages us to hope that other Noblemen and Gentlemen will aid in an effort of such importance to the great mass of the population.

27   BL, Peel Papers, Add. MS 40,550, f. 347.

We refrain from any such remarks on the importance of an effort of this kind, as your knowledge of the density of the population of Manchester, and of the injury inflicted on the health of the poor by the want of ready access to open-air exercise and recreation must render such unnecessary.

Soliciting your kind co-operation and requesting the favour of an early reply

We have the honour to be Sir, your very obedient servants

Malcolm Ross
Edward Watkin, Hon. Secs.
The Right Ho'ble Sir Robert Peel Bart MP London

Subscription List in aid of Public Walks[28]

£1,000 each
Lord Francis Egerton
Sir Benjamin Heywood, MP, Bart
Mark Philips, Esq., MP
Jones Loyd & Co

£500 each
Sir Thomas Potter, Knight
John Brooks, Esq
J. C. Harter, Esq.
Alexander Henry, Esq
Thos Hoyle & Son
Kershaw, Leese and Sidebotham
J. & N. Philips & Co.
Townend & Hickson

£300 each
Elkanah Armitage, Esq.

---

28   Although not referred to in the letter of 30 Aug, the list is filed next to the letter in the Peel Papers and clearly accompanied it.

James Heywood, Esq.
James Smith, Esq.
E.P. Thomson, Esq.
John Hargreaves, Esq.
Samuel Brooks, Esq.

£250 each
Horrocks Jackson & Co
A.G. Murray

£200 each
Alexander Kay, Esq., Mayor
William Harter, Esq.
Robert Gardner, Esq.
James Carlton, Esq.

£105
William W. Wood, Esq.

£100each
The Hon Very Rev the Dean, Dr Ashton
W.R. Callender, Esq.
Richard Cobden, Esq., MP
William Entwistle, Esq., MP

2 Sir Robert Peel to Malcolm Ross and Edward Watkin, 7 September 1844[29]

Whitehall, 7th September

Gentlemen,

Although I have no longer any personal connection with the Town of Manchester by property or other local tie, yet considering Manchester to be the Metropolis of a District to the industry of which I and my Family are under very deep

29   BL, Add. MS. 40,550, f. 351.

obligations and most heartily approving of the wish and benevolent design to provide for those who are doomed to almost incessant Toil the means of healthful recreation and harmless enjoyment, I willingly contribute to the furtherance of that design and offer my cordial good wishes for its success.

I request my name to be added to the subscription which has been commenced for this service for the sum of £1,000.

I am, Sir

Robert Peel

Malcolm Ross, Esq.
Edward Watkin Esq.

Town Hall
Manchester

September 10th 1844

3 Letter from Alexander Kay, Mayor of Manchester, to Sir Robert Peel, 10 September, together with an extract from the minutes of the Public Parks Committee held on 9 September 1844[30]

Sir,

I have the honour to enclose a copy of a resolution agreed to by the Committee on public parks etc. for this town at its meeting on the 9th inst. when your letter addressed to the honorary secretaries was read. And I venture to add that the sense entertained by each Member of the committee then present of the value of your opinion on the subject is very inadequately expressed by the resolution which in compliance with the dictation of the committee I have the honour to transmit.

30   BL, Add. MS. 40,550, f. 353.

I trust I shall not be charged with presumption in thus conveying the feelings entertained by the committee as well as its formal resolution.

I have the honour to be
your very obedient and respectful servant
Alex Kay, Mayor

The Rt Hon'ble Sir Robert Peel Bart MP

Town Hall Committee Room for Public Parks, Walks etc.

Manchester 9th September 1844

At a Special Meeting of the Committee holden this day

Alexander Kay, Esq. in the Chair

Read letter from the Rt Honourable Sir Robert Peel Bart MP dated Whitehall, September 7th 1844, announcing a subscription of £1,000.

Resolved unanimously

That the Committee highly appreciating the opinions expressed by Sir Robert Peel begs to convey to him its most sincere thanks not only for his donation of one thousand pounds in aid of the Funds now raising for the establishment of public parks etc. in this neighbourhood, but especially for the gratifying terms in which he communicated his Munificent Gift in the letter now read.

Extracted from the Minutes by
Malcolm Ross
Honorary Secretary.

4 *Covering letter Lord Francis Egerton to Sir Robert Peel, 26 March 1845*[31]

Confidential
Worsley, 26th March 1845

Sir

I think it would be for your convenience to know beforehand the subject of an interview which you will see by another letter of this date I have to request. Not having had any opportunity of personal communication with the parties, I have at present no further knowledge of their views and prospects than is supplied in the enclosed letter which I forward for your information.

I am faithfully yours

Egerton

Rt hon Sir Robert Peel

5 *Malcolm Ross and Edward Watkin to Lord Francis Egerton, 22 March 1845*[32]

Public walks, Parks, Gardens and Playgrounds
Committee Room, Town Hall, Manchester
22 March

My Lord,

The subscriptions to the fund for the formation of Public Parks etc amount now to the sum of £30,300 and, as a good proportion of the money is already paid into the Bank, the Committee are justified in taking the steps they now contemplate for procuring sites of land. Plots of land of considerable eligibility are offered to us: the total value of those selected by the Sub-

31   BL, Add. MS. 40,563, f. 292.
32   BL, Add. MS. 40,563, f. 293.

Committee as preeminently advantageous is about £60,000. In order therefore to the successful exploitation of the effort it is necessary, following the original intention, to apply to Government for the means of carrying out the work in the most efficient manner, in the hope that a liberal grant may be given.

As it is important that a deputation wait upon the Premier with as little delay as possible formally to make the application, we take the liberty of asking whether your Lordship would be so obliging as to arrange for an interview provided this mode appears best in your much greater knowledge of these matters.

In case of the deputation it would consist of the Mayor, the local members and others waiting upon Sir Robert Peel. The Com'ee would wish your Lordship to lead it.

An early answer would greatly oblige.

We have the honour to be
My Lord
Your Lordship's most obedient servants

Malcolm Ross
Edward Watkin
Honorary Secretaries

The Right Honorable Lord Francis Egerton MP, Worsley Hall

6 Malcolm Ross and Edward Watkin to Sir Robert Peel, 7 April 1845[33]

Public walks, Parks, Gardens and Playgrounds
Committee Room, Town Hall, Manchester
7 April 1845

---

33   BL, Add. MS. 40,563, f. 297.

Sir

As we do not wish to trespass unnecessarily upon time so valuable to the country and it is desirable to place before you a summary of the proceedings upon which the application to be made at the interview which you have done us the honour to appoint for Wednesday next – preparatory to the attendance of the deputation – we take the liberty of enclosing a brief recapitulation of the case which it is desired to lay before you.

Further statements and any explanations which may be needed we shall be prepared to give on Wednesday.

The plan or sketch named in the memorandum will be brought up to London by the deputation as it is too bulky to be sent by post.

We have the honour to be, Sir
with the greatest respect
your most obedient servants

Malcolm Ross
Edward Watkin

Rt Honourable Sir Robert Peel Bart MP
London

7 Memorandum from the Manchester Public Parks Committee to Sir Robert Peel, 7 April 1845

A nearly complete draft of the memorandum below was included in the last pages of Watkin's diary. The version below is that sent to Sir Robert Peel (BL, Add. MS 40563, f. 297). It differs from the version in the diary only in minor detail and the inclusion of the sum raised by the appeal left blank in the draft.

Memorandum of the Committee for the establishment in
Manchester of Public Parks, Gardens and Playgrounds

Manchester, April 7th

The Movement in favour of public places for spacious recreation in Manchester was originated with a view effectively to remedy the great public evils consequent on the absolute want of any public provision of such means of popular improvement.

Having a population of 300,000 souls to serve, and unaided by the existence of common lands or other spaces of ground procurable for the mere cost of laying out and planting, it was felt necessary to obtain pecuniary aid both of the town and the Government.

The effort was resolved upon on the 8th August 1844 at one of the largest Town Meetings ever held in Manchester. A public subscription was then originated and the meeting encouraged by the past practice of the legislature placed upon record its confidence in the readiness of Parliament to assist the effort by a liberal grant.

The Committee elected by the meeting considered it their duty to obtain as large and general a subscription as possible from the inhabitants prior to making an application to Government for aid. They have therefore diligently canvassed the town and applied to persons residing at a distance who from the possession of property or from known predilection were likely to contribute. The result has been that the fund now amounts to £30,746.17.10 contributed by 3318 persons of all classes, in sums varying in amount from 6d to £1,000 – a larger amount, perhaps, than was ever before raised by voluntary donation for local objects in any town or city in the Kingdom. Of this sum £26,000 is already paid into the Banker's hands.

Having now done their utmost in the way of self-assistance, the people of Manchester can without any impropriety lay before the Government the grounds of their claim upon the public purse.

To make the undertaking efficient it is absolutely necessary to have a Park Promenade and a playground on each side of the Town,

to erect rooms for refreshment and shelter,
to provide seats and benches in abundance,
to construct fountains and to secure a plentiful supply of fresh water,
to lay out the grounds in the most attractive mode possible.

From the plots of land offered to the Committee there have been selected as most desirable, land sufficient for 5 public places. The accompanying sketch[34] divides the towns of Manchester and Salford and the outlying townships into two portions – the Northerly one (pink) contains about 170,000 souls – the Southerly (blue) about 130,000. The population of the former consists very greatly of factory operatives and others who especially need facilities for open air recreation, that of the latter comprising large numbers of the labouring with other classes but it is not so dense.

For the use of the population to the north it is proposed to purchase and adapt the lands marked 1, 2, 3 of the several extent, 27 acres, 95 acres and 31 acres; for the use of the population to the south the lands marked 4 (40 acres), and 5 (13 acres).

---

34   Not attached to either version of the document.

The expenditure involved would be about as follows–

	£	£	£	£
Plot No 1				
7 acres now laid out and planted	4,600			
and more from 20 acres in field	6,000			
Altering mansion, making seats, fountains and laying out of 20 acres		2,000		
			12,600	
Plot No 1				
Mansion and 95 acres now laid out and planted	27,500			
Altering house, seats, fountains, fencing		1,500		
			29,000	
Plot No 3				
31 acres land	7,750			
Buildings		1,500		
Laying out, seats, fountains, etc		1,250		
			10,500	
Plots 1, 2 and 3				52,100
Plot No 4				
40 acres land	10,000			
Buildings		1,500		
Laying out, seats, fountains		1,500		
			13,000	
Plot No 5				
13 acres land	19,000			
Buildings		1,000		
Laying out, fountains etc		1,500		
			21,500	
Plots 4 and 5				34,500
Total				86,600

The plot No 5 from various causes is much dearer than any other and as the district in which it is situated is open and diversified and has advantages which a park would furnish, the Committee do not regard its immediate purchase as imperative.

Deducting the cost of it from the estimate it appears that a sum of up to £65,100 or £34,354[35] more than the sum subscribed will be required to continue that measure of success without which the efforts of the inhabitants of Manchester will be in good measure abortive.

The Committee regard the work entrusted to them as a great experiment; and while they anticipate the happiest results from its success, they fear the consequences of its failure. It is a model effort, (the commencement it is hoped of a great national movement), sure to lead to emulous imitation, provided the scale on which it may be completed be sufficiently comprehensive. The Committee fear that a niggardly accomplishment of the object would restrict the enterprise of towns, some waiting to see the conclusion of the works in Manchester before commencing similar undertakings.

They are convinced that nothing less than what they propose will be at all adequate to the pressing needs of the industrious population around them.

The Committee submit that Manchester has special claims upon the Government. It is the metropolis of a most important district where a rapidly growing population is perpetually pressing upon the means of moral, physical, and mental improvement. Its population give a tone to and have a marked influence upon that of the belt of Towns around it.

While Edinburgh, Dublin and London and numerous other places have been frequently and largely aided in their public works from the common purse, Manchester though

35   £65,100 was the cost of plots 1 to 4, towards which £30,746 had been
        subscribed, leaving a shortfall of £34,354.

contributing very greatly to the general revenue has never yet received a farthing for such purposes.

It should not be overlooked that Manchester although made a corporate town within the last six years had no corporate property or fund, and does not possess an acre of common land. It has this year had to burden itself with a debt of two hundred thousand pounds for the purchase of the Manorial rights and further large obligations must be entered into with a view to the efficient working of the corporate body.

Considering therefore the importance of the effort to be completed and the necessity of completing it in an efficient manner, and the impossibility of doing without the liberal cooperation of the Government, the Committee very greatly hope for a sum at least equal to that raised already by spontaneous donations.

8 *Edward Watkin to Edward Tootal, 2 July 1846*[36]

5 Marsden Street,[37] Monday morning (2nd July 1846)

Dear Sir

I think it would be well to state to Sir Robert Peel the following particulars connected with the address forwarded from Manchester on Saturday evening.

The address was agreed upon at 1/2 past 11, engrossed at 12, put on 'change[38] at one and removed from there at 2 o'c.

All parties – Tories, Whigs and Radicals, signed it and no difference of opinion was exhibited.

36   BL, Add. MS. 40,595, f. 66.
37   The office of the Trent Valley Railway.
38   The Manchester Exchange.

The Mayor, most of the Corporation, Banks, Merchants and Manufacturers signed it, and had there been <u>time</u> the <u>number</u> of signatures would have would have reflected the property and influence represented.

You are cognisant of most of these facts and if you will write to Sir Robert on the subject he may be able to estimate the address as it deserves.

I am Sir your obedient servant

E W Watkin

Edward Tootal, Esq.
Weaste House

9 Edward Tootal to Sir Robert Peel, 2 July 1846[39]

Manchester, 2nd July 1846

Sir

I had written to you with some account of the address forwarded to you the other day – it was done most promptly and had it remained a day it would have been most <u>nobly</u> signed.

I trust you will pardon me when I say that the parties will be greatly delighted and honoured by your reply.

Mr Brown comes forward for the Vacancy caused by the elevation of Lord Francis Egerton, which we are all greatly pleased with – and the probability is that your name will be out in 24 hours with an expression of feeling which you are most truly entitled to – the intention to return you for the Southern Division of this County at the next general election without any appeal to you whatsoever. I shall know more in the morning.

39   BL, Add. MS. 40,595, f. 64.

If I may be of any service to you I should be truly grateful if I could perform it.

Mr Westhead[40] is very firm in his determination to support you. I had a long address from him yesterday.

Your kindness to me I shall never forget and can never repay. I look forward to the day when <u>justice</u> at last shall be done to you for the great blessings you have incurred on mankind and upon this country in Parliament.

May the Blessing of the Almighty attend you and yours.

Kindly excuse the liberty.
I am Sir, Yours sincerely

Edward Tootal

10 Sir Robert Peel to Edward Tootal, 3 July 1846[41]
Drayton Manor, 3 July

I have availed myself of the earliest opportunity of which I could avail myself to return an answer to the gratifying address which was sent to me from Manchester. I think it better to have no reserve whatever about the Representation of South Lancashire.

It is more than probable that those to whom the proposal of that Representation to me may in a moment of temporary excitement have occurred would think better of it in calmer moments, but I have no wish to have a compliment paid to me which I could not accept – and though it is rather premature and unseemly to decline that which has not been offered to me,

40   Joshua Brown Westhead, later Brown, was a small ware manufacturer in Manchester and Bury. Moved to Worcestershire in 1847. MP for Knaresborough, 1847–52, and later for York. Like Tootal a director of the LNWR and later deputy chairman.
41   BL, Add. MS. 40,595 , f. 70.

I think it right, after your mention of the subject to say at once I do not think I could undertake the laborious duties which the seat for South Lancashire imposes, and I should not wish to abandon my present constituents while they desire my services.

Robert Peel

Edward Tootal, Esq.

Bibliography

Unpublished primary sources

Chichester, West Sussex Record Office
Cobden Papers

Kew, National Archives, Public Record Office
Home Office Papers
RAIL 638/1 and 1160/32

London, British Library

MSS 43649, 50750	Cobden Papers
MSS 40550, 40563	Peel Papers

Manchester Central Library

MS 373–4273C1	Baker, Thomas, 'An Account of the Manchester Literary Society'
MS f052 L161, 1889–1898	Leary, F., 'History of the Manchester periodical press'
MSF 062 M3	Manchester Literary Society Minute Book
MS 352.7 M5	Malcolm Ross's Scrapbook
MS FF 382 S35	John Scholes, 'Foreign merchants in Manchester, 1784–1870'
M20	Wilson Papers
M219	Watkin Papers

Oldham Archives

28/7, /9, /11 and /22, Oldham Railways, collection of documents relating to the Oldham, Manchester, Liverpool and Birkenhead Junction Railway (Shaw Bookshop Purchase)

Published contemporary sources

Newspapers

Anti-Bread Tax Circular
The Looking Glass
Manchester and Salford Advertiser
Manchester Examiner
Manchester Guardian
Manchester Times
Northern Star
Railway Times

Other

Report of the Minutes of Evidence taken before the Select Committee on the State of Children employed in the Manufactories of the United Kingdom, PP, 1816 (397, 317), III, 555.

Report from the Select Committee on Public Walks with the Minutes of Evidence, PP, 1833 (448, 4), XV, 340.

First Report of the Commissioners of Inquiry into the State of Large Towns and Populous Districts, PP, 1844 (572), XVII.

The return of Sums of Money, by way of loans or grants on public works in England and Scotland, PP, 1843 (124), XXXVIII, 455.

Adshead, Joseph, *Distress in Manchester: Evidence of the State of the Labouring Classes in 1840–2* (London: Henry Hooper, 1842).

Aiken, John, *A Description of the Country from Thirty to Forty Miles Round Manchester* (London: John Stockdale, 1795).

Axon, W. E. A., *The Annals of Manchester: A Chronological Record from the Earliest Times to the End of 1885* (Manchester: John Heywood, 1886).

Carlyle, Thomas, *Chartism* (1842; London: Holerth Press, 1924 reprint).

Catalogue of the Library of Sir Edward W. Watkin MP, Rose Hill, Northenden (Manchester, compiled and printed for private use by J. E. Cornish, 1875; 2nd enlarged edn, Manchester: Henry Blacklock, 1889).

Cobden, Richard, *Incorporate Your Borough, 1837*, reproduced in W. E. A. Axon, *Cobden as a Citizen: A Chapter in Manchester's History* (London: T. Fisher Unwin, 1907).

Defoe, Daniel, *A Tour through the Whole Island of Great Britain, 1724–26*, ed. G. H. D. Cole (2 vols, London: Peter Davis, 1927).

de Tocqueville, A., *Journeys to England and Ireland, 1835*, translated by G. Lawrence and K. P. Mayer, ed. J. P. Mayer (2 vols, London: Faber & Faber, 1955).

Dickens, Charles, *Hard Times* (1854; Everyman edition, London: J. M. Dent, 1907).

Disraeli, Benjamin, *Coningsby* (1844; Everyman edition, London: J. M. Dent, 1911).

Disraeli, Benjamin, *Sybil, or the Two Nations* (1845; Harmondsworth: Penguin Books, 1954).

Engels, Frederick, *The Condition of the Working Class in England in 1844* (London: Swan Sonnenschein, 1892).

Faucher, Leon, *Manchester in 1844: Its Present Condition and Future Prospects* (translated by a member of the Manchester Athenaeum, London: Simpkin, Marshall, 1844).

Gaskell, Elizabeth, *The Letters of Mrs Gaskell*, ed. J. A. V. Chapple and A. Pollard (Manchester: Manchester University Press, 1966).

Gaskell, Elizabeth, *Mary Barton* (1848; London: Penguin Books, 1996).

Glover, Stephen, *The History and Directory of the Borough of Derby* (Derby: Henry Mozley and Sons, 1843).

Goffin, Magdalen (ed.), *The Diaries of Absalom Watkin: A Manchester Man, 1787–1861* (Stroud: Alan Sutton, 1993).

Haydon, Robert, *Diary of Benjamin Robert Haydon*, ed. Willard Bissell Pope (5 vols, Cambridge, Mass.: Harvard University Press, 1960–63).

House, Madeline and Storey, Graham (eds), *The Letters of Charles Dickens* (12 vols, Oxford: Oxford University Press, 1965–2002).

Kay, James P., *The Moral and Physical Condition of the Working Classes Employed in the Cotton Industries of Manchester* (London: James Ridgeway, 1832).

Morgan, Peter F. (ed.), *The Letters of Thomas Hood* (Edinburgh: Oliver & Boyd, 1973).

Neele, George P., *Railway Recollections: Notes and Reminiscences of Half a Century's Progress in Railway Working, and of a Railway Superintendent's Life, Principally on the London and North Western Railway* (1904; Wakefield: E P Publishing, 1974 reprint).

O'Connell, Maurice R. (ed.), *The Correspondence of Daniel O'Connell* (8 vols, Dublin: Blackwater for the Irish Manuscripts Commission, 1978).

Parkinson, R., *On the Present Condition of the Labouring Poor in Manchester* (London: Simpkin, Marshall, and Manchester: Sims & Dinham, 1841).

Pigot and Slater's General, Classified and Street Directory of Manchester and Salford (Manchester: Pigot & Slater, 1828, 1841).

Prentice, A., *Historical Sketches and Personal Recollections of Manchester* (London: Charles Gilpin, 1851).

Prentice, A., *History of the Anti-Corn-Law League* (2 vols, London: W. & F. G. Cash, 1853).

Robbins, Michael, 'From R. B. Dockray's diary', *Journal of Transport History*, 1st ser., vii (1965–66), 1–13, 109–19, 149–59.

Saunders, C. R. (ed.), *Collected Letters of Thomas and Jane Welsh Carlyle* (31 vols continuing, Durham, North Carolina: Duke University Press, 1970–).

Slugg, J. T., *Reminiscences of Manchester, Fifty Years Ago* (1881, Shannon, Ireland: Irish University Press, 1971 edition).

Taylor, William Cooke, *Notes of a Tour in the Manufacturing Districts of Lancashire* (London: Duncan & Malcolm, 1842).

Torrington, John Byng, *The Torrington Diaries*, ed. C. B. Andrews (4 vols, London: Eyre & Spotiswoode, 1935).

Watkin, A. E. (ed.), *Absalom Watkin, Extracts from His Journal, 1814–56* (London: T. Fisher Unwin, 1920).

Watkin, E. W., *A Trip to the United States and Canada: In a Series of Letters* (London: W. H. Smith, 1852).

Watkin, E. W., *A Sketch of the Life of Absalom Watkin: Fragment No 1* (Manchester: Alex Ireland, 1874).

Watkin, E. W., *Canada and the States, Recollections, 1851–1886* (London: Ward, Lock, 1887).

Watkin, E. W., *Alderman Cobden of Manchester: Letters and Reminiscences of Richard Cobden, with Portraits, Illustrations, Facsimiles and Index* (London: Ward, Lock, 1891).

Wheeler, James, *Manchester: Its Political, Social and Commercial History, Ancient and Modern* (London: Simpkin, Marshall & Co., 1836).

Wiebe, M. G. (ed.), *Benjamin Disraeli Letters* (8 vols, continuing, Toronto and London: Toronto University Press, 1989–).

Later secondary sources

Andreades, Sophocles Chr., *A Personal History of the Greek Community in Manchester and its Church, 1843–1990* (Manchester: S. Chr. Andreades, 2000).

Ashton, T. S., *Economic and Social Investigations in Manchester* (London: P. S. King, 1934).

Atkinson, Norman, *Sir Joseph Whitworth: 'The World's Best Mechanician'* (Stroud: Sutton, 1996).

Ayerst, David, *Guardian: Biography of a Newspaper* (London: Collins, 1971).

Bateson, Hartley, *A Centenary History of Oldham* (Oldham: Oldham Borough Council, 1949).

Briggs, A., *Victorian Cities* (London: Odhams Press, 1963).

Briggs, A. (ed.), *Chartist Studies* (London: Macmillan, 1959).

Brown, Lucy, 'The Chartists and the Anti-Corn Law League', in Briggs (ed.), *Chartist Studies*, pp. 342–71.

Chadwick, George F., *The Park and Town: Public Landscape in the 19th and 20th Centuries* (London: Architectural Press, 1966).

Chapman, S. D. (Stanley), 'Financial restraints on the growth of firms in the Lancashire cotton industry', *Econ HR*, 2nd ser., XXXII (1979), 50–69.

Chapman, S. D., 'The commercial sector', in Rose (ed.), *Lancashire Cotton Industry*, pp. 63–93.

Chapman, S. D., *Merchant Enterprise in Britain from the Industrial Revolution to World War I* (Cambridge: Cambridge University Press, 1992).

Clark, G. Kitson, 'Hunger and politics in 1842', *Journal of Modern History*, 25 (1953), 355–74.

Conway, Christine, *Dublin* (New Haven and London: Yale University Press, 2005).

Conway, Hazel, *People's Parks: The Design and Development of Victorian Parks in Britain* (Cambridge: Cambridge University Press, 1991).

Coward, T. A., *Picturesque Cheshire* (2nd edn, London: Methuen, 1926).

Crofton, H. J., *A History of Newton Chapelry*, 2, pt 2, Chetham Society, new ser., 54 (Manchester: Chetham Society, 1905).

Davies, S. J., 'Classes and police in Manchester 1829–1880', in Kidd and Roberts (eds), *City, Class and Culture*, pp. 26–47.

Dean, F. R., 'Dickens and Manchester', *The Dickensian*, 34 (1938), 111–18.

Farnie, Douglas A., 'An index of commercial activity: the membership of the Manchester Royal Exchange, 1809–1948', *Business History*, 21 (1979), 97–106.

Farnie, Douglas A., 'The role of merchants as prime movers in the expansion of the cotton industry, 1760–1990', in Douglas A. Farnie and David J. Jeremy (eds), *The Fibre That Changed the World: The Cotton Industry in International Perspective, 1600–1990s* (Oxford: Oxford University Press, 2004), pp. 15–55.

Fleischman, Richard K., *Conditions of Life among the Cotton Workers of Southeastern Lancashire During the Industrial Revolution, 1750–1850* (New York and London: Garland Publishing, 1985).

Gatrell, V. A. C., 'Incorporation and the pursuit of liberal hegemony in Manchester, 1790–1839', in D. Fraser (ed.), *Municipal Reform and the Industrial City* (Leicester: Leicester University Press, 1982), pp. 15–60.

Grindon, Leo H., *Manchester Banks and Bankers* (Manchester: Palmer & Howe, 1877).

Gunn, Simon, 'The "failure" of the Victorian middle class', in John Seed and Janet Wolff (eds), *The Culture of Capital: Art, Power and the Nineteenth-Century Middle Class* (Manchester: Manchester University Press, 1988), pp. 17–43.

Gunn, Simon, *The Public Culture of the Victorian Middle Class: Ritual and Authority and the English Industrial City* (Manchester: Manchester University Press, 2000).

Heginbotham, Henry, *Stockport, Ancient and Modern* (2 vols, London: Sampson Low, Marston, Searle & Rivington, 1877–92).

Hewitt, Martin, *The Emergence of Stability in the Industrial City: Manchester, 1832–67* (Aldershot: Scolar, 1996).

Hibbert, Christopher and Weinreb, Ben (eds), *The London Encyclopaedia* (2nd edn, London: Papermac, 1987).

Hinde, Wendy, *Richard Cobden: A Victorian Outsider* (New Haven and London: Yale University Press, 1987).

Hodgkins, David, *The Second Railway King: The Life and Times of Sir Edward Watkin, 1819–1901* (Cardiff: Merton Priory Press, 2002).

Howe, Anthony, *The Cotton Masters, 1830–1860* (Oxford: Clarendon Press, 1984).

Howe, Anthony, 'The business community', in Mary B. Rose (ed.), *The Lancashire Cotton Industry: A History since 1700* (Preston: Lancashire County Books, 1996), pp. 94–120.

Jones, Stuart, 'The Manchester cotton magnates move into banking, 1826–1850', *Textile History*, 9 (1978), 90–111.

Kamish, Alon (ed.)., *The Corn Laws: The Formulation of Popular Economics in Britain* (6 vols, London: William Pickering, 1996)., iv: *Free Trade and Religion*.

Kaplan, F., *Dickens: A Biography* (London: Hodder & Stoughton, 1988).

Kargon, Robert H., *Science in Victorian Manchester: Enterprise and Expertise* (Manchester: Manchester University Press, 1977).

Kidd, Alan J., *Manchester* (Edinburgh: Edinburgh University Press, revised edn, 2002).

Kidd, Alan J., 'Introduction: the middle class in nineteenth-century Manchester', in Kidd and Roberts (eds), *City, Class and Culture*, pp. 1–24.

Kidd, Alan J. and Roberts, K. W. (eds), *City, Class and Culture: Studies of Social Policy and Cultural Production in Victorian Manchester* (Manchester: Manchester University Press, 1985).

Lasdun, Susan, *The English Park: Royal, Private and Public* (London: Deutsch, 1991).

Lloyd Jones, Roger and Le Roux, A. A., 'The size of firms in the cotton industry: Manchester, 1815–41', *Econ HR*, 2nd ser., XXXIII (1980), 72–82.

Lloyd Jones, Roger and Lewis, M. J., *Manchester and the Age of the Factory* (London: Croom Helm, 1988).

McCord, Norman, *The Anti-Corn Law League, 1838–1846* (London: George Allen & Unwin, 1958).

McKerrow, James Muir, *Memoir of William McKerrow, D.D., Manchester* (London: Hodder & Stoughton, 1881).

Marcus, S., *Engels, Manchester and the Working Class* (New York: Random House, 1974).

Matthews, R. C. O., *A Study in Trade Cycle History: Economic Fluctuations in Great Britain, 1833–42* (Cambridge: Cambridge University Press, 1954).

Monypenny, William Flavelle and Buckle, George Earle, *The Life of Benjamin Disraeli, Earl of Beaconsfield* (2nd edn, 3 vols, London: John Murray, 1929).

Morgan, Simon, 'Cobden and Manchester', *Manchester Region History Review*, 17 (2004), 28–37.

Morris, R. J. (ed.), *Class, Power and Social Structure in British Nineteenth-Century Towns* (Leicester: Leicester University Press, 1986).

Pearson, Robin, and Richardson, David, 'Business networking in the Industrial Revolution', *Econ HR*, LIV (2001)., 657–79.

Pickering, Paul A., *Chartism and the Chartists in Manchester and Salford* (Basingstoke: Macmillan, 1995).

Pickering, Paul A. and Tyrrell, Alex, *The People's Bread: A History of the Anti-Corn Law League* (London: Leicester University Press, 2000).

Read, Donald, 'North of England newspapers (c. 1700 – c. 1900) and their value to historians', *Proceedings of the Leeds Philosophical and Literary Society*, 8 (1956–59), 200–15.

Read, Donald, 'Chartism in Manchester', in Briggs (ed.), *Chartist Studies*, pp. 29–64.

Read, Donald, *The English Provinces, c. 1760 – 1960, A Study in Influence* (London: Edward Arnold, 1964).

Redford, Arthur and Russell, Ina Stafford, *The History of Local Government in Manchester* (3 vols, London: Longmans, 1939–40), II: *Borough and City*.

Reed, Malcolm C., *Investment in Railways in Britain, 1820–1844: A Study in the Development of the Capital Market* (London: Oxford University Press, 1975).

Rose, Mary B. (ed.), *The Lancashire Cotton Industry: A History since 1700* (Preston: Lancashire County Books, 1996).

Rose, Michael E., 'Culture, philanthropy and the Manchester middle classes', in Kidd and Roberts (eds), *City, Class and Culture*, pp. 103–17.

Saxonhouse, George and Wright, Gavin, 'Technological evolution in cotton spinning, 1878–1933', in Farnie and Jeremy (eds), *The Fibre That Changed the World*, pp. 129–52.

Scola, Roger, *Feeding the Victorian City: The Food Supply of Manchester 1770–1880* (Manchester: Manchester University Press, 1992).

Seed, John, 'Unitarianism, political economy and the antinomies of liberal culture in Manchester, 1830–50', *Social History*, 7 (1982), 1–25.

Seed, John, '"Commerce and the liberal arts": the political economy of art in Manchester, 1775–1860', in Seed and Wolff (eds), *The Culture of Capital*, pp. 45–81.

Seed, John, 'Theologies of power: Unitarianism and the social relations of religious discourse', in R. J. Morris (ed.), *Class, Power and Social Structure in British Nineteenth-Century Towns* (Leicester: Leicester University Press, 1986).

Seed, John and Wolff, Janet (eds), *The Culture of Capital: Art, Power and the Nineteenth-Century Middle Class* (Manchester: Manchester University Press, 1988).

Shapely, Peter, *Charity and Power in Victorian Manchester*, Chetham Society, 3rd ser., XLIII (Manchester: Chetham Society, 2000).

Sharples, Joseph, *Liverpool* (New Haven and London: Yale University Press, 2004).

Simmons, Jack, *The Railway in Town and Country, 1830–1914* (Newton Abbot: David & Charles, 1986).

Swindells, Thomas, *Manchester Streets and Manchester Men* (5 vols, Manchester: J. E. Cornish, 1906–8).

Turner, Michael J., *Reform and Respectability: The Making of a Middle-Class Liberalism in early Nineteenth-Century Manchester*, Chetham Society, 3rd ser., XL (Manchester: Chetham Society, 1995).

Voth, Hans-Joachim, 'Living standards and the urban environment,' in Roderick Floud and Paul Johnson (eds), *Cambridge Economic History of Modern Britain* (3 vols, Cambridge: Cambridge University Press, 2004), i. 268–94.

Wach, Howard M., 'Civil society, moral identity and the liberal public sphere: Manchester and Boston, 1810–40', *Social History*, 21 (1996), 281–303.

Williamson, Elizabeth, Riches, Anne and Higgs, Malcolm, *Glasgow* (London: Penguin Books, 1990).

Wyborn, Theresa, 'Parks for the people: the development of public parks in Victorian Manchester', *Manchester Region History Review*, 9 (1995), 3–14.

Youngson, A. J., *The Making of Classical Edinburgh, 1750–1840* (Edinburgh: Edinburgh University Press, 1966).

INDEX